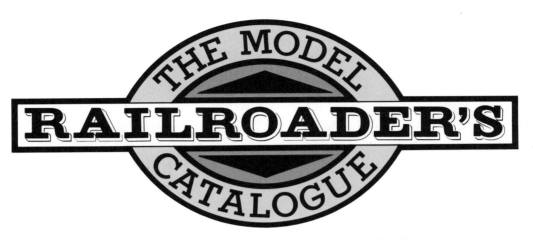

THE MODEL RAILROADER'S CATALOGUE

The Complete Sourcebook for Collectors, Model Builders, and Railfans

by Melinda Corey and George Ochoa

Foreword by Bruce Metcalf, A. C. Kalmbach Memorial Library,
National Model Railroad Association, Inc.

Simon and Schuster
New York   London   Toronto   Sydney   Tokyo   Singapore

A RUNNING HEADS BOOK

Simon and Schuster/Fireside Books,
Published by Simon & Schuster Inc.
Simon & Schuster Building
Rockefeller Center
1230 Avenue of the Americas
New York, New York 10020

SIMON AND SCHUSTER, FIRESIDE and colophons are registered trademarks
of Simon & Schuster Inc.

The Model Railroader's Catalogue
was conceived and produced by
Running Heads Incorporated
55 West 21 Street
New York, New York 10010

Editor: Charles A. de Kay
Designer: Jack Tom
Production Manager: Linda Winters
Managing Editor: Lindsey Crittenden
Photo Editor: Ellie Watson

10 9 8 7 6 5 4 3 2 1

Library of Congress Cataloging in Publication Data

Corey, Melinda.
    The model railroader's catalogue : the complete sourcebook for
collectors, model builders, and railfans / by Melinda Corey and
George Ochoa ; foreword by Bruce Metcalf.
        p.   cm.
    Includes index.
    ISBN: 0-671-74093-8 (cloth)
    ISBN: 0-671-70949-6 (paperback)
    1. Railroads—Models.   I. Ochoa, George.   II. Title.
TF197.C28   1991
625.1'9'0294—dc 20   90-45830
                                                     CIP

Typeset by Trufont Typographers, Inc.
Color separations by Hong Kong Scanner Craft Company, Ltd.
Printed and bound in Singapore by Tien Wah Press (Pte.) Ltd.

To Tim, who is still excited by the sound of a steam engine, and to model railroaders everywhere

ACKNOWLEDGMENTS

A model railroad manufacturer who sent us material asked us not to let this "fall by the wayside, as others have done." We would not, because the fact is that this book could not have been written without him and the dozens of others who gave us information, photographs, and drawings. There are too many of you to list here, but we thank you all.

We would especially like to thank Dick Christianson of *Classic Toy Trains* for his generosity and knowledge; The Red Caboose for all their kind assistance; and Bruce Metcalf of the Kalmbach Memorial Library for his welcome availability whenever we called with questions or requests ("Tell us the history of coupler development," "Where can I get a photo of a Blue Comet?"), for his thoughtful information, and for carefully reviewing the manuscript.

Finally, we thank our editors, Sarah Kirshner and Charlie de Kay, and our photo editor, Ellie Watson, for their patience and support.

CONTENTS

Color illustrations fall after pages 96 and 176.

FOREWORD

Model railroading is magic! I'm sorry, I'd like to be able to give you a more precise and technical description, but after twenty-five years in the hobby, I find nothing else says it quite so well.

This hobby is many things to each of us who invest our time in it. The model railroader has the opportunity to become a model builder, a collector, an artist in three dimensions, a carpenter, an historian, a traveler in time and space, an electrician, a surveyor, a photographer, a solitary laborer, and a gregarious social animal.

This may sound rather awe-inspiring at first, and, unfortunately, some people are frightened away from the hobby before they've even begun for fear they must be an expert in all of these fields to succeed. Nothing could be farther from the truth—many people get their start at a very tender age after discovering a train set under the Christmas tree! You can have a great time with this hobby without taking it any further. The possibility of a deeper involvement, however, is what allows model railroading to become a lifelong hobby—not just a great children's toy.

A large part of the attraction of model trains is the fascination with real railroads. They are very much a part of America—our social history, our industrial technology, our mythology. The brave engineer with his hand on the whistle and the punctual conductor consulting his watch are images as bright in our collective imagination as the powerful locomotive and the little red caboose in which they ride.

But modern railroads are not simply antiquated relics of a previous age. Today's locomotives contain sophisticated electronic controls that raise their price to a million dollars and more. Amtrak, the government-owned corporation that operates nearly all passenger service in the U.S., has carried more people every year since it began; and, despite competition from trucks and airplanes, rails still carry over a third of all intercity freight—including many trucks carried "piggyback." Satellite communications keep dispatchers informed of train locations, and one of the largest computer systems in the country keeps track of every freight car and shipment in North America twenty-four hours a day.

While modelers don't use satellite communications for their model railroad, they do use just about every other tool and technique imaginable—including computers—to enable and enhance their enjoyment of the hobby.

Whether you want to build an up-to-the-minute replica of a modern transportation network or run a fanciful toy train around a miniature "Big Rock Candy Mountain," model railroading has the range and variety to keep you busy for a lifetime. The careful

historian who struggles to get every detail correct can find just as much satisfaction in the hobby as the collector who finds a train just like the one he had as a child or the freelance modeler who lets his imagination run wild.

If I had to pick one aspect of the hobby that makes model railroading special, it would have to be its social side. Model railroading, by its nature, is a group activity. Just as a real train employs an engineer, a conductor, brakemen, tower operators, station agents—an entire crew—model trains can employ the talents of a group. A gang of modelers can all work on the same railroad, passing each other's trains, picking up passengers, and all the while remaining in contact with the others.

Now this book isn't going to take you from blissful ignorance to master craftsman in a single step. A whole shelf of books couldn't do that, though there are plenty of instructional manuals mentioned herein that will help you along the way. In this volume the authors will give you an appreciation of the scope of the hobby; they consider each of the many facets of modeling trains and discuss a range of related activities. The text will also help you to select good basic products from the wide variety available, and point to ways you can get involved and learn more.

The authors explain the hobby in understandable terms—keeping the jargon to a minimum—and include a glossary to explain the special language that you just can't get by without. Furthermore, the text has been carefully reviewed by several expert modelers to verify the accuracy of the wealth of detailed information and the availability of the products mentioned.

Experienced model railroaders can also benefit from this book by using it to review their hobby. You may well find some new products discussed—or even some old products you missed when they first came out—as I did. Has your enthusiasm been slipping lately? Why not try a different aspect of the hobby? From modeling to collecting to railfanning, the possibilities and the challenges of model railroading are as boundless as your imagination.

You don't have to join a club to enjoy model railroading, and you don't have to belong to the National Model Railroad Association before you can buy a train. But it's too much fun to keep all to yourself, so gather your family, your friends, draft your boss if you have to! This book, large as it is, can only give you a good start in model railroading, but that's a start on something very special indeed.

Bruce Metcalf
Library Director
Kalmbach Memorial Library
National Model Railroad Association
Chattanooga, Tennessee

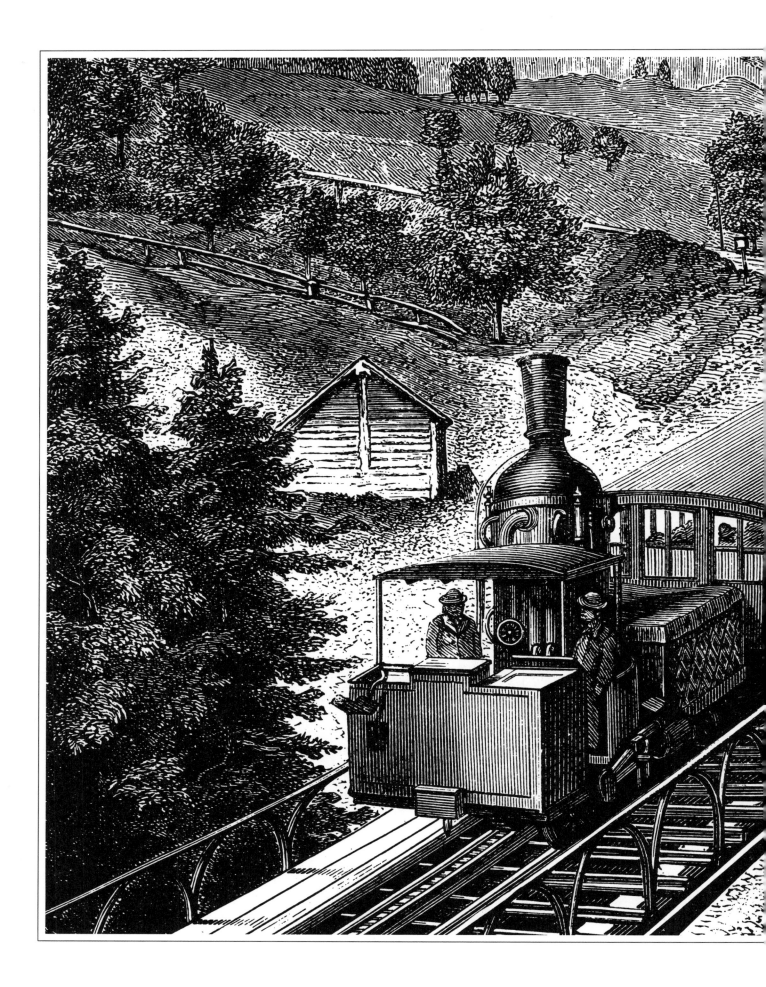

INTRODUCTION
Model Railroading Yesterday and Today

Only a heart of stone can resist a model train in motion. It is smaller than any working machine should be, but represents huge machines, symbols of power and speed. The landscape through which it travels enchants like a fairy tale, but tells of real times and places. Children love model railroads, but it is primarily adults who build them—and who appreciate the ingenuity and care that goes into them.

Model railroaders are not all alike. Some give only a few hours a month to the hobby; others work at it all the time. Some build in clubs, some with their children, and some build alone. Some collect trains but rarely "model" them; some specialize in scenery or wiring; some are jacks-of-all-trades. Some are "armchair" railroaders who read about other people's layouts and imagine a grander one than anyone has ever seen.

The Model Railroader's Catalogue is not tailored to any one type of model railroader. It is a comprehensive account of what is available—products, publications, services—for all railroaders, whatever their level of expertise or involvement. If you are a beginner, it will help you make sense of the array of products found in hobby stores and sales catalogues. If you are more advanced, it will help you plan new stages of work. If you are an old hand, it may suggest aspects

Above: The John Bull, an early prototype locomotive. Constructed in England, it began regular service on the Camden & Amboy Railroad in the United States in 1833. Right: A model of the De Witt Clinton, the first locomotive on the Mohawk and Hudson Railroad. It began pulling stagecoach-type passenger cars in 1831.

of the hobby you are currently missing. For all railroaders, it is meant to help turn a complex marketplace into a treasure-trove of choices.

The plan of the book is simple. The first four chapters describe the basic supplies for starting, developing, and perfecting a railroad. Chapter One covers train sets, locomotives, and *rolling stock**; Chapter Two describes benchwork, track, scenery, and structures; Chapter Three details the tools and supplies needed for *scratchbuilding*, *kitbashing*, and enhancing realism; Chapter Four discusses power sources, wiring, and electronics. The last three chapters cover additional aspects of the hobby. Chapter Five describes the wider world of railroading (publications, clubs, shows, museums); Chapter Six discusses rare collectibles and limited editions; Chapter Seven describes "railroadiana"—artwork, clothing, and housewares for the railroader who has everything else. Extensive appendices feature a glossary of technical terms and a comprehensive sources section that lists each of the manufacturers and organizations—and their addresses—mentioned in the book.

Most experienced railroaders are well-acquainted with the history of the hobby. But for those just starting out—and for those who may not have heard the story for some time—we present a brief biography of the model railroad.

*Terms frequently used by model railroaders will be introduced in italics. These terms are also listed in the Glossary in the back of the book.

Above: A Mogul steam locomotive that began running on the Michigan Central Railroad in 1886. Right: An engraving of the De Witt Clinton, after the replica built by the New York Central for the 1893 Chicago Exposition. The replica is now in the Ford Museum.

MODELS AND TOYS

The first working steam locomotive was a model. Built by William Murdoch, an employee of James Watt, in England in 1784, it was 14 inches high and 19¼ inches long, and ran six to eight miles an hour. The model was so impressive that, according to legend, it frightened the village parson half to death and caused Watt to forbid Murdoch from conducting any more such experiments.

Inventors did continue experimenting, however—using miniature models to test their ideas before building full-size versions. Once full-size versions were built, models were used to demonstrate and promote the locomotives. These models were intricate and expensive, and were not for sale to the general public.

Miniature trains first became commercially available as toys around the 1840s. By that time, railways were spreading throughout the world. The locomotive—large, fast, powerful, crossing vast distances—was capturing the imagination of people throughout Europe and the Americas. In Germany, England, France, and the United States, toymakers started making miniature trains. Some of the earliest ones, like toy soldiers, were made of lead and had no moving parts. Others had working wheels, but had to be pushed or pulled on the floor. The future, however, belonged to the trains that were self-propelling.

Many of the trains ran on clockwork. A British toy train of the 1850s, the Rotary Railway Express, was connected by a wire arm to a clockwork mechanism 18 inches away. When the child (or parent) wound the mechanism, the Express traveled in circles for up to 300 feet before exhausting its power. Other toy trains, like their prototypes, were propelled by steam—but they burned spirits instead of wood or coal. Nineteenth-century British toymakers specialized in steam-driven trains of solid brass known indelicately as "dribblers" or "piddlers" (for the trail of water they left behind on the floor).

Right: A "pull" train of the late nineteenth century. A child pulling the string served as the locomotive force.

Above: The train set under the Christmas tree is a treasured memory of many people's childhoods. This is an HO-scale starter set from Märklin. Opposite: The first operating, full-scale railway locomotive was this 1804 engine by Richard Trevithick. It operated briefly on the tramway of the Penn-y-Darran Iron Works in Wales.

None of the nineteenth-century toy trains would today be considered "model" or "scale" trains—trains that strictly reproduce the proportions and detail of a *prototype*, or real train. In a *toy train*, the smokestacks and wheels might be too big in proportion to the length of the locomotive; small details like handrails might be left out. In a *scale train*, by contrast, the smokestack and wheels are correctly proportioned in relation to the locomotive's length, and all (or most) of the fine details are in place. Theoretically, if you enlarged a *scale* train to the size of its prototype, it would look exactly like the real thing. If you enlarged a *toy train* to that size, it would look like a big toy.

In the United States toy locomotives were only loosely based on any prototype at all. The stylized bodies were large and durable. Many were made of tin plate, painted red and gold, and decorated with hearts and flowers. Later, they were made of cast iron or of wood with lithographed paper—though, among railroaders, *tinplate* remains a syn-

onym for toy, as opposed to scale, trains.

British "dribblers" tended to be more delicate and realistic than American trains. Like many of today's miniature trains, they were based on bygone prototypes—such as the *Planet* of the early 1830s. But with their polished brass and decorative bands, the British toy trains were still toys, and did not duplicate the finish and fine detail of prototypes.

One crucial detail was missing from most toy trains: the track. Most were floor trains, meant to be pushed or driven on the floor. As early as the 1860s, the French company of Emile Favre at E. F. LeFèvre Successeurs provided stations, signals, and sheds made of tinplate to accompany its trains, but track was limited to a circle of tin often with two grooves for the wheels. By the 1880s, some companies were offering straight rails and circular track, but straight lines and circles hardly represented the paths of real trains—curving at odd angles, crossing, diverging.

In 1891, at the Leipzig Toy Fair in Germany, toy tracks changed forever. Germany was the site of a thriving toy train industry—including such companies as Issmayer, Bing, and Carette—that exported its wares throughout Europe and the United States. One company, Märklin, was more well known for its toy kitchen and doll house accessories than for its trains. But at the 1891 Leipzig fair Märklin introduced a series of train sets that marked the birth of the toy railway system.

The trains came in three different sizes, each accompanied by a different *gauge* of track. (*Gauge* means the distance between the rails.) The smallest, called gauge I, measured 1¾ inches between the rails. Gauge II measured 2 inches and gauge III measured 3 inches. As important as the standardization of sizes were the complex kinds of track Märklin offered: sectional pieces with *turnouts* and *crossings*. (A *turnout* [also called a *track switch*] is the place where two tracks diverge; it allows a train to go onto a different route. A *crossing* is the place where two tracks cross each other.) Track components like these allowed for complex maneuvers; the ability to add on extra sections of track meant that the railroad could grow as large as the buyer wanted.

The new railway system was an immediate success. With the addition of stations, tunnels, bridges, and figures (eagerly provided by Märklin), a toy train could become the center of a miniature world. By the early 1900s, virtually every toy train company was following Märklin's lead. By that time, Märklin had introduced a new 1¼ inch gauge, gauge 0 (zero, so-called because the distance between the rails was smaller than gauge I). The gauge eventually became known as "O" (the letter "o").

The advent of electric power brought the next breakthrough in toy trains. In 1897 Märklin introduced train sets that used alternating current—though it continued to offer steam and clockwork motors as well. Märklin and other German exports became popular in the United States, but in the early 1900s domestic manufacturers, such as American Flyer, Ives, Lionel, and Marx, began to rival them.

Founded by Joshua Lionel Cowen in 1900, Lionel, in particular, achieved great success with its line of inexpensive, electric-powered trains. In the American toy-train tradition, they were large, stylized, and durable. In 1906, Lionel started building the trains in a non-standard gauge—2⅛ inches, a little larger than gauge II. In a bold stroke of marketing, Lionel labeled this size Standard gauge. By the 1920s it had actually become a standard and was copied by other manufacturers.

Lionel's trains in the 1920s were *electric outline* rather than *steam outline*—that is, they were modeled after electric-powered prototypes rather than steam-powered ones. Designed in Naples, Italy, they included elaborate, colorful trains like the 381 with its twelve-wheeled locomotive and string of four Pullman passenger cars. Lionel's competitor Ives was not as successful and went bankrupt in 1928. But Lionel, American Flyer, and Marx continued to thrive.

The companies were riding a wave of interest in miniature railways. In 1925, the first model railroad society in America was founded—the New York Society of Model Engineers. In 1934, *Model Railroader* magazine was founded by Milwaukee printer Al Kalmbach. But the adults who were turning to railroading as a hobby were not satisfied with the toy trains that so pleased children. Seeking greater realism, they started building their own models (*scratchbuilding*) and altering existing ones. The time was ripe for a more authentic miniature railroading system to emerge.

1938

THE BIRTH OF SCALE MODELS

The Great Depression of the 1930s initially hurt sales of toy trains worldwide and forced manufacturers to try new approaches. One approach was to miniaturize trains further—making them cheaper to buy. Lionel stopped manufacturing its large Standard gauge and concentrated on the smaller O gauge (as did American Flyer). American toy train makers received a boost from the appearance of luxury streamlined prototypes like the Twentieth Century Limited. These sleek and glamorous vehicles revived the public's interest in trains, and Lionel was soon producing handsome toy versions of the streamliners, including its models of the Union Pacific *City of Portland* and the New York Central *Hudson* locomotive.

One reason that Lionel made some of its trains smaller was to allow them to operate on a smaller *track radius*. *Track radius* is a measure of the curve in curved sections of track. If you assemble curved sections of track into a circle, the distance from the center of the circle to the center of the track is the track radius. The smallest and most popular of Lionel's three sizes of O gauge train sets was O-27 gauge—that is, O-gauge track (1¼ inches wide) with a radius of 27 inches.

If it is unclear why a smaller radius re- quires smaller trains, imagine a city bus trying to turn a corner in narrow streets. Even though the streets are wide enough to accommodate the bus when it is traveling in a straight line, the corner is too tight—that is, its *radius* is too small—to allow the bus to turn. The bus will crash into a street sign or a building if it keeps trying. Similarly, if a railroad car tries to negotiate a curve that is too tight, it may jump off its rails.

On prototype railroads, curves can generally be long and gentle enough to accommodate very long cars (many modern cars are 85 feet long). But the amount of space modelers have available has always been much more limited, even as a small-scale representation. The largest rooms most people have available are too small to model the miles and miles of railroad real trains travel along. The width of the room determines how large track radius can be.

This restriction had been one of the reasons toy trains were usually unrealistic. Remember that the gauge (or width) of O-gauge track—then the smallest track in common use—was 1¼ inches. But, because of practical space limitations, track *radius* was very small in relation to track gauge. (To use the metaphor above, the street was wide enough for a bus but the curves were tight.)

Above: Streamliners figure prominently in this Lionel catalogue cover from 1938. Second from left is a bullet-nosed locomotive; fourth from left is a shovel-nosed one. A Lionel remote-control airplane flies overhead. Opposite: One way that Lionel kept its competitive edge was through skillful promotion. In this 1932 catalogue, real railroad engineers endorse Lionel's line of products.

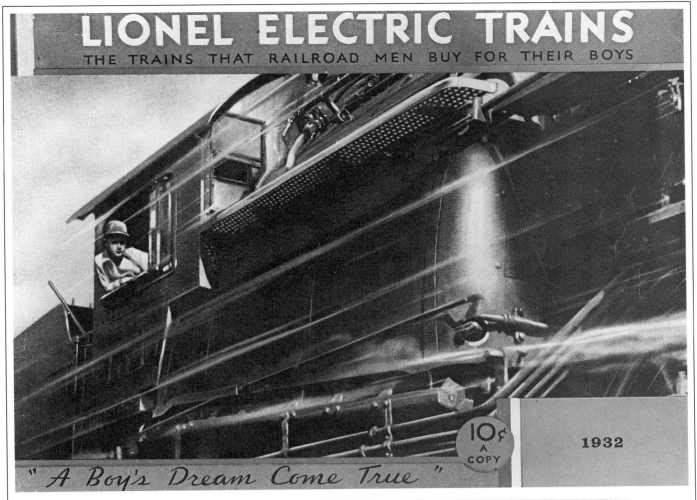

LIONEL ELECTRIC TRAINS
THE TRAINS THAT RAILROAD MEN BUY FOR THEIR BOYS

10¢ A COPY

1932

"A Boy's Dream Come True"

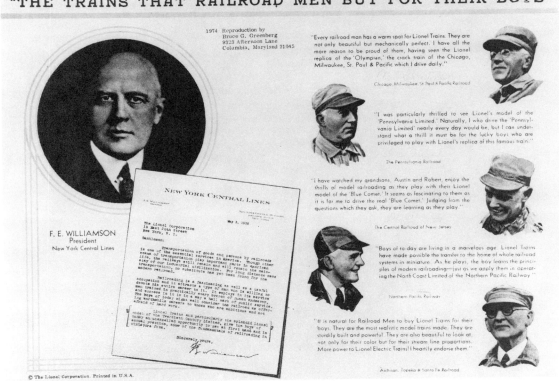

"THE TRAINS THAT RAILROAD MEN BUY FOR THEIR BOYS"

A passenger car had to be wide enough (from side to side) to fit on the track, but short enough (from end to end) to get around the tight curve. This made for a short, fat passenger car with fewer doors and windows than its prototype.

Lionel's O-27-gauge trains were made to fit a smaller track radius than other O-gauge trains. But they were still short and thick enough to look like toys. The real change came in Germany. There, in 1935, Märklin sowed the seeds of yet another revolution when it introduced a new gauge—one now known to us as HO (for "half-O"). At 16.5 millimeters, this track gauge was roughly half as wide as O gauge. This meant that trains could be built much smaller, and would be better able to negotiate tight curves. The individual cars could become longer in proportion to their width—long enough to reproduce the actual proportions of prototype cars.

Opposite, top: Some Lionel locomotives in the 1930s featured sound effects, such as a remote-control steam whistle. Opposite, bottom: Lionel catalogue covers of the 1930s were masterpieces of advertising art. The tools and slide rule in the lower left add a sense of scale. Above: This complex layout representing the New York metropolitan region in the 1930s is presented every Christmas season at New York's Citicorp Center. The layout, designed by Clarke Dunham (lower right), showcases American Flyer, Lionel, and HO-scale trains.

Märklin's leap forward was to build the "HO" cars true to scale. The trains followed a scale of 1:87.1 (that is, they were about ⅟₈₇ the size of the prototype). The windows of model passenger cars were spaced in proportion to the spacing of windows in the prototype; the height of a locomotive's smokestack was in correct proportion to the length of its boiler. These trains were not toys but accurate *scale models*. They soon became a success across Europe, and caused the American toy train makers to take note.

In the late 1930s the American companies introduced their own versions of HO-scale, but the outbreak of World War II put a temporary end to further development. After the war, a booming American economy renewed the public's interest in large trains, and Lionel and American Flyer felt no need to resume their experiments with smaller ones. Märklin, on the other hand, continued to concentrate its efforts on HO—and its efforts paid off. By the mid-1950s, O-gauge trains were getting harder to sell, but HO scale had caught the imagination of customers in both America and Europe. Miniature trains were no longer simply toys for children. They had become the cornerstone of a growing, immensely satisfying pastime—model railroading.

THE GROWTH OF MODEL RAILROADING

As a new kind of realism became possible, hobbyists became interested in evoking an entire world. They carefully studied prototype railroads and strove to re-create track plans, equipment, scenery, and structures. Railroading became a combination of authenticity and imagination, of technical skill and creativity, of attention to detail and to overall effect.

Märklin led the field in providing supplies for the new hobby. At first, German and Japanese manufacturers dominated the American market. In time, American manufacturers joined the bandwagon. Some eventually built large businesses—Atlas, Bachmann, Con-Cor, Walthers. Many others remain small, specializing in one aspect or another—detail parts, supplies for scratchbuilding, miniature people.

New scales were introduced. N scale, about half the size of HO, was introduced to the United States in the early 1960s and quickly gained a large following; today it is second only to HO in popularity. The tiny Z scale, introduced by Märklin in 1972, took miniaturization even further. On the other end of the spectrum, G scale was introduced in 1970 by the West German firm of LGB—with the "G" standing for the gardens where these trains were meant to run.

Toy trains fell in popularity as model trains rose. American Flyer and Marx stopped production; Lionel was sold and resold. Some trains continued to be built to fit the width of track for which Lionel was famous (O gauge) and the smaller width associated with American Flyer (S gauge). But these trains were scale models rather than toys. They were called "O scale" and "S scale" respectively to distinguish them from "O-gauge" and "S-gauge" toys.

In 1986, however, Lionel Trains emerged again as a privately-held corporation enjoying record sales in the "tinplate"-style railways it had helped to pioneer. Reproductions of the O-gauge Lionel and S-gauge American Flyer trains again became part of the model railroading scene.

Other changes happened in the 1980s. Microelectronics and computer software increased the modeler's control over a railroad. Miniature video equipment made it possible to "see" a layout from the engineer's point of view—watching from the locomotive as the train chugs through tunnels and around mountains. Yet for those uninterested in high-tech changes, the basic hobby remains what it has been for decades. Get a locomotive and some cars, lay some track, build some scenery, and watch the train go.

It is often said but worth repeating: model railroading is a hobby that is as simple or complex as you make it. If you are just beginning, it is best to keep it simple. But as you progress, don't be afraid to experiment. Finally, bear this in mind: model railroading can be an art form and a way of life, but fundamentally it is play. Enjoy.

CHAPTER ONE
The Trains

The new model railroader who visits a hobby store or thumbs through a sales catalogue faces one basic problem: an embarrassment of riches. The problem is nowhere more pronounced than in selecting locomotives and *rolling stock* (the cars a locomotive pulls). You thought all you wanted was a simple freight train. But do you want HO or N? Plastic or brass? Kits or ready-to-run? Steam or diesel? Hoppers or tank cars? Southern Pacific or New York Central?

A little knowledge can help you make sense of the enormous diversity in the model train market. As you read this chapter, consider your own needs and desires. How much time, space, and money do you want to invest? Do you want to try out new skills or exercise proven ones? What is the "look" you want for your railroad? Select the trains that best fit your needs—not those of modelers you've read about in magazines.

Right: Ray Tustin at work on his O-gauge outdoor layout in Leicester, England. **Below**: The stuff great models are made of: a prototype Norfolk & Western 4-8-4 streamliner. Photographs like this one, available from Rail Photos Unlimited, are used by modelers to achieve realism on their layouts.

SCALE

The first important decision you face in buying trains is scale. Scale is the ratio of the model to the original (the "real" train which modelers refer to as the *prototype*). This ratio determines the size of your trains and therefore affects the size of the whole layout. Scale also affects how visible your trains are, how realistic your layout will look in a limited space, and how easy or hard it is to get new items.

Today's model trains come in many different scales. From small to large, the most popular ones are Z, N, HO, S, O, and G. (There is actually considerable confusion in the marketplace about what G scale is. See the sidebar on "Large Scale Trains" for details.) The following mnemonic may help the novice remember the order of sizes: "**Z**achary **N**eeds **HO**bbies **S**o **O**rder **G**adgets." Female railroaders can substitute "**Z**enobia" for "**Z**achary."

The most popular scale, HO, is about 1/87 prototype size—a 1:87.1 ratio. Thus a typical boxcar in HO, representing a 40-foot prototype, is 5½ inches long. In a larger scale, O, the same boxcar would be about 10 inches

long, and in Z scale it would be a little over 2 inches.

There are larger scales still—the so-called "live steam" scales that are steam-powered (or gasoline-powered) and are big enough for people to ride. The most popular of these scales are called ¾ inch, 1 inch, and 1½ inch scale. These names refer to the fact that a 1 inch scale train, for example, follows a scale of 1 inch to the foot of the prototype—that is, the model is only 1/12 as big as the original. "Live steam" is a fascinating hobby, but it is outside the scope of this book. For more information see *Live Steam*, a magazine for steam engine enthusiasts, which includes information on historic trains and on how to set up working scale models.

Clearly, scale affects how much space is needed for a basic layout. A basic HO layout fits neatly on a 4 × 8 foot tabletop, but you need at least 5 × 9 feet for an O-scale layout, and perhaps 8 × 16 feet for a G-scale layout.

Before examining the differences between the scales, one important distinction should be mastered: the difference between scale and gauge.

Above: The tiny Z-scale diesel locomotive is dwarfed by the HO-scale boxcar behind it—the result of mismatching different scales. Both items are offered by Kadee's® Micro-Trains® Line.

Opposite, top: A prototype diesel locomotive of the Louisville & Nashville line. **Top:** Another prototype diesel— an SD40-2 locomotive run by the Soo Line. **Bottom:** The Royal Blue, a G-scale passenger train set from Bachmann. This train provided first class service between New York and Washington at the turn of the century.

Above: The Gold Rush Special™ train set from Lionel. This Large Scale™ (i.e., G-scale) set comes with an engineer figure and track sections that form the simplest and oldest layout—the circle.

SCALE AND GAUGE

Although you will often hear the two terms used interchangeably, "scale" and "gauge" are not the same thing. *Scale* is the proportion of a model train to the original. *Gauge* is simply the width of the track measured as the distance between track rails. A given size train belongs on a particular gauge of track. A wider or narrower gauge will not be able to accommodate the train's wheels (unless the *wheelset*—the way the wheel and axle assemblies are mounted—is modified or replaced).

Each of the scales is usually assigned to a particular gauge. The smaller the train, the narrower the tracks on which it rides. Thus HO-scale trains use a track gauge of 16.5 millimeters. The larger O-scale trains use a gauge of 31.8 millimeters. Each of these scale-gauge combinations is meant to represent roughly the same prototype gauge—4 feet 8½ inches, now standard in North America and much of Western Europe. See the sidebar "Summary of Scales" for a chart of standard scale-gauge combinations.

Actual prototype gauges have varied widely: 5½ feet in countries like Spain, Argentina, and India; 1 meter (39.4 inches) in many other parts of the world. Even in the United States, some railroads have been much narrower than 4 feet 8½ inches: only 3 feet, for example, in the Rocky Mountains.

To represent these *narrow gauges*, modelers sometimes put a train (for example, one

that is HO scale) on a gauge of track that is smaller than normal (in this case, N). The train then appears a little too big for the tracks underneath. But as long as the wheels are correctly arranged to fit the rails, the train is an accurate model of a narrow-gauge railroad. Such combinations of larger scales with smaller gauges are discussed further on in this chapter under "Narrow Gauge."

As if the relation between scale and gauge is not confusing enough, one further distinction must be added. Scale and gauge refer not only to types of measurements, but to types of *trains*. A *scale* or "model" train is a realistic rendering of a prototype, following a particular ratio of small to large. A *gauge* or "toy" train is stylized and does not reproduce any prototype accurately. Generally, model railroaders do not concern themselves with toy trains, and toy train collectors are not interested in scale trains. But both kinds of trains continue to be manufactured and sold.

What follow are notes to help you decide which scale is for you. Bear in mind that your decision need not be forever. You can collect trains in as many scales as you want, and build as many layouts as you have room for. At some point you may trade in most of your collection for another scale. Such trades happen every year at hobby shops, at conventions, and through classified ads in model railroad magazines.

SUMMARY OF SCALES

Name of Scale	Proportion to the Prototype	Gauge
O	1:48	31.8 mm (1.25″)
S	1:64	22.2 mm (.875″)
HO	1:87.1	16.5 mm (.649″)
N	1:160	8.97 mm (.353″)
Z	1:220	6.52 mm (.257″)

LARGE SCALE TRAINS

One of the peskiest problems in model railroad terminology comes with the large scales that are usually referred to as "G" or "#1" scale. All of these scales are built to run on 45 millimeter gauge track (#1 gauge), but they do *not* follow the same ratio to their prototypes. In other words, some are smaller or larger compared to the trains they represent, but all fit on the same track. Many of them do so by representing *narrow gauge* prototypes—trains that ride on tracks narrower than is standard in the United States.

There are at least three distinct large scales. From largest to smallest, they are ½-inch, G, and ⅜-inch (also called #1 scale). Here is a comparison:

Name of Scale	Proportion to the Prototype	Scale to Foot (what fraction of an inch represents a foot)
½ inch	1:24	½″
G scale	1:22.6	¹⁷/₃₂″
⅜ inch (#1)	1:32	⅜″

The trains made by LGB are G scale; the trains made by Kalamazoo are ½" scale. The trains made by Con-Cor are off this chart entirely, with a proportion of 1:29.

As you can see, the issue of how to define "G scale" or "large scale" is a thorny one. The only consolation is that most of the makers of these scales have the wisdom to keep their trains compatible. Thus you can link cars from different companies together—even if the scales are slightly different.

Left: Kadee® boxcars in five different scales give an idea of the range of model train sizes. From left to right, the scales represented are O, S, HO, N, and Z.

Right: A brass HO-scale tank car from Pecos River Brass. Note the fine realism of the detail work. Below: This train set in Lionel Large Scale™, the Thunder Mountain Express™, is more stylized and playful than the train above. Passenger silhouettes in the windows are illuminated by interior lights.

Larger Scales (½ inch, G, #1, O, S). The size of large-scale trains is their chief attraction and their chief limitation. The trains are easily visible, with all the detail parts writ large. They are big enough to have some of a "real" train's imposing weight and presence as they clatter over the rails. However, a realistic layout in G or O requires more space and larger *track radii* (a measurement of track curves) than many home-based modelers can offer. The cars will look too big and the trains too short if you try to run a few cars in a small space.

You can find space for a G-scale train if you run it in a garden or yard. Sunlight and natural surroundings can enhance the railroad's realism, but also add wear and tear: if you are going to run the train outside, get weather-resistant models such as those offered by LGB. Manufacturers of G- or

#1-scale trains include Bachmann, Con-Cor, Delton, Kalamazoo, Lionel, and Model Die Casting.

O- and S-scale trains need to be distinguished from their cousins, O- and S-gauge trains. As explained earlier, "gauge" trains are toy trains, following the tradition of the big, stylized trains that reigned in the United States until the mid-1950s. Lionel predominated in O-gauge trains, while American Flyer became famous for S gauge. These are the trains that the original baby-boom children remember finding under Christmas trees. Lionel still produces reproductions and extensions of its own line and American Flyer's.

O-scale and O-gauge trains both use what is called O-gauge track. But *O-scale* trains are as precise and realistic in detail as any other scale model trains. They are em-

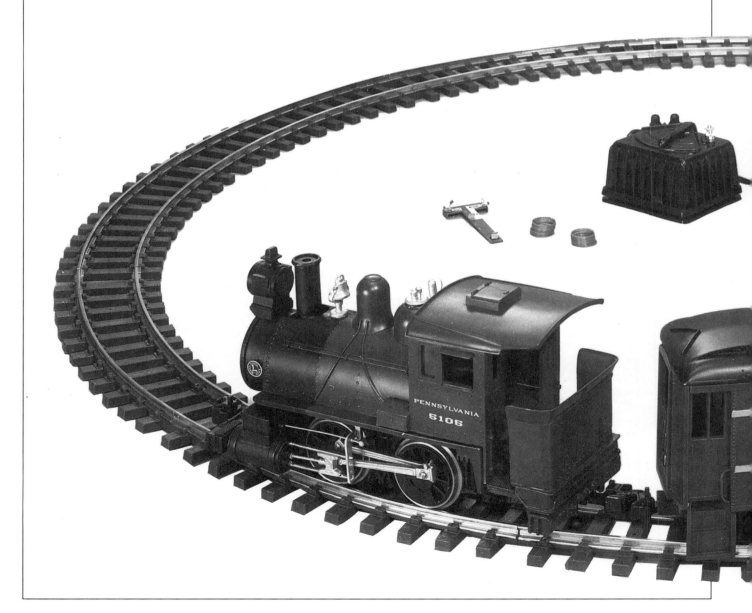

phatically *not* toylike. Many large train manufacturers offer locomotives and/or cars in O scale (e.g., Atlas, Bachmann, Con-Cor, International Hobby Corp., Life-Like, Märklin, Walthers). Other O-scale producers include Mac Shops, MTS Imports, Pecos River Brass, Right-of-Way Industries, Trackside Specialties, W & R Enterprises, and Ye Olde Huff N Puff.

Similarly, *S-scale* trains (precise models) are not the same as S-gauge trains (stylized toys). Companies specializing in S scale include American Models, Pacific Rail Shops, Quality Craft Models, Rex "S" Gauge Models, and Triangle Scale Models.

Even if you buy scale model trains instead of toys, you will find that children react favorably to the large size. A G-scale or O-scale train is easy for little hands to handle and more likely than HO- and N-scale trains to withstand rough play. Partly because of this, O scale maintains a loyal following of nearly

5 percent of model railroaders. G-scale modelers are a much smaller segment, but large enough to have attracted a number of companies to the field and growing fast. S scale is holding its own as a middle road between HO and O, though supplies remain relatively scarce (that very fact makes the scale attractive to scratchbuilders).

One note: Lionel's O-gauge toy trains require special track and wiring—an AC three-rail set-up instead of the DC two-rail set-up required for most scale trains. Reproductions of the S-gauge American Flyer trains run on direct current, but require "hirail track." See Chapter Two for more details on track requirements.

HO. By far the most popular scale, HO is preferred by about 75 percent of American model railroaders. It is not hard to see why: for most modelers, the scale is the perfect compromise between visibility of train detail and conservation of space. A modest HO layout fits on a standard 4 × 8 foot sheet of plywood, but can be detailed enough to please even nearsighted observers.

More train products are available in HO than in any other scale—from ready-to-run cars to kits to detail parts, from trains and track to scenery, structures, and figures. Many train manufacturers (Athearn, Bowser, Life-Like, Mantua, Tyco, and others) concentrate their efforts in HO; so do many of the small companies specializing in detail parts or accessories. Foreign manufacturers such as Faller, Kibri, Märklin, Rivarossi, and Roco also have a wealth of products available in HO. In short, there is plenty to keep the HO modeler, at whatever level of skill, busy for a lifetime.

On the other hand, some people find HO too small or too big. Some want to see more detail without having to bend close; others want to run more trains in a limited space. Those who see modeling as first and foremost a family hobby may find that their children under seven prefer playing with bigger trains. Whatever your devotion to HO, be ready to consider the merits of the other scales as well.

One note about Märklin's HO-scale trains: some run on a three-rail AC-powered track system rather than the two-rail DC-powered track system used by other HO-scale manufacturers. (The third rail is actually a line of stud contacts between the two rails.) This means that Märklin's AC-powered trains cannot run on the same track as your other HO-scale trains. However, the trains are high quality and represent some foreign prototypes that are otherwise hard to find. Märklin's trains in other scales (Z and #1) do run on two-rail DC power.

Opposite, top: A limited edition Z-scale train from Märklin. Representing the California Zephyr passenger line of the late 1940s/early 1950s, it includes an F7 diesel, "vista dome" car, and baggage car. Left: An O-scale GA-65 covered hopper from Pecos River Brass, with square hatches on the roof and Santa Fe markings. The prototype GA-65 first appeared in 1946.

Smaller Scales (N and Z). N scale has gained rapidly in popularity over the thirty years since it was introduced in the United States, and is now second only to HO. Favored by some 20 percent of model railroaders, N-scale trains are a little more than half the size of HO. The details of individual cars are harder to discern, but longer trains can be run in a limited space, and more trains and more scenery can be displayed.

Because of their small size, most N-scale trains come ready-to-run rather than in kits. N modelers who enjoy kitbuilding or scratch-building concentrate on scenery and structures. Fewer items are available in N than in HO, but the number of companies offering N scale is growing. Some companies, such as TJ Models and V-line Locomotives, specialize in N. Companies such as Atlas, Bachmann, Con-Cor, Kadee, Märklin, and Roco also carry N.

Z is the smallest scale—too small for many modelers; a practical choice for others. A Z-scale car is no longer than an adult's thumb; unless you get up close, details are hard to make out. But the details are all the more impressive for that reason: precise, almost microscopic, crafted by machine. An entire layout fits in a briefcase, making it a worthwhile option for modelers who travel.

Very few kits are available in Z, and most models are still based on European rather than American prototypes—reflecting the scale's European origin. (Z was created by—and is still mainly produced by—the German company Märklin.) That is changing as the American market for the scale grows; Kadee, along with Märklin, now offers Z-scale trains in American prototypes. If you have serious space limitations, if you love precision instruments, or if you simply want the latest in miniaturization, consider Z scale.

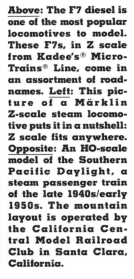

Above: The F7 diesel is one of the most popular locomotives to model. These F7s, in Z scale from Kadee's® Micro-Trains® Line, come in an assortment of roadnames. Left: This picture of a Märklin Z-scale steam locomotive puts it in a nutshell: Z scale fits anywhere. Opposite: An HO-scale model of the Southern Pacific Daylight, a steam passenger train of the late 1940s/early 1950s. The mountain layout is operated by the California Central Model Railroad Club in Santa Clara, California.

Narrow Gauge. An alternative solution to the problem of space is *narrow gauge* (already alluded to in the section on "Scale and Gauge"). Narrow-gauge prototype track, laid since the 1800s, measured as little as 2 feet in Maine and Massachusetts and 3 feet in the Rocky Mountains and Pennsylvania. Trains built for narrow-gauge track were generally smaller in size and in number of cars. Hence, an HO-scale model of a 3-foot-gauge prototype train is smaller and runs on narrower track than HO-scale, standard-gauge trains. The resulting combination of scale and gauge is called HOn3. The "n"

refers to "narrow gauge," the "3" to the 3-foot width of the prototype track. If a 3-foot-gauge prototype is modeled in S scale, the combination is Sn3; if a 2-foot prototype is modeled in O it is On2; and so on. The most popular narrow gauges are Nn3.5, HOn3, Sn3, Sn3½, and On3.

Narrow-gauge railroading has become popular because you can fit bigger cars into a smaller space while still being true to prototype—and because the often mountainous settings of most narrow-gauge prototypes provide a dramatic subject for a layout. More and more locomotives and cars

Below: This S-gauge American Flyer® passenger train set (produced by Lionel) represents the #7 Chesapeake and Ohio, which ran from Chicago to Virginia. The prototype train was double-headed—that is, powered by two locomotives joined back to back. In the model below, only one of the two PA-1 diesel locomotives is powered. Opposite, top: A narrow-gauge caboose in Nn3 scale from Kadee's® Micro-Trains® Line. Opposite, bottom: An example of traction modeling (the modeling of electrically-powered prototypes) from MTS Imports: a brass HO-scale New York BMT "D-type" articulated subway car.

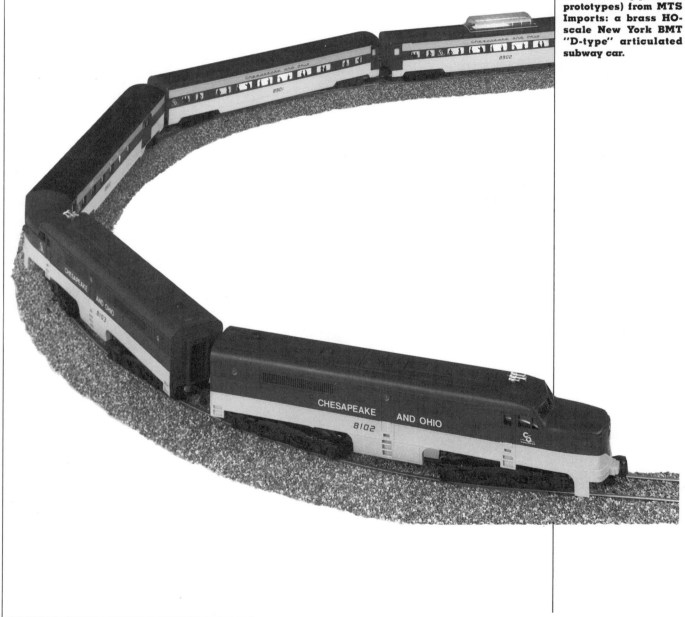

are becoming available in narrow gauge, particularly in Sn3 and HOn3. If you've mastered flat layouts and are interested in trying a mountainous one, narrow gauge may be the best way to do it.

PBL specializes in Sn3. Other companies offering narrow-gauge trains include Funaro & Camerlengo, LaBelle Woodworking Co., Master Creations, Precision Scale Co., S & C Enterprises, V & T, and Ye Olde Huff N Puff.

Cost Considerations: Scale. Generally, the bigger the train, the more expensive it is—since more material is required to pro-

duce it. But a scale's popularity is also a factor. The large market for HO, N, and O scales makes it easy to find a wide range of products at affordable prices in these scales. Most Z-scale trains are imports and require sophisticated manufacturing; hence they tend to be more expensive than their size would suggest.

On the other hand, if your taste runs to the very large (G) or very small (Z), don't settle for a scale you like less. You may not be able to afford as large a collection, but you will have exactly the kinds of trains you want.

Above: An HO-scale Chicago Rapid Transit articulated elevated car. **Opposite:** An HO-scale Philadelphia Suburban Transit interurban. **Below:** An HO-scale IRT R-29 series New York subway train. All models are brass from MTS Imports.

Above: The Prairie Flyer, a G-scale train set from Bachmann. The 2-4-2 steam locomotive comes with smoke and speed-synchronized sound. Below: Lionel's Amtrak Passenger set in O gauge is 9 feet long from the front coupler of the GG-1 locomotive to the rear end of the observation car. The construction is all metal; the car bodies are aluminum. The pantographs, or hinged frames, on the roof of the locomotive can be wired to operate with an overhead power source.

TRAIN SETS VS. SINGLE PIECES

The easiest way—though not the only way—for a modeler to get started is to buy a train set. A typical "starter" set includes at least one locomotive, four to six cars, a snap-together oval of track, and a power pack with connections. You can have the train up and running in about two hours. It is as close to instant gratification as a model railroader can get. (A more complex set may take longer. Bachmann's "Silver Express" diesel train set contains eighty-three pieces, including a bridge and trestle kit, telephone poles, and human figures.)

The problem is that a train set is only a beginning—and it may not be the beginning you want. As you find out more about the hobby, you may decide that the set you bought does not fit in with the railroad you are building, or that the set's quality is not up to the standards you develop later. Since a set can cost five to ten times as much as a single freight car, you may be better off experimenting with a locomotive and a few simple rolling stock kits.

On the other hand, there is something to be said for learning by doing. With a train set, you can be running trains the day you bring the set home—particularly handy if you have impatient children. Finally, a train set can be a bargain if you have a good idea of the prototypes you want to model and choose the set carefully. Look for the same detail and quality—and perhaps the same manufacturer—you admire in cars sold separately.

Atlas, Bachmann, Con-Cor, International Hobby Corp., Kadee, Life-Like, Märklin, and Model Power are among the companies that offer train sets in a variety of scales. A wide range of prototypes are represented by train sets—from Con-Cor's Pennsylvania Railroad steam passenger set in G scale to Märklin's California Zephyr diesel passenger set in Z scale.

READY-TO-RUN VS. KITS

The ready-to-run locomotive or car is attractive for the same reasons a train set is. Take it out of the package, hook it up to the rest of the

train, and watch it go. Still, many people have no interest in a car if they didn't put it together themselves—from a kit, from scratch, or by kitbashing (combining two or more kits or ready-to-run models). See Chapter Three for more on scratchbuilding and kitbashing. Herewith, several things to think about in deciding whether to assemble it yourself or buy it ready-to-run.

Cost/Availability. Good-quality, ready-to-run models of popular prototypes are affordably priced, but easy-to-build kits tend to be still cheaper. (A *craftsman* or advanced kit, however, can be several times the price of a ready-to-run, since the detail and materials are of higher quality.) The real savings with kits come with prototypes that are uncommon. A hard-to-find freight car or locomotive (a loco to modelers) from a long-forgotten fallen flag (a defunct railroad line) may be prohibitively expensive in a ready-to-run model—if it is available at all. If you are willing to buy kits, your field of choices becomes far wider.

Time/Difficulty. A simple "screwdriver" kit with most parts painted, requiring only a screwdriver, glue, and a razor blade, will take you all of fifteen minutes to complete. Harder kits, with wooden parts that require sanding and fitting, will require more tools and a few hours. Craftsman kits of rolling stock can take all day or longer, depending on your skill and experience. Locomotives are even harder. If you start with simple kits, you will improve with practice. If you buy mostly ready-to-run, you won't even have to try.

Satisfaction. Most modelers agree that a kit is more satisfying than a ready-to-run. The harder the kit, the prouder you will be when you place the model on the layout. It is a model-building hobby, after all. A ready-to-run is bought and paid for, but a kit-built model has a little bit of you in it.

Quality. Intermediate and craftsman kits tend to have higher-quality parts and materials than the average ready-to-run car. If properly assembled and painted, your kit-

built models may be the best ones on the railroad.

The number of companies offering ready-to-run locomotives and rolling stock is legion. Besides the companies named in the discussion of train sets, it includes American Models, Brawa, Finestkind MDL's, Kato, Mantua, Rivarossi, and Roco.

Athearn's name is often associated with easy-to-build kits that are of consistently high quality. Other companies producing easy-to-build kits include Details West, Eastern Car Works, Model Die Casting, Pacific Rail Shops, and Walthers. LaBelle Woodworking Co. has been a highly regarded maker of all-wood craftsman kits since 1952. Other producers of wood craftsman kits are Gloor Craft, John Rendall Scale Models, and Ye Olde Huff N Puff. Craft kits in metal and/or plastic are offered by many companies, including Bowser, Cannonball Car Shops, Funaro & Camerlengo, Master Creations, Model Die Casting, Peco, Tichy Train Group, Tiger Valley Models, and Wabash Valley.

Below, top: Lionel's 027-gauge Cannonball Express™ train set includes a 2-4-0 steam locomotive with chugging sound effects, a flatcar, a boxcar, an open-top hopper, and a caboose. Road signs, telephone poles, and an extension bridge are also included. **Below, bottom:** Another 027-gauge train set from Lionel. The Freight Flyer™ includes a Conrail boxcar and a gondola with removable canisters.

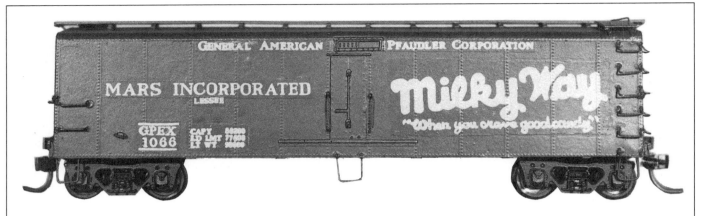

GENERAL AMERICAN — PFAUDLER CORPORATION

MARS INCORPORATED
LESSEE

milky Way
"When you crave good candy"

GPEX
1066

Racine

WAGON & CARRIAGE CO

RACINE, WIS

Above: A finely-detailed HO-scale model of a GPEX 40-foot steel milk car, from Funaro & Camerlengo. Below: An HO-scale boxcar from LaBelle Woodworking Co. The realistic appearance of this car shows what is possible with a top-notch craftsman kit.

QUALITY AND COST

The following factors all affect the price of your locomotives and rolling stock—and may or may not affect the quality. It is up to you to decide which factors are important—depending on your tastes and how much you want to spend.

Details. The better the model, the more authentic and complete its details will be. Different companies may model the exact same prototype (A GE U30C diesel locomotive, for example), but some companies will be more accurate than others. In designing models, these companies will carefully research original plans and photos of the prototype. Proportions will be exactly to scale; the paint job and lettering will be accurately rendered. The numerous *detail parts* will be reproduced with care. (*Detail parts* are the small parts—such as handrails, steps, and lights—that are attached to a model to make it more true-to-life.)

Naturally, more detailed models tend to be more expensive. But bear in mind that even an inexpensive, relatively plain locomotive

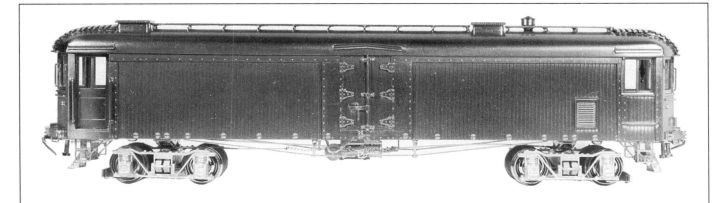

or car can be given a new life through the use of detail parts bought separately (valve gear, break wheels, etc.). These parts can be attached to a model with glue, solder, or screws, making a "superdetailed" train out of a simple one. A new paint job and decals can also improve an unsatisfactory model. (See Chapter Three for more information.)

Some trains are designed to be worked on. NorthWest Short Line, for example, offers a "Spartan Series" of locomotives in On3 scale that conform to the basic lines of narrow gauge trains without being specific about details. You add the detail parts yourself, allowing the locomotive to represent any of a number of prototypes.

Materials. In an age when everything from watches to tableware is disposable, plastic often means low quality. This is simply not the case in model railroading. Most model trains are plastic (usually injection-molded styrene), even those of extremely high quality. What matters is the level of detail in the molds used to make the trains and the workmanship in assembling parts.

Rolling stock is usually all plastic, but

Above: An HO-scale brass model of a mechanical reefer, from MTS Imports. The prototype car first appeared on the Chicago North Shore & Milwaukee line in 1926.

many locomotives, such as Atlas' and Athearn's, have metal main frames with plastic bodies. Craftsman kits are often made of wood, with metal or plastic detail parts. Wood, of course, was the material used in most actual rolling stock until well into this century, and may therefore seem more "true to prototype" than plastic. But once a freight car is painted and *weathered* (that is, once it has been treated with washes and other techniques to simulate the effects of weather), plastic may be just as realistic as wood.

Metal is generally more expensive than plastic and is often considered a "prototypically correct" material (that is, true to the original) for modeling locomotives and modern rolling stock. In fact, however, model trains rarely use the metals that their prototypes were made of. Master Creations and Tiger Valley Models use a zinc-cadmium alloy (easy to drill) in their locomotive kits. Bowser uses lead, zinc, and brass. Mac Shops uses aluminum to represent the stainless steel Budd passenger cars of the 1940s and 1950s.

Brass is the metal of choice for most of the highly detailed, investment-quality trains imported from Japan and South Korea. These cars and locomotives may each cost hundreds of dollars; for the money, you receive a showpiece for your collection that may increase in value (see the section on "Limited Editions" in Chapter Six). If you are looking for a model of a certain hard-to-find prototype you may only be able to find it in brass—such as the New York IRT subway cars and Chicago elevated cars marketed by MTS Imports. Other brass manufacturers or importers include Pecos River Brass, along with Model Power, NorthWest Short Line, PBL, Precision Scale Co., S & C Enterprises, Trackside Specialties, and W & R Enterprises.

An alternative to standard materials is the ultra-thin resin used in Westerfield's Golden Age Line. The level of authentic detail in Westerfield's kits is comparable to brass; a wide range of prototypes are available; and the kits are about one fourth the price of brass (though more expensive than most craftsman kits).

Below: An N-scale model of a 40-foot Southern Pacific boxcar from Kadee's® Micro-Trains® Line. Opposite, top to bottom: 1) A piggyback flatcar—a flatcar carrying a highway trailer—in N scale from Kadee's® Micro-Trains® Line. 2) From Funaro & Camerlengo, an HO-scale 40-foot auto car. 3) Also from Funaro & Camerlengo, an HO-scale GPEX 40-foot wood milk car with Borden's lettering. Compare to the steel milk car on page 48.

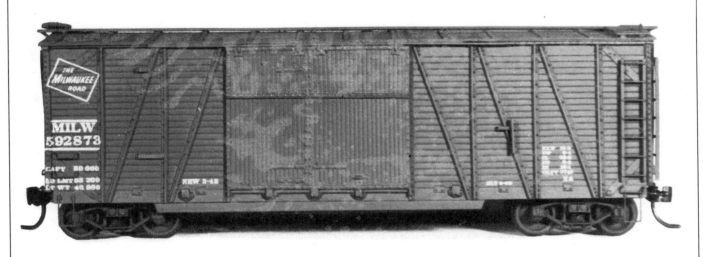

Below: A Lionel Classics replica of a 1930 Lionel Standard Gauge freight train. Special features include an operating headlight and whistle and an operating searchlight car.

Special Features. There are some features that are virtually standard on most trains; others are less common and will cost you more. Operating headlights are now commonplace on locomotives; this simply means that the headlights turn on. In addition, many locomotives have *directional* or *reversing* headlights. This refers to the fact that, in the real world, many diesel and some steam engines have been "double-ended," with a headlight on either end so that the locomotive can run in either direction. With a reversing headlight, one headlight goes on when you run your model locomotive in one direction, the other goes on when you run it the other way. It is a handy and "prototypical" feature.

A *constant intensity* headlight means that

the headlight won't dim when the train starts or accelerates. A *flywheel drive* means that the locomotive's motor assembly contains a flywheel, a relatively heavy wheel that helps smooth the flow of power. This promotes realistic starting and stopping and helps prevent your train from stalling over "dead spots" (electrically inert places on the rail). A locomotive with all wheels powered is one in which all the wheels rotate in response to the motor. This increases a locomotive's *tractive power*—its ability to pull a long train.

All of the features above are fairly common and worth having. Some features, however, are judgment calls. Trains with *sound effects* built in are generally more expensive than other trains. These trains provide you with chugging and whistles for your steam

engine, turbo and horn sounds for your diesel. The price can be high—particularly for high quality. Bear in mind you can add sound effects to your railroad later. See the section on "Sound Effects" in Chapter Four for more details.

Whether to get a locomotive with *smoke* is a matter of taste. The smoke in these locos is produced by a vial of nontoxic "smoke fluid" (or occasionally tablets). You pour the fluid into the smokestack; an electrical heating element heats the liquid and generates "smoke." In some locos, the chuffing of the smoke is timed to match the turning of the axles. Some people love the way this looks; some don't. One drawback is that the smoke leaves a residue on the rails that can interfere with electrical pickup. As with sound effects, you can buy smoke effects separately

if you decide you want them later: companies like Seuthe and Vollmer sell "smoke generators" that can be mounted in existing locos.

You may choose to go the minimalist route and get as few features as possible. For example, "dummy" or unpowered locos are available with no motor at all; these can be used in a train with multiple locomotives (fairly common in long prototype trains). You can buy unpainted locos, or freight car kits that lack *trucks* and *couplers*. (*Trucks* are the wheeled carriages on which a piece of rolling stock rests; *couplers* are the hooks that join one car to another). Paint, trucks, and couplers can be added later. This is perhaps the best route if your main reason for the hobby is a chance to work with your hands.

Below: Lionel's 027-gauge Midnight Shift™ train set comes with cable reels for the gondola and fences for the flatcar. Opposite, top to bottom: 1) The sound effects in Lionel's O-gauge B6 switcher include an electronic "bell," a "chuff" sound, and a whistle. 2) Lionel's #44E Freight Special replicates an O-gauge classic. The headlights are reversing; the boxcar and hopper hatches open and close. 3) A Lionel O-gauge Union Pacific Dash-8 40C diesel locomotive with a flashing warning light.

CHOOSING TRAINS: SOURCES

When shopping for locomotives and rolling stock (and for any other model railroad merchandise), consult the following:

the Walthers catalogues—*The World of HO Scale, The World of N & Z Scale,* and *The World of Large Scale Trains* (published annually; comprehensive product listings and prices in each scale; available at most hobby dealers and from Walthers)

NMRA Buyer's Guide to Model Railroading (published by the NMRA [National Model Railroad Association]; complete listings of manufacturers and publishers by scale and by type of product)

For information on prototype trains—useful in selecting models and in knowing which cars are compatible with which—consult:

Model Railroader Cyclopedia (Kalmbach Publishing Co.)—Vol. 1, Steam Locomotives; Vol. 2, Diesel Locomotives

NMRA Data-Pack—information on trains and their operations; available only to NMRA members

Trains—a magazine for *railfans* (fans of prototype railroads) widely read by modelers

Creative Layout Design by John Armstrong (Kalmbach Publishing)

For general advice on the hobby of model railroading, three steps are recommended:

Join the NMRA. Their conventions and meetings, along with the array of information they offer, will be a constant source of ideas and encouragement. See Chapter Five for details.

Get a general manual on the hobby such as Robert Schleicher, *Model Railroading Handbook* (Chilton).

Order a sample copy of one of the following magazines (or pick one up at your hobby shop or magazine store), and subscribe to one or more of them:
Model Railroader
Railroad Model Craftsman
Classic Toy Trains

Below: Lionel's Large Scale™ Frontier Freight™ train set, with bright Santa Fe markings, includes an 0-4-0 steam locomotive, a flatcar with stakes, and engineer and fireman figures. Opposite, top: Lionel's 027-gauge Silver Spike™ set. Two FA-1 diesel engines pull this passenger train, which includes a combine, vista dome car, and observation car. Opposite, bottom: Lionel's O-gauge CP Rail Limited Freight set. An SD-40 diesel engine, with electronic horn and illuminated number plates, pulls a boxcar, reefer, gondola, hopper, log car, and caboose.

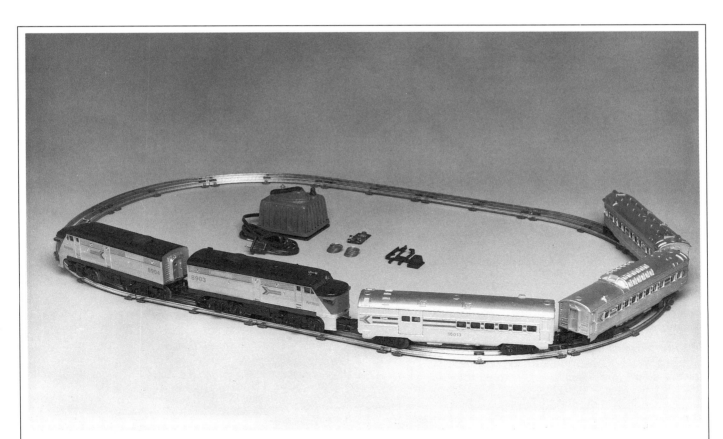

LOCOMOTIVES

When you choose a locomotive you choose a time and place. The more specific you get, the more you narrow in on a particular setting. Choosing steam as opposed to diesel will put you anywhere from the 1830s to the 1950s, but choosing a streamlined 4-6-4 Hudson puts you in Depression-era New York. Your rolling stock and accessories should be consistent with that time and place. Fortunately, many locomotives stay in use in many parts of the country for decades. If you follow the widespread practice of dating your layout in the early 1950s, when railroads were converting from steam to diesel equipment, you can combine a number of different types of equipment.

Locomotives are classified by several attributes, including **Motive Power**, **Function**, **Design Elements**, and **Official Names/ Nicknames**.

Motive Power. Three kinds of power are commonly used to drive prototype trains: steam, diesel, and electric (also called traction). Steam power lasted for more than 100 years, from the 1830s through the mid-1950s. Coal, wood, or oil, stored in a tender (a car attached to the locomotive) heated water in a boiler, which produced steam, which turned the wheels. In the 1940s and 1950s, steam locos were rapidly replaced by diesel-electric (usually called "diesel") locos. These burn diesel fuel to generate electricity to drive the motors.

Electric railroads also use electricity, but they derive it from an outside generator. The current is carried to the cars by a third rail or along an overhead wire. Since the 1890s, electric power has propelled streetcars (or trolleys), interurban trains, and even some mainline railroads. Streetcars have all but disappeared, but electric power is still used in rapid transit systems, commuter lines, and a few mainline railroads, including parts of Amtrak.

Diesels and electrics are commonly referred to by horsepower (hp). The EMD MP15, for example, is a 1500 hp diesel switcher. Another important characteristic of any loco is its maximum speed. The Big Boy 4-8-8-4 steam locomotive, for example, had a maximum speed of 80 miles per hour. Other identifying features include the shape of the forward end ("bullet-nosed," "bulldog") and the location of the cab ("cab-forward," "cab-center").

Function. Trains have served two basic functions: carrying cargo (*freight trains*) and carrying people (*passenger trains*). Some locomotives are built specifically for one function or the other, while others are "gen-

eral" or "multi" purpose. Locos have often been further specialized for mainline, branchline, or shortline service. (A *mainline* is a long-distance, heavily-used route; a *shortline* is a short-distance route; a *branchline* is a part of the railroad that branches off from the mainline to service a town or industry or connect with another line.) *Switchers* are locomotives designed primarily for yard duty—switching cars from one track to another.

On this page and opposite are various classic trains, displayed on aluminum shelves designed and offered by Rail Rax. **Opposite:** An EMD SW series diesel switcher on the top shelf; three steam locomotives with different wheel arrangements below it. <u>Left</u>: The classic Lionel trains on these shelves include (top down) bullet-nosed Union Pacific, shovel-nosed Hiawatha, and four bulldog-nosed F-series diesels.

Below: A ready-to-run Weyerhauser Tank Mallet Logger 2-6-6-2 steam locomotive from Mantua.

Design Elements. One design element that is commonly used to classify steam locomotives is *wheel arrangement*. A 4-6-2, for example, had four wheels leading, six driving, and two trailing. That means there were four small *pilot* wheels guiding the locomotive at the front, six large wheels driving the locomotive forward, and two small wheels supporting the *firebox* (the place where fuel was burned) at the back.

Simpler locos (such as a 2-6-0) had no wheels trailing. More complex ones, called *articulated locomotives*, had two separate sets of driving wheels that were joined by a pivot to help the locomotive get around curves. A 4-8-8-4 locomotive had four leading wheels and eight driving wheels on its *leading* or forward frame; eight driving wheels and four trailing wheels on its *trailing* or rear frame.

Official Name/Nickname. Diesel-electric locos are often referred to by the manufacturer's name and a model number: the EMD GP7, for example, a diesel made by the Electro-Motive Division (EMD) of General Motors in the 1950s. Other locos are best known by a nickname or by the railroad for which they were first built—e.g., the Union Pacific Big Boy of 1941.

Ready-to-run model diesel locomotives are usually cheaper than steam locos. Diesel railroads often have two or more engines working together at the head of one train for greater pulling power. Very long prototype trains (as long as 250 cars) have "multiple units" at key points throughout the train for better handling. "Dummy" or unpowered model locomotives (less expensive than powered units) can be bought to simulate multiple units on your layout.

Modeling an electric-powered trolley system or interurban has the advantage of taking up little room and allowing smaller track radii. You also get the interesting period detail that comes with modeling a streetcar or an elevated train. Some modelers even incorporate a traction layout into a larger layout depicting a steam or diesel line.

As you read more about railroading, you will discover that there were thousands of types of prototype locomotives. Some are available only in kits; some require kitbashing or have to be scratchbuilt. The locos in the sampling below are available in most scales in both kits and ready-to-run models.

Steam

- *2-6-0 Mogul—freight, post-1840s*

- *2-8-2 Mikado—freight, post-1860s*

- *4-4-2 Atlantic—passenger, late 1800s*

- *4-6-2 Pacific—passenger and express freight; designed for the Pennsylvania Railroad; first built in 1915*

- *2-8-8-2 Mallet—freight, first built 1919*

- *0-8-0 switcher—heavy duty, late 1920s and 1930s*

- *4-6-4 Hudson—passenger, high-speed; first built 1927 for the New York Central System*

- *streamliners—passenger trains of the 1930s, such as the 4-6-4 Hudson, with sheet metal shrouding the superstructure; the loco thus became "shovel-nosed" or "bullet-nosed"*

- *4-8-8-4 Union Pacific (Big Boy)—the largest steam locomotive ever built; heavy freight, articulated; first built 1941*

Left: A prototype EMD GP38-2 diesel switcher with Norfolk Southern markings.

Diesel

- *ALCO RS series (RS1, RS3, RS11)—road switchers, introduced in 1941; used for passenger service and light freight as well as yard duty*

- *EMD F series (F3, F7, F7A, F9)—streamlined cab diesels for passenger and freight use, first introduced in 1945 to replace steam locos*

- *ALCO PA1—heavy passenger service; built in 1946; very popular with railfans*

- *EMD GP series (GP7, GP9, GP38-2)—"General Purpose" switchers used for everything from yard switching to mainline freight service; introduced in 1949*

- *GE U50B, U50C—General Electric "cab-forward" diesel; built in the early 1960s; heavy freight or passenger service*

- *EMD SD45—road switcher; EMD's most popular diesel loco from 1965 to 1971*

- *EMD SD40-2—high horsepower (3000 hp) road switcher, introduced in 1972; common on American railroads throughout the 1970s and 1980s*

Electric. Steam and diesel trains are undoubtedly more popular to model than electric ones, but electric or traction modeling has its adherents. Manufacturers offering traction models include Access Models, Alpha Models, Bachmann, Berkshire Car Shop, Bowser, GHB International, LaBelle Woodworking Co., LGB, Märklin, MTS Imports, Q-Car Co., Roco, Russ Briggs Designs, Walthers, and WP Car Corp. Popular prototypes include:

- *LVT Liberty Belle Trolley—built by Jewett Car Co.; operated between Norristown and Allentown, Pennsylvania, from 1912 to 1939*

- *BMT Standard Car, New York—designed in 1913; in use until 1972*

- *Boston Elevated Railway Type 5 Trolley—popular trolley design developed in the early 1920s; similar cars used in Pennsylvania*

- *IRR Interurban Trolley—Indiana Railroad cars that operated between Louisville and Ft. Wayne, Indiana, from 1931 to 1941*

- *PCC Trolley (President's Conference Commission)—streamlined streetcar in use in Brooklyn from 1936 to 1956; also used in Boston, Philadelphia, Pittsburgh, Cleveland, Toronto, and elsewhere*

- *IRT R33 subway cars, New York—built by St. Louis Car Company in 1963–1964; assigned to service at the New York World's Fair*

- *Chicago Transit Authority (CTA)—2200 series elevated line; built by the Budd Company; first delivered 1969*

- *European-style trams—widely used in Europe; now being tested in the United States*

- *San Francisco Bay Area Rapid Transit (BART)—in service since 1972*

- *Washington, D.C., Metro—in service since 1976*

Above: Märklin's HO-scale model of the EMD F7 diesel, with the Burlington Northern roadname. One unit is powered, the other unpowered, to represent a double-headed train. Below: An HO-scale brass model of a Baldwin Westinghouse Class B-1 locomotive, with steeple cab.

ELECTRIC (TRACTION) MODELING

For further information, consult these books:
   Traction Guidebook for Model Rail-roaders (Kalmbach Publishing)
   Model Traction Handbook by Paul and Steven Mallery (Vane A. Jones Co.)

The following magazines may also be helpful:
   Traction and Trolleys Quarterly (Vanishing Traction Products)
   Traction Prototype and Models

Above: One of Märklin's most famous traction models: the Crocodile in gauge 1. This train was a heavy-duty articulated locomotive of the Swiss Federal Railroad. Märklin's Crocodiles were first presented in O and 1 gauges at the Leipzig Spring Fair in 1933.

Below: A single-dome tank car, carrying diesel fuel, in N scale from Kadee's® Micro-Trains® Line.

ROLLING STOCK

The same basic kinds of rolling stock—boxcar, gondola, coach—have persisted over the years, but their details have changed. Thirty-six foot wooden boxcars were popular in the early part of this century; 40-foot all-steel boxcars were common from the 1930s to the 1960s; more recently, 86-foot boxcars have appeared. Even within a time period, there are differences. Some steam-era wooden boxcars had vertical ribs reinforcing the sides; some had outside bracing. Some hoppers have "ribbed" sides; others have smooth "offset" sides—the outer walls bulging to increase carrying capacity. Reefers (refrigerated cars) and some boxcars have "plug" doors—large, tightfitting doors that help maintain the temperature inside.

The many varieties of rolling stock fall into three broad categories: freight cars, passenger cars, and non-revenue equipment (cars designed for maintenance or crew use). The list at right gives you an idea of what's available.

Freight Cars

- *boxcar*—box-shaped, entirely enclosed car typically used to transport packaged products, but sometimes used for bulk loading

- *gondola*—open-top car used to haul scrap metal, pipe, and other bulky commodities

- *flatcar*—a car with no sides used for carrying lumber, machinery, pipes, etc.

- *bulkhead flatcar*—a flatcar fitted with walls on the ends to prevent shifting of loads

- *hopper*—a car that unloads through doors on the bottom; used for granular or loose items; may have from one to six bays or compartments

- *open-top hopper*—a hopper open at the top; used to carry coal, sand, ore, and other commodities that don't need protection from the weather

- *covered hopper*—a hopper with a roof; used to carry sugar, flour, and other items that need protection from the weather

- *stock car ("cattle car")*—car used to carry livestock; has open, horizontal slats to allow circulation of air

- *refrigerator car ("reefer")*—insulated boxcar capable of keeping perishables cold; blocks of ice were used from the 1880s to the early 1960s; mechanical refrigeration became the norm after that

- *tank car*—a cylindrical, watertight car for transporting liquids such as milk, corn syrup, chemicals, and oil; may have one or more domes or hatches at the top

- *piggyback flatcar*—a flatcar carrying a highway trailer (which can later be hitched to a truck)

- *container car*—a flatcar carrying a standardized container or large steel box; the container can also be carried by ship or truck

- *well car*—a container car with two containers stacked one on top of the other; a depressed central section or well gives the car extra clearance when going through tunnels or over bridges

The pictures on this page give some idea of the diversity of freight cars. Top to bottom: 1) Lionel's Pennsylvania auto carrier in O gauge comes with six die-cast metal vehicles on board. 2) A 40-foot steel milk car in HO scale from Funaro & Camerlengo. 3) An open-top wood hopper, in HO scale from Funaro & Camerlengo. Note the "angle" or "zee" steel bracing on the sides. 4) A covered steel hopper, in HO scale from Funaro & Camerlengo. Note the vertical ribs reinforcing the sides.

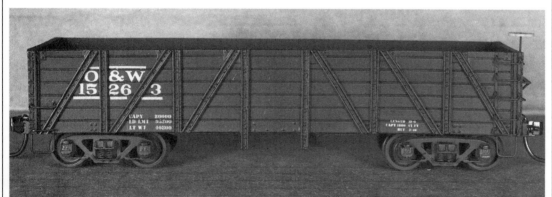

Passenger Cars

• *coach—a car with windows and seats*

• *sleeping car—a car with beds*

• *dining car—a car with a kitchen at one end and tables at the other, served by waiters*

• *cafe car—a food car with limited, quick service*

• *food-service car—a self-service food car with vending machines*

• *dome car—has a raised, glassed-in roof section for viewing the scenery*

• *baggage car—carries passengers' baggage*

• *combine—a car divided into two or more parts to fulfill different functions, such as coach and baggage*

• *bi-level commuter coach—coach with an upper gallery for commuter runs; first built by Pullman-Standard for use in the Chicago area in the 1950s*

• *Superliners—full line of passenger cars used by Amtrak on Western routes*

Non-Revenue Equipment

• *MOW ("maintenance of way")—general term for cars used by a crew repairing rail or laying new tracks; often adapted from old or obsolete rolling stock*

• *tool car—a MOW car used to store tools*

• *bunk car or camp car—a MOW car used to house personnel during major railroad projects*

• *cook's car or kitchen car—the car where food is prepared for the crew during major projects*

• *office or business car—used by company officials while on inspection tour of a line*

• *rail "detector" car—automatically records the condition of the track surface alignment or locates flaws in the rail*

• *locomotive crane—a self-powered crane, often large enough to lift locomotives*

• *snow plow—used to clear snow from tracks*

• *caboose—last car on a freight train; used as living quarters for the crew; with an elevated cupola or bay window from which workers can monitor the cars ahead*

These brass, HO-scale models from MTS Imports represent the kinds of passenger coaches most familiar to urban commuters. Above: A New York City IRT R-22 subway car. Below: A Chicago Transit Authority 2201-2350 series elevated car.

Two common types of non-revenue equipment: the caboose and the crane. <u>Right, top:</u> This brass, O-gauge B & O caboose from Right-of-Way Industries runs on three-rail track and features a Seuthe smoke generator. <u>Right, bottom:</u> A brass, HO-scale Brooklyn Rapid Transit crane car from MTS Imports.

ROADNAMES AND OTHER LETTERING

Union Pacific, New York Central, Baltimore & Ohio—the names of the famous lines are music to a railroader's ears. If you are just starting out, the music may be unfamiliar, but you will soon grow to know it. Many lines use the same equipment (GP35 diesel locos, Budd coach cars) but each has its own distinct color scheme and lettering.

Names of railroads are not the only lettering to be found on model trains. Reefers and tank cars have often carried brand names advertising products from perishables (Borden) to pickles (Heinz 57 Varieties) to gasolines (Mobil).

You don't necessarily have to get trains with your favorite roadname or brand name painted on. If the roadname you want for a particular model isn't available, just get the type of locomotive or car that is appropriate for that line. You can then paint the colors on yourself, and apply the roadname with decals or dry transfers. You may even choose to call your railroad by a made-up roadname rather than a real one—and have it custom-lettered on all your equipment. See Chapter Three for more on decals, dry transfers, and custom decal services.

Roadnames, of course, have changed over time, as have the routes traveled by the various lines. Magazines and books on the prototypes can help you keep track of which line ran where and when. To help you get started, here are some of the most prominent railroads of 1906—and what had become of them by 1986.

1906	1986
Chicago, Milwaukee & St. Paul	renamed Chicago, Milwaukee, St. Paul & Pacific Railroad
Northern Pacific	part of Burlington Northern Railroad Co.
Union Pacific	part of Union Pacific System
Denver & Rio Grande	part of Denver & Rio Grande Western Railroad
Philadelphia & Reading System Pennsylvania Railroad New York Central & Hudson River Delaware, Lackawanna & Western	part of Consolidated Rail Corp. (Conrail)
Baltimore & Ohio Chesapeake & Ohio	merged into Chessie System, which became part of CSX Corp.

Below: A coal-carrying twin-bay hopper in N scale from Kadee's® Micro-Trains® Line. The dramatic lettering makes the car stand out. **Opposite, top:** One of the most common and versatile kinds of rolling stock—a "basic" 40-foot wood boxcar. This HO-scale version from Funaro & Camerlengo features New York Ontario & Western lettering. **Opposite, middle:** The streaked logo of the Denver & Rio Grande is a popular marking. This is a narrow-gauge (Nn3) gondola from Kadee's® Micro-Trains® Line. **Opposite, bottom:** Recognize this car? It's the same GPEX 40-foot wood milk car that appears on page 51 with Borden's lettering. A fresh coat of paint and a few decals transform it into a moving billboard for Nestle's. In HO scale from Funaro & Camerlengo.

Foreign Lines. You need not restrict yourself to American prototypes. Some of the most interesting model trains are those based on foreign prototypes. Märklin makes models of German, Belgian, Dutch, and Swiss lines, along with the famous Orient Express. Roco, an Austrian company, produces models based on Austrian prototypes—and also prototypes from France, Spain, Luxembourg, and Italy.

For Anglophiles, the British company Peco offers a handsome selection of British prototype trains and publications. If you are contemplating a Canadian layout (or one set on the United States–Canada border), look at the rolling stock offered by C & S Scale Industries.

Top: The rolling stock in these two photos includes gondolas, a boxcar with brakesman's cab, and a flatcar with a swiveling cradle for fastening cargo. Middle: Märklin's digitally-controlled dance car, with five dancing couples, in HO scale. The roadname is the German Federal Railroad. Bottom: To add local color to a turn-of-the-century German layout, include this HO-scale truck from Märklin.

At the top of this page are foreign-prototype models in Z scale from Märklin. **First row:** A depressed-center flat-car loaded with an industrial transformer. **Second row:** Assorted rolling stock—a telescoping car, a boxcar, a beer car, and a tank car—with German roadnames. **Bottom:** A gondola and a boxcar bear the roadnames of German provincial railroads, in HO scale from Märklin.

TRAINS: A SELECTION

You now know the broad outlines of the model train market. But the fascination of the hobby lies in the particulars—the variety of bright, colorful, odd, and breathtaking products that look even better when they move than they do on the shelf. Here is just a selection of the most interesting products currently available. Some are limited runs and may not be available when you go shopping—but products just as fascinating will be.

● *New York Central Twentieth Century Limited passenger train—similar to the train John Barrymore and Carole Lombard rode in the 1934 movie Twentieth Century (Limited Editions, HO)*

● *World War II Pullman troop car (Precision Scale Co., O scale)*

● *narrow-gauge mine train—an electric loco with three mine cars (side-dumping hoppers) for use in mine shafts (Ye Olde Huff N Puff, HOn3)*

● *German Federal Railroad dance car—with five dancing couples and a rotating disco light; digitally controlled (Märklin, HO)*

● *Ringling Bros. 36-foot elephant car (Model Die Casting, HO)*

● *circus flatcars, ticket cars, cage cars (TJ Models, N)*

● *Civil War Train Set—your choice of Union or Confederate (Kalamazoo, collector's edition, #1)*

● *Cardinal's Train Set—a New York Central train painted Cardinal Red, specially commissioned to carry Roman Catholic cardinals from New York to Chicago for an international meeting in 1926 (Con-Cor, collector's edition, HO)*

● *Presidential Special Train Set—4-6-2 Pacific loco with working smoke unit, coaches, and caboose;*

presidential seal and flags on caboose; for "whistle stop" campaigns in the days of Teddy Roosevelt (Model Power, HO)

● *Work Train Sets—two sets of cars for your railroad's "maintenance of way" personnel; Set #1 includes a bunk car, a kitchen car, and a work flat; Set #2 includes a crane and a caboose (Walthers, HO)*

● *Heinz Reefers—series of insulated cars that ran from 1894 to about 1930; lettering on sides included slogans such as "Heinz Baked Beans—When Dinner Time Comes" (Westerfield, HO)*

● *digital sound-equipped stock cars—with cow, horse, pig, and chicken sounds (Right-of-Way Industries, O scale)*

● *BL2 diesel locomotive—a short-lived engine introduced in 1948 and soon replaced by the GP7; painted black with the yellow stripes of the Western Maryland Fast Freight Line (Life-Like Proto 2000 series, HO)*

● *searchlight car—flatcar with two working searchlights; reproduction of O gauge train from the 1920s and 1930s (Lionel, O gauge)*

● *Budd dome-buffet coach—one-piece aluminum body beautifully simulates the Budd cars of the 1940s; a whole line of similar Budd car kits available (Mac Shops, O scale)*

● *#50 diesel—narrow gauge loco used by the Denver & Rio Grande Western; orange, black, and silver lettering with diagonal "tiger stripes" (PBL, Sn3)*

● *log cars—flatcars with logs and chains; all-wood craftsman kits (John Rendall Scale Models, HO)*

● *Great Northern Empire Builder streamlined observation car—orange and green, with dome (Mantua, HO)*

● *Blatz Old Heidelberg Beer reefer—red and yellow with black lettering and three-color logo (Kadee, N)*

● *Borden's Milk tank car (Funaro & Camerlengo, HO)*

Above: Two S-gauge, American Flyer® PA1 diesel locomotives from Lionel. This locomotive has a miniature Rail Scope™ video camera mounted inside, allowing modelers to see their layouts from the engineer's point of view. **Opposite, top:** For the collector, the joy of model trains comes from obtaining rare and valuable models such as this distinctive American Flyer refrigerated car from the 1940s. **Opposite, bottom:** A self-powered track maintenance car, with crew figure, in O gauge from Lionel. The car operates by itself on a spur of track, traveling back and forth between two bumpers.

CHAPTER TWO
Getting On the Right Track

You may have had some idea of the era and the part of the country you wanted to evoke when you bought your locomotive and rolling stock. Now that you have your train, you can actually begin to create your world. In this chapter, we'll show you all the parts you need, from tracks that carry the train to tunnels through which it travels to train stations where it stops. Again, in every scale, there is much to choose from; again, the work can be as simple or as time-consuming as you wish, with everything from ready-made items to craftsman kits to scratchbuilding materials at your disposal.

TRACK PLANS

Before you buy track and accessories, you need to think about *track plans*. A track plan is simply a paper blueprint of your layout, which reflects the design as well as the measurements for the track, buildings, and scenery (see sidebar on track planning radii for details).

As you begin to consider your plan, think about how you want to feature your train. Do you want a simple oval on a table next to a Christmas tree? A super-realistic layout of a train climbing through the mountains to silver mines? Don't be discouraged if you want a complicated layout in a limited space: You can build nearly any kind of industry and town in any style of track plan.

Below: Z-scale layouts are so small that they can travel easily; here, the busy executive who hates to leave his or her layout at home has the best of both worlds with the layout in a briefcase. Bottom: In this typical model railroad layout, all created from Life-Like products, two trains circle a small town. A layout like this is a good way to introduce yourself to modeling.

There are several long-proven track plans—oval, figure 8, loop-to-loop, dogbone, folded dogbone, point-to-loop, and point-to-point. They are used because they work: they provide room for the accessories you need. Here are a few types of layouts using these familiar patterns:

• *An oval with a larger scale locomotive and boxcars is perfect for a family with small children under seven years of age. You don't need great verisimilitude; you need a train that can be appreciated by a child with an often short attention span. Here, weathering is not as important as bright color. As a young father told us, "I spent a lot of money on a complicated train set, but it was too much for my four- and five-year-olds. They couldn't get interested in it."*

• *An HO-scale layout in a railroader's basement can be the site for the fulfillment of a lifelong dream. It's a permanent fixture, to be added to as time permits. The basement provides plenty of room for the HO-scale trains and for the creation of natural features like mountains and industries like logging. Says one established modeler, "When we looked at houses, my wife had her checklist and I had mine. I wanted a railroad basement."*

• *A Z-scale model-in-a-briefcase is perfect for the*

modeler who travels but can't be away from his trains. Half of all Z modelers work on portable layouts, and an average Z-scale layout can be carried easily. The small space may not allow for an intricate track design, but it does invite the modeler to concentrate on scenery.

These are just some ideas to get you started. For additional ideas, you may be interested to know the three most popular eras for modeling:

The 1950s. This is the transition period, in which both steam and diesel motive power was used. It allows for great flexibility in locomotive and car choices—and is distant enough to seem nostalgic.

The present time. It allows, perhaps requires, constant updating of cars, which provides added interest to modelers and viewers. This period of time is especially popular with new and young modelers.

The era in which you were 12 years old. Nearly everyone's world looked better at that age.

Above: Your layout need not feature a town. It can be centered on an industry or, as in this layout, a train yard. Note the mirror beneath the freeway overpass, which gives the illusion of longer tracks. Below: A stereotypical model railroader at home.

For Better or For Worse®   by Lynn Johnston

TRACK PLANNING TEMPLATE

A *template*—a standard planning piece that serves as a stencil for where the parts of your layout will fall—is a good and practical way to start your design.

Templates come in a variety of forms. There are paper cutouts of tracks, which appear in some catalogues, such as those by the William K. Walthers Co. More substantial metal or plastic templates are sold in hobby stores. Some, like the metal templates produced by Custom Railway Supplies, in ⅛ actual HO-scale, are meant to be used with graph paper. Others, like the plastic track planning templates in HO and N by Con-Cor and CTT, and in HO by Roco and Hobby Craft Specialities, and in three-rail O scale, S, and G, by Greenberg Publishing Co., are to be used with graph paper.

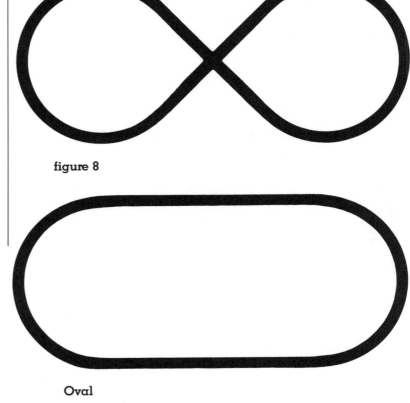

figure 8

Oval

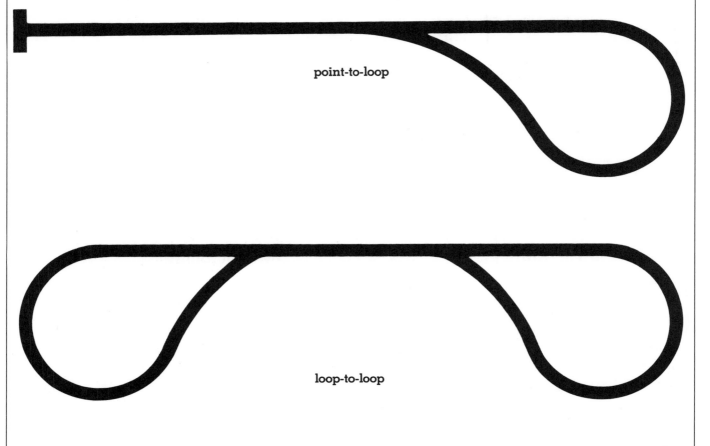

point-to-loop

loop-to-loop

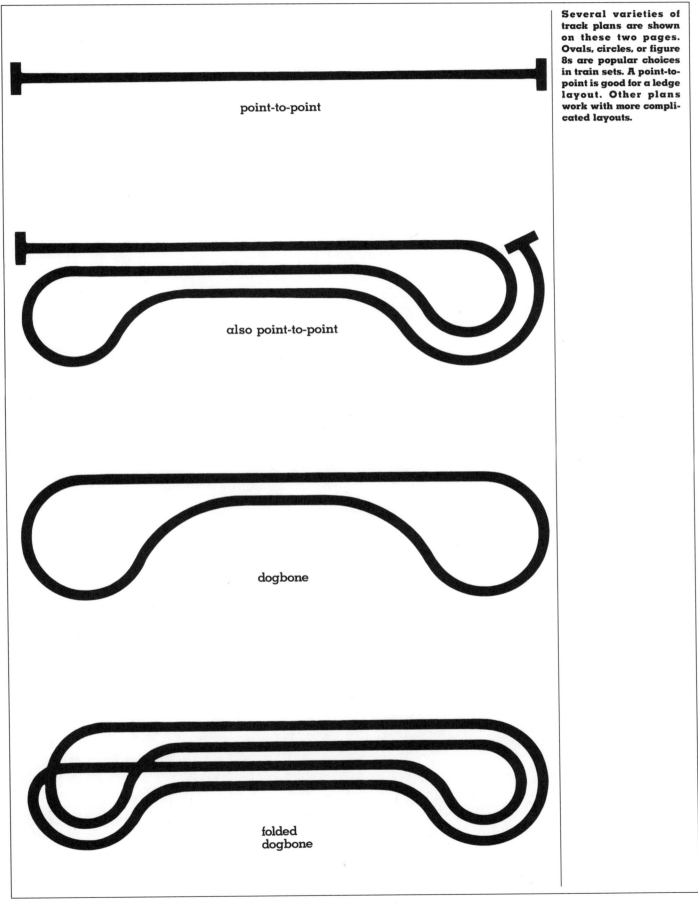

point-to-point

Several varieties of track plans are shown on these two pages. Ovals, circles, or figure 8s are popular choices in train sets. A point-to-point is good for a ledge layout. Other plans work with more complicated layouts.

also point-to-point

dogbone

folded dogbone

CITIBANK STATION: THE ULTIMATE LAYOUT

Few layouts are as complex and evocative as the pre–World War II world created in Citibank Station, at the Citicorp Center in New York for the Christmas season.

Inaugurated in 1987 and already visited by half a million people, Citibank station is a three-sided layout, each side representing a different New York scene from fifty years ago. For example, on the first side of the 1989 layout was the skyline of mid-Manhattan in the 1930s, as seen from the terminal and yards at Weehawken, New Jersey, just across the Hudson River. Passing through Weehawken were passenger trains coming from the Catskills, streetcars shuttling between Weehawken and New York, and tired trains being repaired in the train yards. In the middle section was a thriving logging town along the Hudson River Valley; its name, Generak, was invented for the layout, but the town is meant to reflect any of a number of upstate New York logging, paper, and mining communities during the 1930s. The main street was busy, with stores, a hotel, and a movie theater; trains coursed the hills and valleys; farms could be seen from afar. The final side represented a 50th anniversary celebration of the 1939 World's Fair, with the famous Trylon and Perisphere, the centerpieces for the Fair's "World of Tomorrow" theme. Local businesses and the terminal for the New York Central mainline, which came in to Grand Central Terminal, completed the scene.

Above: In this 32-foot high Victorian train depot at Citicorp Center in New York, dozens of historical model trains course across New York–area landscapes. **Right:** Citibank Station designer Clarke Dunham surveys one part of his layout—the re-creation of Weehawken, New Jersey, as it looked fifty years ago. In the background is the skyline of Manhattan, seen from the Hudson River side, as it is being approached by the trolley (center). In the foreground, the New York Central passes on its way out of the city.

This is "a world in memory," said Citibank Station designer Clarke Dunham, "Nostalgia is a primary destination." Dunham brought much experience in re-creating such worlds to his work on Citibank Station: He is a Tony-nominated Broadway set designer, whose credits include *Bubbling Brown Sugar* and *Candide*. Dunham designed and built the first Citibank Station for the 1987 Christmas season, and he has refined and rebuilt it for every holiday season since then.

One of the many distinctive features of the layout is the use of a variety of train scales and gauges to simulate perspective. Running simultaneously are fifteen different model railroads using three types of trains—Standard-gauge American Flyer, O-scale Lionel, and HO-scale trains, many of which are the streamliners of the 1930s. Other fea-tures include the use of *fast time*, in which a long period of time is compressed into a much shorter timespan. At the 1989 Citibank Station, a timed lighting system simulated the movement of an entire 24-hour period in Weehawken and New York City within five minutes.

Dunham sees trains as a "symbol of individualism." "The power of the trains," he says, "was harnessed by the little guys, like the engineer. Even now, no one remembers the name of the president of Illinois Central, but they remember that Casey Jones was the engineer." As for his own Citibank Station, he hopes people will "remember the entire experience," with perhaps a few understanding that "Citibank Station is a trip in time to a different America, one from which we have much to learn."

Below: To celebrate the fiftieth anniversary of the 1939 New York World's Fair, the 1989 Citibank Station layout for Citibank Station featured a stop at the Fair. Note the re-creation of the Fair's symbols, the Trylon and the Perisphere.

Track Planning Tips. Here are a few additional tips from professional designers and lifelong modelers:

● *Keep your first track plan flat. A multi-level system—with trains winding up and down mountains, for example—may be too complex for a first attempt.*

● *If you choose a prototype railroad and scene, don't be afraid to use modeler's license in adapting it for your layout. Almost no one models a prototype exactly. You adapt a railroad, taking into account space, aesthetics, your skills, the time you want to give to it. You may try to closely model a prototype railroad's track plan, or use a more conventional, stylized one. To do so, use selective compression and shorten a main street, a mountain range, or, if you are using lighting effects, a period of time, as was done at Citibank Station. Select the most interesting details of town's central industry—its richest mine, for example—when planning the layout. An oval design can show the pickup of ore, its loading onto cars, and its delivery to the next station.*

● *Think of a design that can grow. Even if you don't plan to expand on your layout now, you may want to do so in the future, so consider how your layout might accommodate an extra mountain range, major industry, or set of trains. As we have said, no modeler believes a layout is ever completed.*

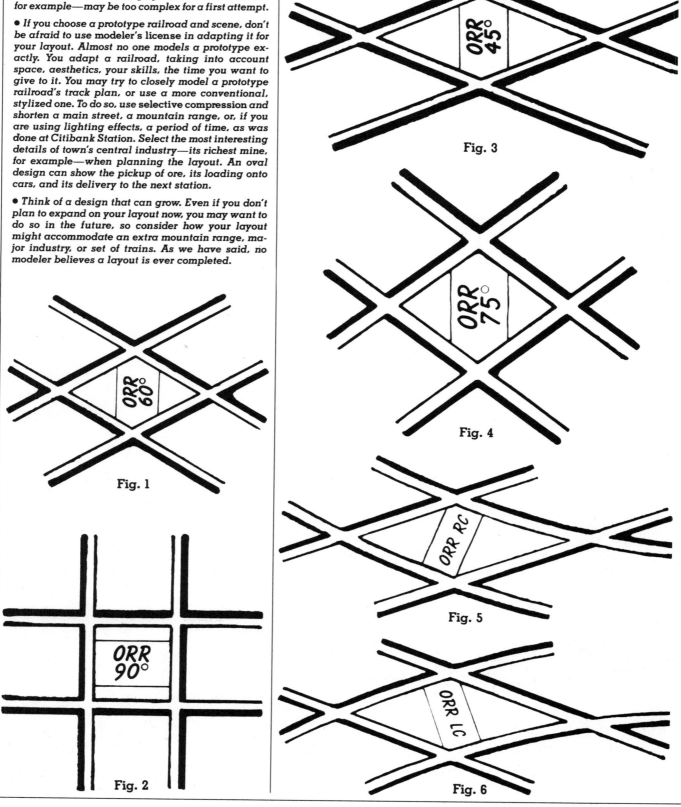

Fig. 3

Fig. 4

Fig. 5

Fig. 6

Fig. 1

Fig. 2

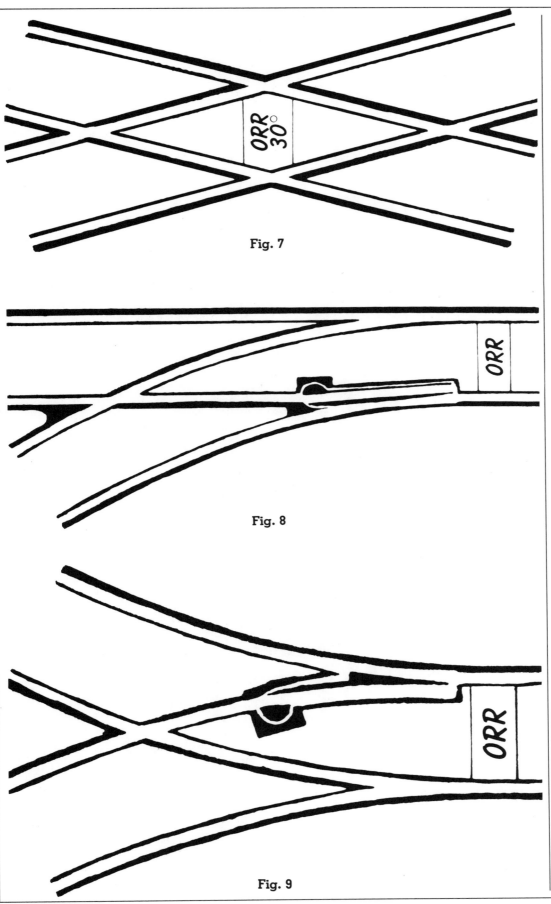

Fig. 7

Fig. 8

Fig. 9

No matter what kind of train crossings you use in your layout, you can find track switches and crossings to fit. The examples on these two pages from Richard Orr include curved track crossings (Figs. 5 and 6), straight track crossings for city streets (Figs. 1, 2, 3, 4, and 7), and single-tongue track switches for city streets (Figs. 8 and 9).

You can also be inspired by successful plans of other modelers in such magazines as *Model Railroader*, *Railroad Model Craftsman*, *Narrow Gauge and Short Line Gazette*, or the magazines devoted simply to one gauge, like *N Scale*, *Sn3 Dispatch* and *Garden Railways Magazine* (large scale). There are also several books on the subject, particularly those published by Kalmbach Books and Carstens Publications. In addition to suggesting design ideas, these books will show you how to do things like set up proportionally correct *grades*, so that your tracks slope at the same percentage as those in your prototype scene.

Books of successful track plans are also useful. Atlas produces two—*Blueprints for Atlas Snap-Track HO Layouts* and *A Clear Guide to N Gauge Fun*. There are also several from Kalmbach Publishing: *101 Track Plans for Model Railroaders*, *18 Tailor-Made Model Railroad Track Plans*, *Track Plans from Sectional Track*, *Track Planning Ideas from 'Model Railroader'*, and *N Scale Model Railroad Track Plans*. From Carstens Publications, there is *Complete Layout Plans for All Model Train Sets*. For Lionel, American Flyer, and other toy train enthusiasts, there is *Great Toy Train Layouts of America*, from TM Books, Inc. (see Chapter Five for more details).

Right: Model trains in a variety of scales and gauges cross through the Hudson Valley in this scene from Citibank Station, the annual holiday layout at Citicorp Center, New York.

BENCHWORK

The word *benchwork* refers simply to the wooden frame that supports a layout. However, this seemingly simple element is as important to the layout as the trains. In the past, benchwork may have meant the floor beneath the Christmas tree. Now it is agreed that, with the exception of outdoor garden railways, the floor or ground is a problematic site for a layout. This is because the floor generates dust and debris and causes operational complications. Train layouts function best when raised above the floor, usually on a specially-built table or a module placed upon a pre-existing table.

Materials for benchwork are relatively simple-precut sheets of plywood, soft pine, and Homasote®, a home insulation product made of recycled newspapers.

Plywood is available in several thicknesses, for various types of layouts. Both the ⅜- and 5/16-inch thick plywood are ideal for the handmade tabletop that will be supported by pine frames and legs. Whichever thickness you choose, buy wood of the highest quality possible. Above all, do not use bargain lumber; it will be green, may tend to warp with time, and have knots that can keep track from being level.

Homasote® is available in precut pieces at some hobby stores and in larger pieces at good home improvement centers.

Nails and screws should not be used for attaching the Homasote® or plywood; they work loose from the layout over time, and cause the layout to rattle. Instead, contact cement should be applied over the entire surface being mounted.

This information does not cover any of the finer points of benchwork construction. For more details, talk with fellow modelers and hobby dealers; for reference, a useful book is *How to Build Model Railroad Benchwork* (Kalmbach Books).

Below: A Santa Fe F7 diesel passes through the mountains.

Below: The gauge 1/½-scale Ogden Botanical Railway in Denver, Colorado.

TRACK

It is comforting to know that track is one of the few elements not greatly affected by the time period in which you set your layout. In some ways buying track is simple: you decide whether you want *ready-made track* or *scratchbuilding materials*, then you find the products that fit the scale or gauge in which you are working.

The only technical point you need to keep in mind before you buy track is that there are several *codes* or heights of rail. This is because prototype (or "real-life") railroads ran on different sizes of rail: Main line railroads ran on one height of rail, branch lines on another. By using a variety of model track sizes, your model railroad can simulate these differences.

Each code is identified by a number. The number represents the actual height of model rail to ⅟₁₀₀₀ of an inch. Here are some codes commonly available for the following scales:

HOn2½	Code 63	.063-inch high
HOn3	Code 70	.070-inch high
HO	Code 83	.083-inch-high
HO	Code 100	.100-inch high
O- or S-gauge hi-rail	Code 220	.220-inch high

Despite this somewhat bewildering array of types of track, your first acquaintance with track will probably be simple: It will come with your first train set. The rail with the snap-together track of most HO train sets is made of brass and is usually code 100. As you continue modeling, you will find that some modelers prefer code 83 or 70 rail because its height is closer in proportion to that of prototype American railroads. You may also learn about *transition track*, short sections which allow you to easily connect different codes (code 83 and code 100, for example) of track.

The most commonly used type of track is *ready-made track*, also known as *sectional track* because it is sold in pieces to fit your design needs. The type of track is manufactured in HO scale by a number of companies, including Atlas, Tru-Scale, and Model Power. The *ties*, which secure the rail, are usually plastic, sometimes wood; the rail is brass, nickel silver, or steel. Nickel silver track is commonly sold separately (from a train set). It is preferred by most modelers over brass because while both brass and nickel silver are alloys of copper, nickel silver provides better electrical contact. Some modelers and most scratchbuilders choose wood over plastic ties, because the prototype ties themselves are made of wood.

As mentioned, sectional track is sold in pieces. These pieces, usually straight or curved, measure from a few inches (often 9) to several feet; they attach or snap together and can be added to or moved. As a rule, sectional track is designed to expand the circle of track found with most train sets.

If you are not sure exactly what shape your track is going to take, you can keep all design possibilities open by using *flexible track*. This track is a popular choice for creating curves without buying curved track. Flexible track is often made with a pliable plastic tie strip, such as the Flex-Track made by Atlas for HO- and N-scale, and it can be integrated with ready-made straight and curved snap-together sections.

The only concern with using flexible track is maintaining proper curve radii. To make alignment easy, use an *alignment gauge*. This plastic or metal gauge fits between rails to show whether you are keeping to the correct radius of the curve. Among the companies that produce gauges are Wallace Metal Products, Rail Craft, and Precision Scale Co.

You can also *scratchbuild* your own track—that is, lay the track tie-by-tie and hand-spike the rails down. This is time-consuming and may be difficult to learn, but it allows you to achieve the ultimate in prototypical reality. To build track, you need individual ties, built to fit the gauge in which you are working. They can be purchased pre-stained from Rail Craft, among others, and are made of fir, redwood, basswood, or styrene plastic. Choose the wood or plastic that suits the look you are aiming for; all are equally easy to work with. Thrifty or industrious modelers may want to cut their own ties from strips of pine or other softwood.

After you have laid the ties, attach the tie to the rail with ebonized steel spikes. For attaching the spikes more easily, there are special tools, like the magnet tip LaBelle In-dustries Spiker and the Kadee Spiker. To fit all popular scales, the spikes are available in the following sizes: ¼-, ⁹⁄₃₂-, ⁵⁄₁₆-, ³⁄₈-, ⁷⁄₁₆-, and ½-inch. In addition to the track, scratchbuilders also need dyes, glue, needle-nose pliers, and rail, usually made of nickel silver.

Finally, to maintain the conductivity of the rail surface, *track cleaners*—liquid cleaners, abrasive blocks, and track cleaning cars—are available from Walthers and Con-Cor. Some modelers use a simple office pencil eraser to clean tracks of dirt and debris.

For more information on types and varieties of track and rail, visit your local hobby shop. See Chapter Three for more details on scratchbuilding and track.

ROADBED AND BALLAST

In prototype railroads, track is supported by a roadbed; the ties are supported and stabilized by small rocks or stones called *ballast*, which raise the level and provide drainage. Model railroaders add their own *roadbed* and ballast to simulate the prototype.

There are many types of roadbed. Textured rubber roadbed is available precut for HO, S, and O gauges from Rick Johnson and AMI, Inc. It is available in six-inch to thirty-foot sections and is beveled along the edges to approximate the slope of the roadbed around the prototype. Some of the advantages of working with this roadbed are its sturdiness and its ability to reduce noise. Rubberized cork roadbed, from Model Power, among others, comes in mottled colors, and may more closely approximate the feel and color of actual roadbed. Some modelers feel it is not as sturdy as rubber roadbed; others appreciate that cork is flexible and easy to cut. Both types of roadbed need to be trimmed at turnouts and crossings with a modeler's knife (see Chapter Three).

There are also other kinds of roadbed, such as those made of uncured rubber, wood, vinyl, and Homosote®. Each has its champions and detractors; check with individual companies for details.

Ballast (the name for the small rocks that support the ties in a prototype) consists, in model railroading, of fine sand, rock, sawdust, or other material in shades of red, brown, gray, and black, which simulate stones and ores. Con-Cor's many ballast colors include iron ore and buff; Life-Like's run the gamut from gravel to red stone. As with every other train element, ballast varies in size to fit its scale. Although you may think a stone is a stone, *do not* substitute alternate scale ballast for your scale. You'll have a track that seems to be supported by either boulders or grains of sand.

Opposite: Rod Wentler's and Petria MacDonnell's O-gauge layout of the Creston Garden Railway in Berkeley, California.

To keep from disrupting the mechanism of the train from underneath, ballast is anchored to the track with any of a variety of glues (see Chapter Three), applied in a thin coat and/or sprayed in a mixture of glue and water. Dry ballast cement is also available from Life-Like and others. It is mixed with the ballast, applied, and sprayed with water. The mixture dries to a solid that adheres to the roadbed. See your hobby dealer for details.

For first-time modelers, ballast can also be created very simply—with spray paint along the tracks. A variety of track, grass, ore, earth, and rust paint colors approximate the mixture of the natural and industrial colors of ballast.

TRACK ACCESSORIES

Turnouts. A *turnout*, also known as a *track switch*, is the section of track where two tracks diverge. At a *right-hand turnout*, a train can go straight ahead or to the right; at a *left-hand turnout*, it can go straight ahead or to the left. A turnout's operation—determining whether a train goes one way or the other—is handled either manually or electrically, by remote control. Manual turnouts can be converted into remote control models by adding a *switch machine* (see Chapter Four).

Turnouts are offered by nearly every company that produces track, and they are available in kits or fully assembled. They may run on a straight line or on curves of varying degrees, to match the curves of your track plan. *Wyes* (Y-shaped turnouts that allow a train to go either right or left but not straight ahead) and three-way turnouts (that let a train go straight, right, and left) are available for more complicated layouts. Some ready-made plastic track has nickel-silver rail and prototypical "all-rail" *frogs*, the part of the turnout where rails cross each other as they break into two tracks.

Among the many manufacturers that make turnouts are Darr's Scale Models, which offers turnouts in all scales, from Z to G; Atlas, F & M Enterprises, and BK Enterprises, which feature turnouts in scales N through O; and LaBelle Industries, Precision Scale, Richard Orr, Kato, Roco, Peco, and Model Power, among others, specialize in HO and/or N. For more information on the wiring aspects of turnouts, see Chapter Four.

Below: This head-on shot of an HO-scale diesel switcher in the industrial switching area of a layout by Bruce Cameron features a flat backdrop decorated with printed buildings. The switcher body is a brass 44-tonner, which has been repowered with a mechanism from a Bachmann 44-tonner. Opposite: Code 83 nickel silver HO track turnouts made by Shinohara for Walthers. The turnouts are part of a complete track system made by Shinohara which simulates the 137-pound mainline rail used by many railroads. Note the "all-rail" frogs.

Turntables. A *turntable* is a rotary platform that allows a locomotive to turn around completely or directs it to a specific stall or track. Model railroad turntables operate in one of two ways—manually or electronically.

From Atlas is a manual turntable in HO that indexes precisely to twelve positions 30 degrees apart. It has a manual crank operation and can be motorized for remote control operation with an Atlas Turntable Drive Unit. The drive unit is sold separately.

Also available to the modeler in most scales are operating turntable craft kits. Those in HO from Diamond Scale Construction, for example, are made of basswood, with metal castings and bronze bearings. Bowser also offers an HO turntable kit.

Just as in prototype railroads, in model railroading, there are different turntables in different uses. Among those available from Diamond Scale Construction and Bowser are steel girder turntables, steel truss turntables, timber truss turntables, and gallows turntables. Each of these turntables is used for trains of different lengths, weights, and dates of construction. Historically, the gallows turntable is the oldest type. In modeling, it is used for older trains or for light duty service. Timber truss turntables (supported by wood) were developed later, but are used in modeling for the same purposes as the gallows turntables. The steel truss and steel girder turntables, which are, as their name implies, supported by steel, are more modern. They can be used in modeling for trains meant to be heavier and/or longer or more modern.

Motors and gear boxes attach to the underside of the pit where the turntable stands and make turntables operational. They are available separately from the kit manufacturers mentioned above.

Left: The narrow-gauge town of Sierra Vista, created by Gilbert Freitag.

Grade Crossing Signs. Most people learn about railroad grade crossing signs from behind the wheel of a car, as they wait for a train to pass. The crossings are a necessary and unavoidable part of real life, and are just as necessary to a realistic train layout.

As with prototypical crossings, model railroad crossing sign sets are designed in a number of ways. There are gates with flashing lights or without, lighted crossings without a gate, and overroad crossings with lighted overhead gates. Space, design, and era will determine which crossing you choose.

Crossing sets are usually made of plastic and are assembled easily. Con-Cor offers a variety of grade crossings in HO, with some in O and N scale. Other manufacturers include N-Way and Train Tronics.

Bachmann offers complete ready-made crossings in both nonoperating and lighted operating crossing-sign models in HO scale, as well as plastic dual crossing gate kits. Simple plastic gates and unlit crossing signals are also available in HO from Bachmann and Life-Like. Nonoperating brass crossing signals are manufactured in HO from Model Power, and in die-cast metal and brass from Walthers. Your choice of plastic or brass will be determined by both aesthetics and finances: brass is attractive and sturdy, but plastic is more affordable. Whether you choose a nonoperating or operating system depends on how much electrical work you want to do.

If you want an automatic crossing system, it is available in HO from Train Tronics. It will run several sets of crossing signals with correct switching. Pola offers an LGB level crossing that opens and closes by its own remote-operated electric motor. Other choices include a set of automatic crossing signals, by Circuitron, which has its own alternating flasher and a detector for oncoming rolling stock. It is powered by a 2 × 3 inch printed circuit board and uses tiny optosensors, mounted between the rails, to detect oncoming trains.

Below: A steam engine from the Whiteshell Division of the Canadian National Railway passes while a truck waits in this HO-scale layout of the Canadian prairie by Stafford Swain.

Right: This 2-8-2 Mikado steam locomotive from Märklin is an example of the smallest scale—Z. Only 4½ inches long, the model represents a prototype common in the United States at the turn of the century. **Below:** Lionel's O-gauge *Hiawatha,* one of the great prizes in toy train collecting, was produced in 1935. A reproduction of this shovel-nosed streamliner was offered by Lionel in 1989.

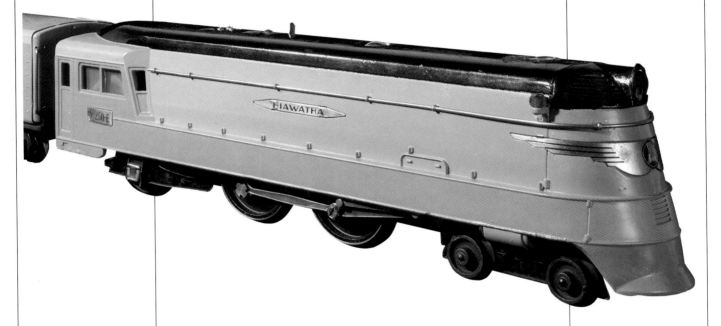

Left: Bachmann's "Big Haulers"—a line of G-scale train sets—include this set, the Rocky Mountain Express. The 4-6-0 Consolidation steam locomotive features smoke and sound synchronized to the train's speed. The rolling stock includes a boxcar and tank car, and the set comes complete with track, trestle, and power pack.

Right: Bachmann's Lumber Jack train set in G scale comes with 0-4-0 steam switcher, flatcar, and caboose. A log load (not shown) for the flatcar is also included in the set.

COAL CREEK LUMBER COMPANY

1

Above right: Mantua's Goat 0-4-0 Camelback Switcher in HO scale accurately represents the little steam switcher that was once the workhorse of yards and wharfs around Philadelphia, Reading, Pottstown, and Wilmington. This loco comes ready-to-run with a choice of roadnames, or in undecorated kit form. Right: Mantua's ready-to-run articulated logger 2-6-6-2-T in HO. The locomotive's two frames—each with six driving wheels—are pivoted together for ease in negotiating curves.

WEYERHAEUSER TIMBER COMPANY 127

Above: There is probably no toy train as instantly recognizable as this red, silver, and yellow Santa Fe F diesel unit from Lionel. First introduced in 1948, the O-gauge locomotive was Lionel's best seller. It has been reissued numerous times over the years. **Left:** The Thunderbolt Express train set, another of Bachmann's "Big Haulers" in G scale. The set's bright colors, big size, durable construction, and simple oval track make it perfect for children. The 4-6-0 Consolidation loco comes with smoke and speed-synchronized sound.

Top: American Flyer produced this S-gauge model of General Motors' EMD GP7 diesel locomotive in 1950. The paint scheme for the model was inspired by GM's demonstrator unit; note the yellow and red GM insignia on the cab. **Above:** This 2-8-2 Mikado in HO scale is a brass import from Westside Models. It was custom painted by Lee Sperry, a professional model painter with Reed's Hobby Shop in La Mesa, California. **Left:** An HO-scale Athearn F7 diesel, painted in the colors of the Southern Mountain, races over a trestle bridge. The Southern Mountain is the private railway of photographer Don Mitchell. The bridge is part of the Mission Empire Railway System, built by the Convair Club in San Diego.

Clockwise from left: 1) The Southern Pacific Daylight, a steam passenger train of the late 1940s—early 1950s, emerges from a mountain tunnel in this HO-scale layout. The layout is operated by the California Central Model Railroad Club in Santa Clara. The train was built by Bill Decker; the scenery is by Mike Kotowski and Rich and John Croll. 2) A 4-6-2 Pacific steam locomotive in HO scale from Mantua. The prototype Pacific was first built in 1915. This model features the colors of the Canadian Pacific. 3) A narrow-gauge 2-8-2 Mikado in HO scale from Mantua, with the logo of the Great Northern Railway and a vandy tender. 4) Märklin's classic LMS E 800 in 00 gauge (the original name of the gauge that became HO). Introduced in 1938, this 4-4-0 steam locomotive with tender was part of the revolution that established scale model railroading as we know it today.

Above: This Lionel O-gauge 773 Hudson was offered in 1950, Lionel's Golden Anniversary year. The prototype was the popular 4-6-4 Hudson introduced by the New York Central System in the 1930s. Not as detailed as the classic Hudson produced by Lionel in 1937, the 773 still ranks as one of Lionel's finest. **Below:** This HO-scale Athearn FP 45 was built by Marty Green of the La Mesa Model Railroad Club in California when he was 13 years old. The Santa Fe passenger train would have operated in the 1960s–1970s. The layout represents California's Tehachapi Pass and is located in the San Diego Model Railroad Museum in Balboa Park. The scenery was constructed by John Rotsart. **Right:** In another section of the Tehachapi Pass layout, an Athearn SD-40T, built by Brenda Bailey, exits from Tunnel No. 1. The locomotive is a "tunnel motor," with radiator vents designed to keep the engine cool while the train passes through tunnels. The gallows-like structure is a "telltale." The wires hanging from the archaic nineteenth-century device warned crewmen on the roofs of cars to get down before the train entered a tunnel. **Bottom:** These RS3 diesel engines were converted into Altoona (left) and Dewitt (right) RS3 engines using conversion kits from Tiger Valley Models. These locomotives were introduced by Penn Central in the 1970s and run by Conrail until the mid-1980s.

Above: C. C. Crow's HO-scale craftsman kit of the Great Northern Passenger Depot in Bellingham, Washington, circa 1910. The kit features thirteen original Hydrocal® castings from master craftsman Clint Crow, with details from Grandt Line and basswood roof trusses from Northeastern. Representing a brick and stone prototype, this popular model is about $10 \times 5 \times 4\frac{1}{2}$ inches in size. **Left top:** AMSI, a specialist in landscape materials, is perhaps most highly regarded for its palm trees. These California-Washingtonia and date palms come in an assortment of sizes that can be adapted to layouts in any scale. **Left middle:** More palm trees from AMSI. The coconut palm on the far left is 6 inches high; the one on the far right is $1\frac{1}{2}$ inches high. **Left bottom:** Palm trees are put to good effect in this N-scale scene depicting the Santa Fe train station in San Diego circa 1940s. The replica of the station was built by George "Pete" Peters; the scene is part of the Pacific Desert Lines layout built by the San Diego Society of N Scale (SDSONS) in the San Diego Model Railroad Museum. Note how a traction model (the streetcar at far right) is incorporated into the layout.

Clockwise from top left: 1) An HO-scale Atlas S2 diesel switcher pulls up for loading at the Liberty Milling Co. The paint and Microscale decals were applied to the train by Don Mitchell. The carefully weathered building is a freelance model (not representing any particular prototype) scratchbuilt by Cris Hollinshead. The 1950s scene, depicting the southern California town of Castaic, is part of a former layout of the La Mesa Model Railroad Club. 2) This crossing is part of an HO-scale layout of the Canadian prairie built by Stafford Swain of Winnipeg, Manitoba.

The layout depicts the Whiteshell subdivision of the Canadian National Railways. Notice how action is implied by the placement of the truck: the truck driver must "wait" while the train passes. 3) This HO-scale Victorian Mansion from I.S.L.E. Laboratories is part of I.S.L.E.'s "Old Hometown Series" of building fronts. Made of low density urethane foam, the mansion features clear plastic windows that can be lighted from be-

hind. 4) The Rutherford B. Hayes Coachworks in HO scale from Master Creations. The building was created as an example of the most common business failures of the early 1900s. The painstaking detail includes rotted boards, collapsed iron fences, overgrown weeds, and assorted junk.

Signals and Detection Units. Aside from the familiar crossing gate and sign, there are many types of *signals* to control the movements of trains. A sampling of types of signals includes:

● bridge units, *which attach to a road overpass or signal bridge. A die-cast version is available from Walthers*

● dwarf units, *small ground-based units usually used to control movement in trainyards. A die-cast version is available from Walthers, and a prepainted LED version from Monongahela Innoventions*

● brass HO block signals (semaphore, target, and colorlight) *from NJ International, painted and wired with bulbs*

● signal bridges, *which support signal heads above two or more parallel tracks, and are used in congested areas, from Bachmann, Oregon Rail Supply, and Model Power*

Products related to signals include:

● plastic and metal operating signal towers *in kit or fully assembled in HO-scale by NJ International, and in N and Z scales by Dimi-Trains.*

● an authentic switchman *in his own building, who emerges as a train approaches in an HO kit from Life-Like.*

● brass switchstand signals *in HO by Tomar Industries, which rotate 90 degrees and are wired with bulbs or LEDs.*

A model train signal can function in three basic ways. It can be nonoperating. It can be lighted by means of colored bulbs, but not necessarily indicating track conditions. If it is lighted it may be connected to a *detection unit*, which, like the Circuitron railroad crossing system mentioned earlier, detects trains and generates correct color indications.

For more information on the wiring of signals and detection units, see Chapter Four.

Rerailers. A *rerailer* is a section of track that facilitates the moving of cars onto the rails. For example, it helps to move trains from repair areas onto the track. Available in most scales, rerailers are made in plastic by a number of companies, including Tru-Scale Models. Rerailer ramps are portable plastic wedges that help move cars onto the track. Rix Products and Kadee are two manufacturers that offer a rerailer ramp that fits any brand of HO track.

Left: Part of Jack Verducci's gauge 1½-scale train line, in San Mateo, California.

NATURAL SCENERY

Now that you have chosen the size of the layout, the track plan, the trains, and have an idea of how you want the layout to look, it is time to build the environment in which the train runs. This means both the natural and the man-made world.

Trees and Forests. All kinds of trees are available for the modeler's world of greenery, from oaks to maples to willows to pines to palm trees.

As with structures and all other elements of model railroading, trees and shrubs are available in two forms—ready-made or in kits. Usually the kits have two basic parts—the trunk and the foliage. The trunk, often made of a pliable metal, is packaged flat, and is bent into shape. Foliage comes in a roll or ball, from which you can pull portions to make the tree as full as you wish. The foliage is attached with a light coating of glue. Both ready-made and hand-assembled trees are full and realistic. Modelers who choose to build their own trees usually do so because they want to control the amount of foliage or bend of the tree, in order to more accurately represent the tree's age or the season.

Among the many types of tree kits available are 2- to 4-inch hardwood and pine-wood forests, in bags of twenty-four trees from Woodland Scenics. The trunks are made of bendable metal, the foliage of lacy plastic. Specialty trees, such as ornamentals, fruit trees—orange and cherry—are available for an orchard, as are flowering trees to line a residential street. For a memorial park or natural forest area, there are big, old trees that add age and dignity to your creation. To model shrubs and add more foliage to already existing trees, lichen and foliage clusters are available in a number of different colors.

Ready-made flexible polyethylene trees are offered by Plastruct, Inc., for G, O, HO, and N scales. Choices include familiar neighborhood and forest choices like the elm, oak, poplar, conifers, and cypress, as well as the palm tree for a California or Florida scene and cactus for a southwestern train line.

Inventive modelers can make their own trees from actual dried foliage. For example, dried goldenrod or baby's breath, broken into scale-size pieces and spray painted with model railroad paint, are extremely realistic simulations of forests or shrubbery.

For more information, see books on railroad scenery, such as *Scenic Modeling Made Easy* (Faller).

Below: Trees and earth from Form-a-Mountain™. Opposite: With proper maintenance and care classic model trains, such as this 1927 standard-gauge "Banker's Special" from Ives, can last for generations. This heirloom train still runs among the natural scenery of its garden layout.

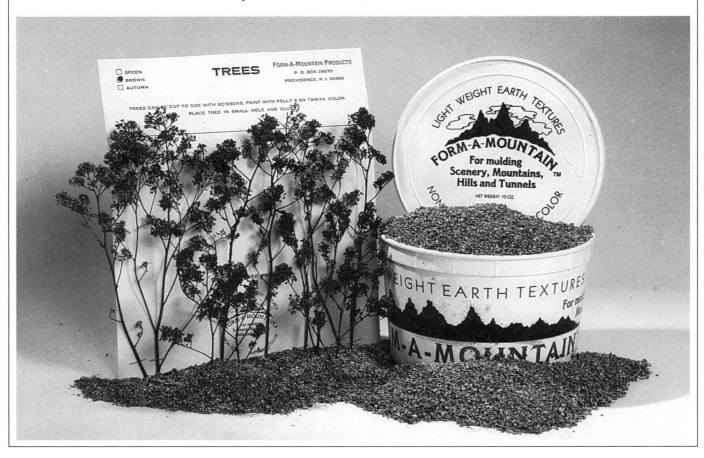

Opposite: With modelers' plants, hedges, and flowers, an indoor layout can look as realistic as this outdoor gauge 1/1½-scale layout of the Minnetonka Valley Railway by Mike and Susan Decker, framed by marigolds and natural grasses. Below: A variety of grasses and lichen grow along the slope of the mountain in this layout. Ground cover and trees in different colors show the change in seasons.

Plants and Hedges. Just as they do for your lawn or local park plants and hedges add height, texture, and color to the ground cover of your layout—and you can find the same variety you do in your local garden shop. Here is a sampling:

• *HO-scale hedgerow scenes of eighteen trees, six bushes, two colors of foliage, and two colors of turf, as well as lichen to use for modeling HO-scale brush and foliage for different types of plant life, from Woodland Scenics,*

• *flocking materials in HO that allow you to cover the ground with either summer flowers or fallen leaves, from Vintage Reproductions,*

• *HO-scale cactus to use in a desert layout, from MLR Manufacturing,*

• *flowering 1¼" bushes and a choice of small, medium, or large hedges to place in a park or backyard, from Faller.*

Grass, Ground Cover, and Lichen. At the base of all natural landscaping is the ground cover, and in model railroading it can be as plain or complex as any natural setting.

Spray paint provides the easiest simulation of ground cover. Spray paints are made in an array of colors in shades of grass and natural foliage. Grass green paint can be used for sunny residential areas, gray-green paint with spots of black for soot for the areas near the railroad tracks, yellow green for arid areas. The only trick is to apply the paint lightly—there is no way to remove a too-generous portion of soot black from a sheet of plywood benchwork. (See Chapter Three for details on paints and painting accessories.)

Another way to cover the ground is with a grass mat. Con-Cor offers a 50 × 99 inch paper grass mat for HO-scale layouts, and Plastruct makes sheets of flexible green plastic ground cover for large-scale layouts. Life-Like offers realistically textured, nonmagnetic, reusable plastic mats for HO layouts. The paper backing allows for easy cutting to fit around various track designs. For those who want to add more texture to their ground cover, Woodland Scenics offers rolls of densely textured plastic turf in a variety of colors and thicknesses. The coarse turf is especially good for meadows or low-growing brush. It can be cut easily and attached with glue.

For visible leaves of grass, Woodland Scenics also sells natural hair field grass. It comes in four colors and can be cut and gathered into bunches before being inserted into place and attached with glue.

To provide meadows and gardens with the welcoming colors of the season, there are premixed flower foam packs from AMSI Scale Model Supplies. There is the Spring Color Pack, with white, canary, bluebell, and coral shades of foam, summer color packs of fuchsia, delphinium, rose and violet, and fall packs, with red, gold, orange, and plum foams. Also available are terrain brush, in 12 × 12 inch pieces and ground foam in three grades—fine, medium, and coarse. Fine grade can be used for grass or small scale models, medium for large scale ground cover or foliage, and coarse for small shrubs or mass small tree plantings. Vista Scenic Hobby Products offers pine-scented lichen in several seasonal shades and in small and bulk packages. From Con-Cor, there is lichen in fall red, dark green, and sunset orange.

Above: John Wenlock's O-gauge steam Clwyd and Dee Railway layout in Wrexham, Wales. For more examples of indoor layouts with manmade scenery, see pages 103–104 and 177–182.

Rocks, Rock Faces, and Mountains.
Although rocks, be they mountains surrounding a railroad or boulders fallen by the side of the road, don't offer the glamour of a 1920s dining car, for example, they do inspire passion. There's a satisfaction in building or finding a realistic rock face that surpasses nearly every other element of scenery building; in addition, it serves the practical purpose of hiding modeling equipment. It may not be easy to find or build a truly prototypical rock face for your layout, but it need not take the obsession of Richard Dreyfuss in *Close Encounters of the Third Kind,* who destroyed his living room to recreate an alien landing site.

Here are a few suggestions: Rock faces come in three forms—ready-made, built from mountain-building material, and scratchbuilt. By far the simplest way to produce rock faces is to use mountain paper or buy ready-made mountains. Both are available from Life-Like. Realistically colored, Life-Like Mountain Paper can easily be shaped into rolling hillsides or mountain tunnels. Life-Like's premade rocky backgrounds in N, HO, and O scales, are made from lightweight Lifoam®, and formed into realistic ridges and hills.

More common is the use of building material or scratchbuilt forms. Hobby store building material usually consists of a foam-like substance. One such material, made by Mountains in Minutes™, uses a two-part liquid system; the liquids mix to create Polyfoam, a lightweight rock. The rock is available in several types of formations, including Colorado Red Rock, Royal Gorge, Kittanning Slope and Agway Canyon Wall. It can be cut with a razor saw into the shapes you need for your layout. You can also design your own rock formations, using molds made from actual rocks, or a base built of cardboard and wire.

Below: The dream of many modelers is to build a realistic-looking mountain like the one through which this diesel locomotive travels.

Above: The types of natural rock castings offered by Mountains in Minutes™ are, from left, Agawa Wall, Kittaning, Royal Gorge, red rock, and, below, embankment. The 4 square foot foam walls are duplicates of actual rock formations. The embankment, with its natural red rock finish, can be carved with a modeler's knife.

Another type of mountain material, Form-a-Mountain™, made by Form-a-Mountain Products, is a nontoxic, nonmagnetic, fireproof earth texture compound. After being mixed with water, the mixture can be applied with a putty knife to any mountain framework.

If you choose to scratchbuild your own mountains you face a multi-part process. First, you have to build a mountain *form* of chicken wire, or screen wire, or cardboard and rolled-up newspaper secured with masking tape. Then cover the form with plaster-soaked paper towels and allow it to dry. A popular material with which to build the mountain is a molding plaster like Hydrocal, which creates a hard shell, eliminating the need for permanent support. This is a complicated activity: For details, talk to your hobby dealer or to fellow modelers.

Ponds, Lakes, and Waterfalls. A realistic body of water can add a strong, clean beauty to your layout and transport you to the Pacific coastline, Great Lakes or Rocky Mountains.

Precast lakes or waterfalls are usually constructed of some type of plastic. To gain the greatest degree of verisimilitude, choose one with lively, believable color and texture—or add your own touches.

Here are a few other suggestions:

● *Plastruct offers a wide variety of colors and types of bodies of water in their plastic streams and waterfalls. There are three colors—aqua, deep blue, and clear—to match your body of water and three levels of water activity—calm, choppy, and agitated—for the type of weather or time of day you want to present.*

● *Faller offers a complete lake construction kit for HO scale, with a rippled plastic sheet and blue landscape paper.*

● *hannes fischer has plastic water sheets—in clear blue and brackish shades.*

● *Color-Rite makes a kit for a semi-transparent 62 × 26 inch plastic waterfall.*

● *Vintage Reproductions offers tints for finishing touches, in five shades that add color, sparkle, depth, foam, and froth to a wild body of water. There are also more sedate sparkling water tints, and for placid summer scenes, a kit with lily pads and pond scum.*

You can also scratchbuild your lakes with clear resin, available from Chemco Resin Crafts and others. For details, consult one of the books on model railroad landscaping, including *How to Build Realistic Model Railroad Scenery* (Kalmbach Publishing Co.).

Left: The Mountains in Minutes™ model landscape kit lets you create a realistic, finely detailed rock formation. Its main ingredient, Polyfoam, can be molded into shape or poured directly onto the layout and carved into a desired shape. Opposite: An example of the natural-looking mountains you can build with Mountains in Minutes™. Note the variations in the surface.

BACKDROPS

An easy way to extend the horizon of your layout and make it seem more realistic is to add a *backdrop* of sky, earth, and scenery. Available in most scales, these printed backdrops are color lithographs that can be attached to the wall behind your layout. Backdrops are available that portray retaining walls and ramps, urban scenes, industrial scenes, and rural scenes, from farm to woods to forest to mountain. Some backdrops are designed to be cut and applied to blue (sky) background; others can be placed in front of the prepainted sky and cloud backgrounds. Instant Horizons™ backdrops in HO from Walthers are 24 × 36 inches; MZZ sheets are 11½ × 16½ inches; Detail Associates Rail-Scenes run 22 × 8½ inches in HO scale, half that in N. A Rail-Scene System instruction book is available from Detail Associates.

STRUCTURES

Buildings give trains a world to blend in with, contrast to, and just pass by. Of course, there is variety in the type of building, amount of detail, and similarity to actual buildings. One company, for example, has created a replica of a Baltimore firehouse (Life-Like), another company a specific actual Pittsburgh office building (City Classics). There are the Texaco gas stations and Kentucky Fried Chicken drive-ins that pinpoint a layout in time and bring back memories. There are also the houses—either the ones you remember having lived in or the ones you wish you had.

Buildings for model railroading come in injection-molded styrene and other plastics, wood, and metal. They can be bought ready-made or in a kit. The only exception is Z scale, which is so small that, at least up until now, it only offers ready-made buildings.

Some building kits are simple ones that take less than an hour to construct. More difficult craftsman-type kits, consisting of both unfinished wood, plastic, and/or metal, can take several nights of assembly time, in addition to aging or weathering the building. In some kits, parts must be cut to size. Some kits are also suitable for *kitbashing* and extending (see Chapter Three for details.)

Industrial Buildings. Since most railroads were built to serve industry, industrial buildings are a key part of any layout. These structures represent two categories of businesses: manufacturing and service industries.

Manufacturing Industries—When every town had rail service, few things were more important than the movement of the commodities they produced—oil, coal, and lumber. In HO scale, Mil-Scale offers the "Jacobs Coal Company," an easy-to-assemble coal yard made of basswood. In O gauge, Trains of Texas offers an Old West industry—the blacksmith shop—in a kit of wood with plastic details for the Blackhawk Blacksmith Shop. A complete diorama of another western livelihood—the prospectors' camp, complete with prospector figures and accessories—is also available from Trains of Texas.

Opposite: The Freitags' realistic mountain range is a combination of a hand-carved rockface and a colorful backdrop. Below: Two popular HO-scale injection-molded styrene structures by Design Preservation Models: Each modular system has four walls of a kind, windows, doors, and clear adaptable window material.

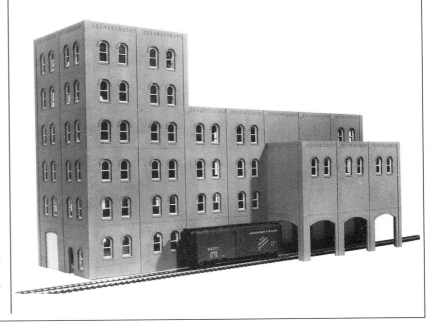

Model Power presents easy-to-assemble kits in HO-scale for turn-of-the-century facsimiles of two well-known American businesses—a Budweiser Brewery and a General Electric Company building. Also available is a stone and gravel unloading station, the end of the process for a town with an active quarry. For the serious HO-scale modeler interested in realism, there is a failed business of the early 1900s—the Rutherford B. Hayes Coach Works. The high-quality kit features laser cut wall sections, injection molded parts, resin castings, metal castings, dry transfers, and color graphics.

Service Industries and City Buildings— Over the years, service industry buildings have run the gamut from plain backwoods offices to huge hotels, and all are available for the model railroader. To re-create older scenes, Trains of Texas offers O-scale wood craft structures with cast plastic details for the old-time Gilpin Hotel and the Fraternal Order of Knights of Pythias hall. For the HO-scale modeler, GRS Model Brass offers a realistic scene of decades ago—a hobo camp diorama. From Woodland Scenics in HO are more turn-of-the century structures—in kits of white metal castings. These include an old pharmacy, gazebos, even outhouses. There are also complete struc-

Above: This O-scale high-quality polyurethane model of Birdie's Tavern is part of Design Preservation Models' "Lunde Landmarks" series. Note the attention to detail, particularly in the columns and window lettering. **Left:** This model of Baltimore's Woodlawn Police Station represents a now demolished city landmark. The manufacturer, Life-Like, has produced a number of model Baltimore buildings. **Opposite, top:** International Hobby Corp. brings the carnival to town with the HO-scale kits for a ferris wheel (left) and a Sky Wheel (right). **Opposite, bottom:** Easy-to-assemble Design Preservation Models kits of townhouses for your urban layout. The injection-molded styrene kits are available in color or white.

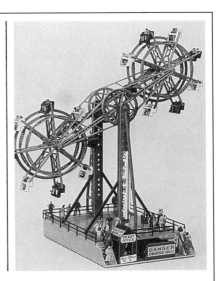

ture scene kits, like the Maple Leaf Cemetery, with its twenty-eight headstones, a Memorial Park, and the Otis Coal Company. Model Power produces simple kits for small-town fixtures like the YMCA, the Post Office and Bank, and the Railroad Hotel. In N, HO, S, O, and G scales from Master Creations are close-to-prototype replicas of a small-town office, a city office building called 111 West 43 Street, Best Auto Garage, and an old-time town center called the Grand Hotel. These high quality kits are made of a combination of white metal and photo etched parts.

International Hobby Corp. offers HO and N plastic kits for quaint modern storefronts and shops like O'Weed's Greenery and Rita's Antique Shop. For the playful modern

layout in HO, International Hobby Corp. also offers unpainted carnival kits, with favorite rides like the Ferris Wheel and Sky Wheel. For the now-gentrified older part of town in a modern HO- or N-scale layout, International Hobby Corp. offers a series of brownstones converted into a Medical Arts building and T-Shirt and Gimmick Shop. Design Preservation Models presents an O-scale Birdie's Tavern and Kirsten's Corner Cafe, as well as an HO-scale Pam's Pet Shop and a Skip's Chicken & Ribs. Model Power also makes plastic kits in HO for a common modern sight—a once-abandoned building being refurbished under an urban renewal project. Another modern sight is the nuclear power plant: for that, Heljan offers a kit in HO for a plastic replica of Three Mile Island.

Burning buildings can add a touch of drama to your layout. With an N-scale plastic kit from Model Power, you can set a seven-story building "ablaze" with light from a 12-volt power pack (sold separately). Another separate kit for the firehouse sends trucks to the rescue. You may not want to send trucks to rescue Life-Like's HO-scale Internal Revenue Service building on fire.

Houses. Victorian, suburban ranch, brownstone, and colonial houses are all available to give life to your railroad layout. International Hobby Corp. makes plastic kits in HO and N for their line of Homes of Yesterday and Today, including rows of Brownstone Mansions, colonial homes, and gingerbread houses. Woodland Scenics offers an original touch with an abandoned caboose converted into a home. Also available are kits for suburban homes to recreate today's housing developments.

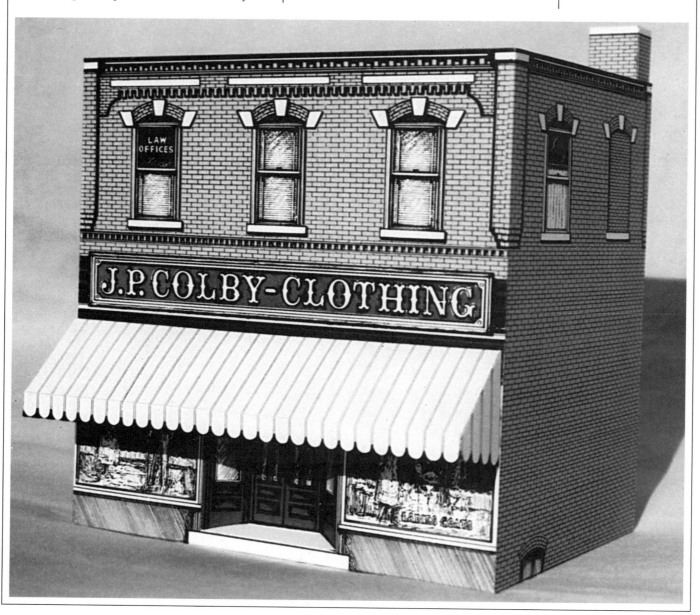

Opposite: This finely detailed, easy-to-assemble O-scale clothing store by Pioneer Valley Models is ideal for a turn-of-the-century layout. Houses, apartment buildings, and various storefronts are also available. Right: For a handsome small-town block, try this HO-scale Victorian mansion from I.S.L.E. Laboratories. Placing a light behind the plastic window makes for a charming late-night effect. Bottom, left: This HO-scale molded pre-colored plastic water bridge from International Hobby Corp. is easy to build and richly detailed. Bottom right: For your N- or HO-scale layout, this kit for the Cheyenne Coal Bunker from International Hobby Corp. provides a good focal point. This true-to-prototype kit is molded in several colors and needs no additional painting.

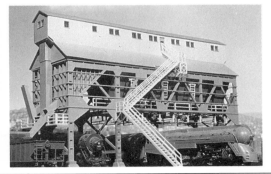

Right: A late 1920s HO-scale residential town street, composed of two Scale Structure Ltd. kits: the first for row houses and a gas station, and the second for metal cast fences and electric street lamps.

Train Stations. No layout would be complete without a train station, and there are many varieties available to the modeler. In HO from Mil-Scale is a basswood kit for the traditional flagstop station, used in the past by branch lines, mainline commuter, and trolley lines. From John Rendall Scale Models comes an HO-scale all-wood kit for an old Canadian train station, Victoria Station. Another small-town touch is the trolley terminal, which can be made by kitbashing the N-scale car repair trolley shed, available from Mil-Scale. Model Power also makes a simple kit in HO scale for an old-fashioned railroad station from the early twentieth century—the kind that has now been converted into a museum or local information center.

Opposite, top: At the train station with the Peter Dobson Line, in O gauge from Sandy, England. Opposite, bottom: This ½-scale wood model of Fiddletown Station from S&C Enterprises is a high-quality, handcrafted addition to your layout. Right: A steam locomotive crosses a trestle bridge.

Bridges and Viaducts. Bridges and viaducts make exciting and creative additions to your model train layout.

Among the many bridges to choose from are the wood trestle and Hermosa Creek bridge kits from Trains of Texas. The wood trestle bridge is available in HO, S, and O; the Hermosa Creek Bridge is for narrow gauges—On3, Sn3, and HOn3. Mil-Scale produces a basswood snow shed kit in HO. Found mainly in the western mountains, the sheds shield trains from winds that can oth-

erwise push snow drifts deep enough to close rail lines. A concrete trestle kit in HO and N, the modern version of the wood trestle, can be used in a layout with late steam or diesel era pikes.

Finally, GarGraves Trackage Corp. makes a Lift Bridge, specially designed for a round-the-room layout. When the layout is up and running, the bridge crosses the doorway to create a track that encircles the room completely. When the layout is not in use, the bridge lifts up and can be put away.

Below: A Pacific Electric car on a bridge in this layout by David Cox. Opposite: Modelers can discover exciting new layouts to champion from a variety of sources, such as this late nineteenth-century engraving of lower Manhattan and the Brooklyn Bridge.

Wall Panels, Tunnel Portals, and Tunnels. Walls can divide your layout into sections and hide wiring that trees and mountains do not cover. A retaining wall around a hillside trailway also adds realism and allows you to set up another level to your layout, one that recalls the walled hills of European towns and city hills.

Walls, panels, and portals are usually constructed of urethane foam, rigid plastic foam, dental stone, or specially treated paper. They range from the simple plastic retaining wall by hannes fischer to the variety of more detailed plastic retaining walls offered by AIM Products that resemble cut stone, poured concrete, field stone, and random stone. Mountains in Minutes™ and Noch offer stone walls with stairways to hold steep banks or reinforce embankments and move from one level of a layout to another.

Tunnel portals, often paired with retaining walls, can simulate timber, cut stone, concrete, or random stone construction, as do those in HO scale by GLR Industries. The portals offered by Mountains in Minutes™ mix tones of golden brown and burnt umber, one an HO-scale model of an actual Canadian Pacific Railroad portal. From Campbell Scale Models is a Timber Tunnel Portal kit; Chooch Enterprises and AIM Products both offer double track tunnel portals. Rugged-looking blasted rock portals in HO are available in high density plaster from AIM, and painted and weathered polyurethane from Chooch Enterprises. Concrete and timber double-and-single-track portals are available in Z scale from Znic-detailZ/Limited Editions.

Ready-to-use tunnels originally became popular with toy train layouts, and are used now mainly when modelers don't need or don't want to build their own mountain and tunnel. Preconstructed tunnels are usually made from colored plastic or foam. While most of these tunnels are ready-to-use, some require minor kit-building. Among the types of tunnels available are those in HO from Noch, which can be straight, curved, or built with a surrounding pond and creek. Also available are HO double track tunnels, one going under a bridge, another through a snow-capped mountain, and one under a castle on a hill. Constructed foam tunnels from Life-Like and Noch are also available in a variety of styles, including one that travels through a quarry.

Above: A curved tunnel made of durable Lifoam® by Life-Like is especially useful to beginning modelers. Below: The exquisite results of scratchbuilding one's own wall—a handcarved stone panel by C. C. Crow. Opposite, top: A finely detailed model of the Rutherford B. Hayes Coach Works from Master Creations shows the failed business in disrepair and disarray. Opposite, bottom: This HO-scale layout features a picket fence with realistic details.

Fences. To create a park, churchyard, or pen for farm animals, your layout needs a fence. There are many to choose from—most of them plastic, some wood or metal. Here is a sampling:

• a colored plastic G-scale garden fence, perfect for a World War II victory garden or to line a country church walkway, from Con-Cor;

• white plastic picket fences in HO, made to surround a nearby farmhouse or an old-fashioned family home, from Atlas;

• an HO-scale chain link fence to surround livestock, from Builders in Scale;

• precut wood kits to fit a farm scene with a cattle-style fence for the livestock and a rustic fence for around the ranch, from Sugar Pine Models;

• the plank-style fence, with one plank left unattached, recalls the fences kids once used to hide out from their parents and scoot off into adventure, from Sugar Pine Models;

• Italianate wrought-iron fences for city brownstones, in HO from Faller, Vollmer, or MZZ;

• a corrugated iron fence kit in HO containing the city junkyard, from Alloy Farms.

Structure Accessories. These are the finishing touches that surround typical buildings, which lend personality and idiosyncrasy to your newly created town, and create a greater sense of reality.

Here is just a sampling of the many accessories available:

• *lighted Esso and Gulf gasoline signs, and Christmas trees in G scale from Model Power;*

• *brass lighted lamp posts, traffic signals, and movie posters (from films of 1924–1940, like Lost Horizon, or 1940–1960, like Rebel Without a Cause) in HO and N from Model Power;*

• *full-color roadside billboards in several scales from Bachmann;*

• *turn-of-the-century metal park benches, mailboxes, water pump and tub in O gauge by Bowser Manufacturing;*

• *shovels, five-gallon containers, and gas pumps in white metal castings in HO scale by Master Creations;*

• *mini-modules of HO-scale trackside railroad yard or auto yard junk, made of ready-to-paint white metal castings by Woodland Scenics;*

• *round and square telephone booths in Z scale from Znic-detailZ/Limited Editions;*

• *Burma-Shave sign kits (remember these?) of metal castings in HO, S, O, and G featuring actual signs used between 1933–1951, from Selley Finishing Touches. Messages include "She kissed/the hairbrush by mistake/she thought it was/her husband Jake" and "He saw/the train/and had to duck it/kicked first the gas/and then the bucket!"*

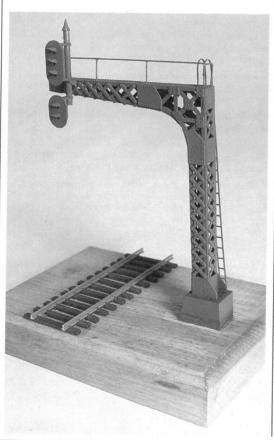

Above: No Sn3 narrow gauge layout would be complete without a coal tower to transfer coal into the locomotive tender, and this **PBL Coal Tower Pilot Model** is one of the most finely made examples offered. Handcrafted in brass, it is based on a prototype in Chama, New Mexico, and is offered in both static and operating versions. The operating version includes a control unit and a plaster coal bin. **Left:** Once electric signals began to be used at the turn of the century, almost every railroad in America had signal bridges like this HO-scale model from Oregon Rail Supply. With its cantilevered design, it can fit more easily into difficult locations than the double-legged style. The model is based on the Chesapeake & Ohio bridge at Peach Creek, West Virginia. **Right:** This LGB outdoor steam layout features a grade crossing in action.

Above: This all-wood HO-scale craftsman kit for the Haliburton Enginehouse by John Rendell is based on the structure built in 1878 for Canada's Victoria Railway. The kit features parts of board-on-board pine and basswood and Grandt Line detail parts. Left: To bring a touch of reality to your highway scenes, period highway billboards are available from Bachmann. This HO-scale billboard is lighted from above.

FIGURES AND ANIMALS

People and animals can make any layout look real, lived in. Otherwise what is the point of the carefully weathered barns, the cluttered train station, the benches in the town park? People and creatures make the difference between a still life and a living town; and in model railroading, as in life, there are more than enough types of people to choose from.

Like trains, figures come in all scales, all eras, and a variety of activities—at work, at play, seated, standing, running the train. City and farm figures are available, as are Gibson Girls, high-hatted dandies, miners, oilmen, hobos. There are commuters of by-gone eras in topcoats and fedoras, latter-day versions in down jackets and running shoes.

Some figures are painted; others can be painted with nontoxic paints. The only constants are the materials with which they are made: molded plastic (styrene or polyethylene) and/or metal (usually white metal castings). They are almost always unbendable as is: the standing employee waiting for the Union Pacific in one layout cannot become a seated passenger waiting for dinner in another. The only way to bend these figures is to heat them over a flame. This is a tricky and potentially dangerous process. Before attempting it, speak to your hobby store owner or other modelers.

Above: Buford and Roscoe pump their way down the track on this operating hand car from the Large Scale™ line by Lionel. Using the tools they keep on board, they can repair breakages along the Lionel Line. **Left:** In model railroading, as in life, figures come in all shapes and sizes. These HO-scale plastic figures from Bachmann show people of all walks of life—traffic cop, waiting passenger, laborer, porter, baker, and child—and in various positions.

Here is a small sampling of the figures available: From Lytler & Lytler, there are turn-of-the-century ladies and gentlemen, laborers, merchants, even a young couple wooing in a rowboat. From Preiser, there are HO-scale Gay Nineties bathers, modern people climbing the stairs, and an ice cream man with a hand cart. The early half of the century—up through the transition period of railroading—is well represented by hand-painted metal figures in O scale by Bowser Manufacturing. There are men in topcoats, newspaper boys, cigar store Indians, and a group of Scotties with their own fire hydrant to decorate a Main Street sidewalk.

From the 1950s, Micro-Metal offers in HO not only a group of bobby-soxers at a jukebox but a scale-sized Marilyn Monroe with a press entourage. Con-Cor in O-gauge offers packs of plastic passengers and workers—even beatniks—some painted, some of which you can paint yourself.

The modeler who prefers to concentrate on painting the trains, not the figures, can find custom-painted white metal figures by Lytler & Lytler from June's Small World. The "Rag-timer"™ collection in HO includes the Bald Blacksmith, the Logger, and the Gold Panner. In S scale are the Conductor, the Dowager, and the Cat and Mouse on Crate. In O gauge, there is the turn-of-the-century look, with the Gibson Girl, Dapper Dan and Red Cap—everything you need for a busy congregation around an exiting train at a station. Trains of Texas offers O-gauge Texans and track gang figures in cast metal.

Other manufacturers and distributors of figures include G-R-S Model Brass, International Hobby Corp., Plastruct, Inc., Trackside Specialties, Busch (imported by F & M Imports), and Woodland Scenics. For the modeler who must have easily bendable figures, Master Creations offers HO-scale men at work, made of unpainted metal, with movable arms and legs.

Opposite: this HO-scale 1970 Plymouth Hemi Cuda from Magnuson Models, with its Mag wheels and wide tires, is perfect for a drag strip in a pre-Watergate era layout. Above: To celebrate the booming post-war economy, place this HO-scale 1948 Ford Coupe from Magnuson Models in the driveway of someone's new suburban split-level. Left: A late 1960s Oldsmobile, a pre-war "rag top," and several cabs from Magnuson Models are all you need for an HO-scale big-city scene.

VEHICLES

Few things set a place in time like automobiles and trucks. The vehicles you choose for your layout will pinpoint it to the decade.

The level of detail varies in vehicles. Some HO vehicles, pressed from metal, have no moving parts; others from plastic can roll freely. Some more complicated vehicles, like fire engines, come in a kit, ready to assemble. Here is a sampling:

The pre–World War I era is represented in a 1914 HO-scale Purina Mills grain truck made of white metal castings by Woodland Scenics. For the World War I Main Street, there is the unpainted 1918 HO-scale Pierce-Arrow and 1920 Olds Truck by Master Creations. Also unpainted are the buses, trucks, and boats in G, O, HO, and N, made by

Opposite, top: A tank car unloading gasoline at a garage is a mainstay of modern layouts. Above: These reproductions of 1930s American cars are perfect for a Depression-era layout. Left: This S-scale pickup truck waits for the train to pass. All parts of the layout—train, gas station, and pickup truck—are available from JAKS Enterprises.

Plastruct Inc. In O gauge in metal, there are unpainted bicycles and tricycles. In N and Z, Holgate & Reynolds offers sturdy metal unpainted pre–World War II cars in sets of six, including the Model T, a station wagon, pickup truck, and three sedans. They can be traveling down the highway while the New York Central speeds along across the way.

To add drama to your layout, Model Power offers die-cast metal hooks and ladders and rescue helicopters. Some of the fire engines have movable turntables and articulated ladders to reach a burning building's highest windows. These trucks are available in HO and O. For the modeler interested in assembling a firefighting train, a Firefighters' set is offered, including an HO-scale gear-driven locomotive, boxcar, caboose, and a firefighting team.

Right: These architecturally correct Pittsburgh office building kits from City Classics are perfect for your big-city layout. The tile-front 102 Penn Avenue (right) and iron-front 101 Grant Street (left) are based on Pittsburgh building prototypes. They are made of easy-to-use injection-molded styrene, with cast metal chimneys, vents, and roof hatch details. Both can be easily kitbashed.

CHAPTER THREE
Achieving Realism

Realism is something you work at, not something you buy. To be sure, there are a number of products that can help you make your railroad more realistic. But they require a commitment of time, labor, and attention. That commitment might mean weeks of research into prototype railroads. It might mean hours spent *kitbashing* locomotives—combining two or more different kits into one to get the exact locomotive you want. It might mean the careful application of detail parts—grabirons, brakewheels, pipe fittings. It might mean building rolling stock from sheets of wood, plastic, or metal (*scratchbuilding*). It might mean creating a beautiful color and letter scheme, then smearing it with rust- and grime-colored paint to simulate the effects of weather (*weathering*).

The aim of all this effort is to make your railroad look more "real"—more true to the prototype. The aim is also to make it

particular—not just any model train, but *this* train on *this* layout, with a certain history, serving this silver mine or that steel mill, carrying this cargo on a particular day. The details you give to your railroad must be not only realistic but interesting and visually pleasing. You may have to stretch the facts a little; you may have to compress details. You may have to invent details that imply action (for example, a totalled vehicle and a flashing tow truck implying a car accident). In short, it isn't enough to "copy" an existing railroad, following rules from a book. Rather, you use your own imagination, judgment, and skill to create an entirely new railroad, based more or less closely on existing prototypes.

As your railroad becomes more realistic, you will find that it also becomes more personal: an expression of your tastes and interests. Here are the products and resources that can help you to make your railroad more realistic and to make it your own.

Below: To model this prototype railroad scene accurately, you'd need to reproduce the rust on the rails, the texture of the ballast, and the lettering on the NATX tank car. Islington Station Products provides HO-scale decals to model the prototype rolling stock on this and the opposite page. Opposite, top to bottom: a Fort Vancouver Plywood boxcar, a UTLX tank car, an XTRX covered hopper, and a Georgia Kaolin tank car.

SOURCES

The best sources of ideas on scratch-building, kitbashing, and the other topics discussed in this chapter are the model railroad magazines, such as *Model Railroader* and *Railroad Model Craftsman*. Every issue is packed with suggestions for new craft projects and examples of successful ones. General how-to-books, such as Schleicher's *The Model Railroading Handbook*, also contain useful information. More specialized books include *Kitbashing HO Model Railroad Structures* (Kalmbach) and *Prototype Railroad Color Guide* (AMS).

In addition, some manufacturers, such as Clover House, Mil-Scale, and Model Builders Supply, offer catalogues or manuals that can help you make optimum use of their products. Other examples are "Hobby & Craft Guide to Air-brushing" (Badger), "Styrene Handbook" (Evergreen Scale Models), "Painting Miniatures" (Floquil), and "Basics for Beginners: A Guide to Model Railroading" (Life-Like).

TOOLS AND SUPPLIES

Very simple rolling stock kits require nothing more than a screwdriver and a razor blade or hobby knife. But as the kits become more complex, and as you become more creative in combining kits and building from scratch, you will need to start collecting tools and supplies.

Basic Tools. The following are the basic tools you need for scratchbuilding and for assembling craftsman kits. They are available from your dealer and direct from many suppliers, including A-Line, Atlas, Clover House, Con-Cor, Micro-Mark, Model Power, NorthWest Short Line, Walthers, and X-Acto.

- *thin-bladed hobby knife (such as those made by X-Acto) for fine cutting*
- *small utility knife, with replaceable blades, for heavy cutting*
- *razor saw*
- *miter box (a device for cutting wood at a precise angle)*
- *rail nippers (for cutting rail)*
- *diagonal cutters*
- *single-edge razor blades*
- *NMRA Standards Gauge (O, On3, S, OO, HO, HOn3, N) to check wheels, track, and clearances*
- *pin vise (for holding small drills)*
- *tweezers*
- *miniature drill and drill bits*
- *needle-nose pliers or jeweler's pliers*
- *jeweler's files*
- *miniature screwdrivers*
- *miniature putty knives*
- *modeler's pins (to hold parts in place during gluing)*
- *taps (for forming threads to receive screws)*
- *toothpicks*
- *eyedropper*
- *emery boards or sandpaper*
- *scriber (for scoring styrene sheets in preparation for breaking)*
- *steel rule in scale feet and inches*
- *small square*
- *cutting surface, either hardwood board or a self-healing plastic cutting board (sold in arts supply stores)*

Motor Tools. If you've ever tried to cut a large lawn with a manual lawnmower, you know why power tools were invented. Power tools reduce the amount of effort you need to spend on a project and can make the results look neater and more professional. This is why motor tools are widely used in model railroading. A motor tool (such as those sold by Dremel, Mascot, Miniplex, and Model

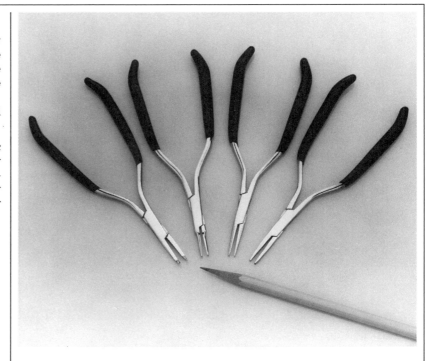

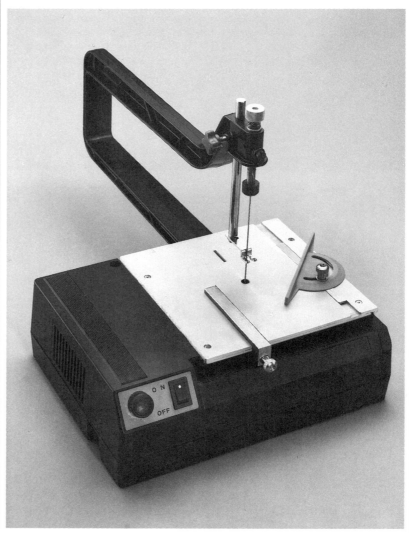

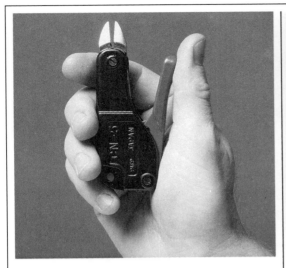

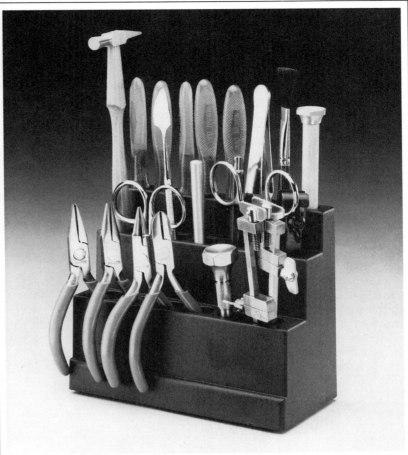

Opposite, top: Stainless steel micro-pliers from Micro-Mark for bending and positioning delicate parts. Opposite, bottom: the Micro-Lux Multi-Saw from Micro-Mark, for precision cuts on wood, metal, and plastic. Top: Micro-Mark's sprue cutter is designed to cut sprues, or waste plastic, from plastic parts. It will also cut thin wire and wood strips. Above: Micro-Mark's angle plate holds small parts together at a perfect 90° angle. Above right: As your tools multiply, you might consider getting an organizer, such as this three-level one from Micro-Mark. It stores 21 tools in 3 × 6 inches of workspace.

Power) typically comes with several bits—for cutting, sanding, grinding, drilling. The tool causes the bit to rotate far more quickly and evenly than a manual tool—and with much less effort on your part.

Dremel's Moto-Tool is highly regarded for its high-speed capability—up to 30,000 revolutions per minute. Lightweight and durable, the Moto-Tool comes in constant speed and variable-speed models. The variable-speed model allows you to do both high-speed operations (such as drilling) and low-speed ones (such as polishing). With a grinding stone, it can smooth imperfections in an engine casting. With cutter attachments, it can cut gaps in rail (important in wiring your railroad) or remove a cheap locomotive part for replacement by a more realistic one. Dremel's Freewheeler is a cordless, rechargeable version of the Moto-Tool.

Another kind of power tool you might consider getting is a power saw. Micro-Mark, for example, offers a power miter/cut-off saw that cuts metal, plastic, and wood. The Micro-Lux Multi-Saw, also from Micro-Mark, accepts most standard jeweler's and coping saw blades for precision cuts even on tiny parts. (A *coping saw* or *scroll saw* is used for cutting intricate patterns.) Dremel produces both table saws and scroll saws.

Adhesives. There are almost as many glues on the market as there are objects to glue. The kind you select depends on the material you're working with—wood, plastic, metal—and your own preferences with regard to speed, strength, convenience, and safety. Cyanoacrylates (also called ACC or "super glue") set in seconds and can be used on virtually all materials, but they also bond skin instantly and should be used with care. Two-part epoxy glues can also be used for nearly all materials, though these adhesives set more slowly. "White glue" (polyvinyl) or "yellow glue" (aliphatic resin) is best used on wood or paper.

Krazy Glue for Wood (available from Mil-Scale) is ideal for wood kits and scratch-building. Pliobond from Rail Craft Products is especially recommended for gluing hand-laid rail to ties. Satellite City's line of nontoxic cyanoacrylate adhesives include "Hot Stuff" (with a 3–5 second bonding time), "UFO-Thin" with a slightly longer bonding time but without odor, and "UFO-Thick" to fill small gaps between parts. Other companies offering adhesives include Ambroid, Bond Adhesives, Hobsco, Model Builders Supply, Plastruct, and Testors.

Soldering tools and supplies. Soldering is a way of bonding metal parts that relies on heat rather than cement. In soldering, filler metal (solder) is heated until it melts and forms a bond between two surfaces. The solder is usually sold in rods that resemble stiff wire. Modelers use soldering for two basic functions: electrical work and construction. Electrical soldering, which involves the joining of wires and terminals, is discussed in Chapter Four. Construction soldering—used to build items from scratch or attach parts from different kits—is discussed here.

Construction soldering is fairly easy with brass, copper, nickel silver, and tin, and much harder with aluminum, iron, and stainless steel. Most of the filler metals used in soldering are 60 percent tin and 40 percent lead; these are considered medium strength, with a medium melting point. Silver solder (actually a silver alloy) is stronger, but its higher melting point requires more heat—as much as 1600°F. (You may hear the process of soldering at temperatures above 840°F. referred to as *brazing*. Silversoldering is brazing or soldering with a filler metal made of silver alloy.)

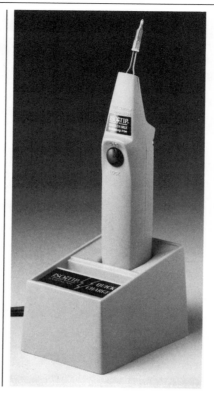
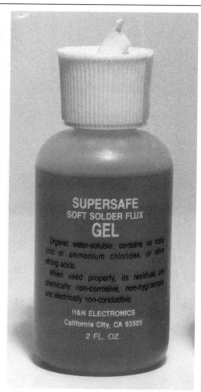

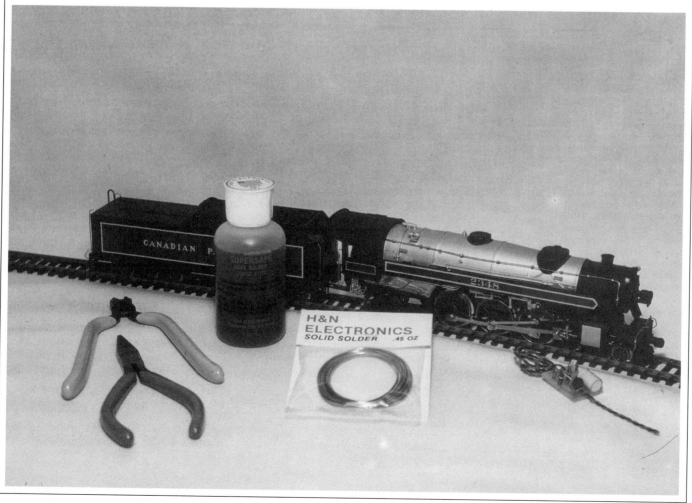

Microflame makes excellent butane torches that are small enough to carry in your pocket but hot enough for delicate silversoldering projects. Microflame also offers solder and *flux*. Flux is a compound that chemically cleans the surfaces to be joined, preparing them for soldering.

The safest kinds of flux to use are rosin or resin; these are inert at room temperature. Acid-based fluxes are also available, but these are hazardous to use. They are, however, useful for working with the difficult materials named above—iron, aluminum, and stainless steel—which otherwise refuse to bond. It might be wise for a novice to glue such materials with cyanoacrylates rather than waste time trying to solder them.

Simplex and Micro-Mark offer soldering torches. Electric soldering irons are sold by X-Acto and K & S Engineering. Another method of generating heat is electrical resistance, created by a low-voltage current. PBL's HOTIP line of tools and accessories makes use of this method. Kester, Erfin, and Radio Shack sell solder and flux; so do H & N Electronics, NJ International, Scale Scenics, and Tix.

Opposite, top left: Micro-Mark's cordless soldering iron heats up in five to ten seconds. **Opposite, top right:** H & N Electronics produces organic, noncorrosive soldering flux in gel and liquid form. **Opposite, bottom:** flux and solder from H & N Electronics.

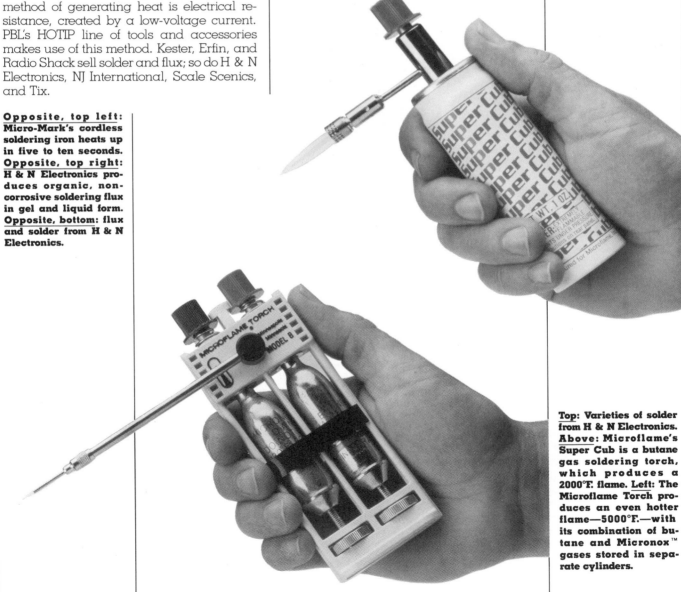

Top: Varieties of solder from H & N Electronics. Above: Microflame's Super Cub is a butane gas soldering torch, which produces a 2000°F. flame. Left: The Microflame Torch produces an even hotter flame—5000°F.—with its combination of butane and Micronox™ gases stored in separate cylinders.

Lubricants, cleaners, and cleaning tools. Like any machine with moving parts, your locomotive needs to be kept lubricated. Lubricants for gears, bearings, wheels and motors are offered by many companies, including Atlas, LaBelle Industries, Life-Like, Model Power, Peco, Precision Scale Co., and Woodland Scenics. Some lubricants are safe for plastic and painted surfaces; some are meant only for unpainted metal.

Nearly every modeler has seen a train refuse to start because a speck of dust or a film of oil is blocking the flow of current. To keep your trains in motion, you need to keep the rails clean. To help you, companies like Bachmann, A. J. Fricko, Life-Like, Roco, Simplex, and Tru-Scale all offer track cleaning solutions. Cleaning tools are also widely available in many shapes and sizes. Walthers, Wallace Metal Products, and NJ International make track cleaning blocks. Tru-Scale offers an eraser-type track cleaner. Kadee's Speedi-Driver Cleaner Brush cleans dirt from loco driver treads. F & M, Andrew J. Fricko, LaBelle Industries, and Model Power make track cleaning cars. Virnex Industries makes an adapter that fits on an Athearn switcher and converts it into a track cleaning loco; a device from Scale

Shops does the same for boxcars.

Miscellaneous. Some hobbyists seem to enjoy collecting tools almost as much as they enjoy collecting trains. For them, a tool is not only a useful means to an end, but interesting for its "gadget" value. The following items are both useful and interesting:

- *rail spiker—for hand-laying track (Kadee)*

- *duplicutter—cuts exactly the same size part out of two or more styrene sheets (the Chopper does the same for strip wood [NorthWest Short Line])*

- *riveter—creates embossed "rivets" in the sides of steel-prototype models (NorthWest Short Line)*

- *track test car—made of clear plastic so you can see track problems under the car (Tru-Scale)*

- *halogen lights—to reduce glare while working (Simplex)*

- *drill press—for precision drilling, shaping, and routing (Dremel)*

- *part-picker—holds small parts during assembly and starts small screws in hard-to-reach places (Clover House)*

- *eye loupe—jeweler's magnifying glass (Clover House)*

- *angle plate—holds small parts edge to edge or edge to surface at a 90° angle (Micro-Mark)*

- *sprue cutter—to cut sprues or waste plastic from injection molded plastic parts (Micro-Mark)*

Only long experience with tools can produce layouts as realistic as these. Above: Part of the Stony Creek & Western Railroad, an HO-scale layout by Gil Freitag, Sr., and Jr., of Houston, Texas. This is the freight house and chemical plant in the town of Arapahoe. Opposite: An automobile and locomotive meet at a crossing on Stafford Swain's HO-scale layout of the Whiteshell subdivision of the Canadian National.

SCRATCHBUILDING

Perhaps the best way to make sure your railroad is both realistic and personal is to build it from scratch. In scratchbuilding, sheets of wood, metal, or plastic are used to construct rolling stock, locos, or structures. Detail parts, paint, and lettering are added later. It may take many evenings of work, but the completed car or building will be entirely your own creation. Scratchbuilding allows you to model prototypes that are unavailable in kits. It also lets you invent a unique item, perhaps one that blends several prototypes and bears your own fictional roadname.

The best way to prepare to be a scratchbuilder is first to work with craftsman kits (discussed in Chapter One). These require many of the same cutting and fitting skills needed for scratchbuilding. Kitbashing and working with detail parts, both discussed below, also will help you prepare for scratchbuilding. In the end, however, it comes down to you, your tools, and one or more of the following raw materials. Leading suppliers include C & S Scale Industries, Clover House, Evergreen Scale Models, Holgate & Reynolds, Model Builders Supply, Northeastern Scale Models, Plastruct, Precision Scale Co., Vintage Reproductions, and Walthers.

Wood. Wood has wide appeal because it is an authentic material: actually used by prototype railroads for ties and rolling stock, carried as cargo, and employed in structures. Clover House offers wood in the form of scale lumber, poles, ties, and barrels. Basswood, a hard wood, is suggested for most railroading purposes; California pine and redwood are softer materials preferred for ties. Northeastern Scale Models also sells scale lumber, along with wood molding, panels for miniature structures, and wood strips and sheets. Other wood manufacturers include Ace Balsawood Co. and House of Balsa.

Metal. Metal is another authentic material, though its chief structural virtue—hardness—can make it difficult to work with. The most popular metal is brass, sold in sheet form for building locos and cars, in wire form for piping and rods, in tube form for smoke stacks and car loads. In addition, some companies, like Clover House, sell metal mesh to simulate security and ventilator screens. Chains—for brake chains and tying down loads—are sold by Clover House, Builders in Scale, and Campbell Scale Models. Precision Scale Co. and Vintage Reproductions also sell metal supplies for scratchbuilding.

Plastic. Plastic is not usually an authentic material, but it is a handy one. It can be quite realistic when used to simulate painted structures; with some sanding and paint, it can even represent weathered wood. Styrene is the most popular plastic: it is inexpensive, durable, easy to cut and paint, comes in many sizes, and can be cemented to any other material. Styrene comes in sheets, strips, rods, and tubes. Other plastics, however, are sometimes called for—such as polycarbonate (or Lexan®), a clear plastic used for windows. (Real glass for windows is also available from Clover House, but is not recommended for large panes.) Suppliers of plastic include Clover House, Evergreen, Grandt Line Products, and Model Builders.

Finishing Materials. Finishing touches are important in scratchbuilding. To add a final touch to raw wood, metal, or plastic, you may decide to use textured patterned sheets of paper or plastic. Model Builders Supply offers these sheets in 120 different colors, patterns, and scales—depicting brick, stone, roofing, tile, and more. Evergreen offers sidings for freight cars, passenger cars, and corrugated and clapboard structures. Evergreen's "sidewalk" plastic comes with light grooves to simulate sidewalks. C & S Scale, Holgate & Reynolds, and Plastruct also make finishing materials.

More examples of skilled scratchbuilding. Opposite: The town of Quin's Bend, from the Freitags' HO-scale layout of the Stony Creek & Western Railroad. Below: Houses and trains at Provo, from the Freitags' layout.

KITBASHING

If you don't want to build a car or loco from scratch, but you're not satisfied with what's available in kits, the solution is obvious: kitbashing. Also called cross-kitting, customizing, or converting, this is a process in which you combine parts from two or more kits to produce a new model. A 1988 article in *Railroad Model Craftsman*, for example, describes how one modeler combined parts from an Athearn SD9 and a Tyco GP20 to produce an HO scale SD18—a rare diesel loco built for the Chesapeake & Ohio in 1963. Structures can also be kitbashed. Mil-Scale's "Jacobs Coalyard" structure, for example, can be combined with an ice supplier structure to simulate a once common sight: retailers who sold coal in the winter and ice in the summer.

Modelers' magazines are a good place to get ideas for kitbashing; as you learn more about prototypes, you will get ideas of your own. To help you along, some companies sell *conversion kits*, which provide virtually everything you need to convert one model to another. C & S Scale Industries makes an N-scale conversion kit that converts a Con-Cor 50-foot gondola to a Canadian-prototype wood-chip car. Rara Avis offers kits to convert their G-scale flatcar into a gondola or bulkhead car.

Locomotives are even more popular as subjects for conversion kits. Conversion kits from V & T Shops can transform a Model Die Casting HO-scale Shay steam loco into an Sn3 or Sn2 Shay. V-Line Locomotives specializes in classic loco conversion shells in N scale.

DETAIL PARTS

One way to make a locomotive or freight car more realistic is to add *detail parts*. Sometimes called "superdetailing parts," these simulate the complex array of external components on prototype trains—steps, valves, pumps, pipe fittings, grabirons (or hand rails). Inexpensive trains, whether kit-built or ready-to-run, are often lacking in these fine details; if the details do exist, they may not be up to a modeler's standards. Either of these reasons may motivate a modeler to buy detail parts. For a scratchbuilt or kitbashed project, detail parts are a simple necessity.

Detail parts are available not only for trains, but for buildings and scenery. Detail parts are usually made of plastic, "lost wax" brass (referring to the casting process), or "white metal alloy."

Train parts. A steam engine needs valve gear, smoke box parts, domes, a stack. Any kind of train needs air hoses, brake wheels, wheel sets. Trains also need steps—pilot steps, tender steps, stirrup steps for freight cars, passenger safety steps. Other detail parts include grabirons, whistles, bells, horns, marker lights, headlights, brake cylinders, number plates, pumps, gauges, doors, and pipe fittings. When you're done with the train, don't forget the crew—they need waterbags, oilcans, wrenches, and scoop shovels.

Numerous manufacturers are eager to help you shop for these and many other parts. Precision Scale Co. carries over 15,000 different parts for HO, HOn3, O, On3, G, and 1 scales. These are described in several thick

Above: The realism of this steam locomotive on Stafford Swain's HO-scale layout of the Canadian prairie is due in part to the abundance of small, authentic-looking detail parts—hand rails, piping, valves.

and fascinating catalogues. Detailing kits are available to simplify the job of detailing a particular car or loco.

Trackside Specialties has been in the business of selling mail-order detail parts for 30 years. Some of its lost wax brass items—in HO, HOn3, O, On3, and O-27—have been acquired from the stocks of import companies such as Sunset and Westside. Trackside Specialties also offers kits for scratchbuilding a new loco from the parts of other locos.

Northeastern Scale Models sells roofs and floors for freight and passenger cars in N through O. Trackside Details specializes in G scale. Detail Associates' catalogue features handsome photos of its HO diesel loco details and N scenic details. Jaks Enterprises has two divisions that offer detail parts: Finestkind MDL's in S scale and Scale Structures Ltd. in HO and N scale. V & T offers parts in S and Sn3.

Flatcars, hoppers, and gondolas in any scale need cargo. Loads of lumber, machinery, coal and other products add interest to your rolling stock—and also add weight, which makes the cars more stable. Kadee offers lumber loads for N-scale trains. Virnex sells all-metal, well-detailed flatcar loads, including ship propellers, strip steel coils, and diesel generators. Other load manufacturers include C & S Scale Industries and Chooch Enterprises.

Bowser offers the Cal Scale line of lost wax brass castings, along with many other HO and O detail parts. In addition, Bowser makes HO detail kits and superdetail kits for particular locos, such as the Mantua 2-6-6-2. Master Creations also makes superdetail kits earmarked for particular locos; each contains white metal and brass pieces. Cannon & Co. offers entire cabs, hoods, and hooddoors for HO EMD diesel locos.

Structure and scenery parts. A superdetailed train only looks at home in a layout where the scenery is equally detailed. Plastruct and Model Builders Supply provide fine structural details like staircases, hand rails, and chain link fencing. For the roofs of buildings, Model Builders Supply makes seventy-five sizes and styles of skylights. Woodland Scenics offers Scenic Details, finely crafted HO kits that include mailboxes, crates and barrels, tombstones, and industrial junk. Detail parts from Alloy Forms include 55-gallon drums, a window air conditioner, junk autos, and a doghouse.

Clover House offers eye bolts and rings for heavy timbers, girders, and concrete (used to anchor cables and chains). Clover House also sells glass beads designed to simulate the insulators on overhead wires (such as

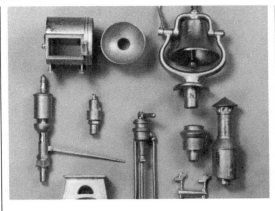

telegraph lines and high voltage lines).

Other manufacturers of detail parts—for trains and/or scenery—include Details West, Evergreen Scale Models, F & M, Holgate & Reynolds, Model Die Casting, Rara Avis, Scale Scenics, Tiger Valley Models, Tomar Industries, V & T Shops, Walthers, Westerfield, and Ye Olde Huff N Puff.

Left: These finely-made detail parts are all you need to make your ½-scale brass locomotive and cars complete. The parts include (clockwise from top left): headlight and reflector; bell kit; passenger car roof vents; smoke box door clamps; loco cab brake valve stand; conductor's passenger safety step; steam whistle and pop valve. Except for the white metal alloy safety step, all parts are brass. Below: Plasti-Kote spray paints produce finishes that resemble granite, asphalt, grass, and soil.

OPERATING PARTS

Most detail parts are "dummies": they only need to *look* authentic. But some parts need to act right as well as look right. These include trucks and couplers, and, perhaps most critically, motors. Just as the external parts that come with a standard loco may be unsatisfactory, the motor that comes with your loco may not run as efficiently as you want it to—or it may wear out over time. In either case, it can be replaced. Here are some of the leading manufacturers of motors, trucks, and couplers.

Motors and Motor Parts. The names of motor parts—gears, flywheels, connector clips, armatures, brushes—are arcane to some modelers but music to other modelers' ears. That is why many companies offer both complete motors and parts. Athearn offers a complete line of motors and motor parts, as does A-Line/Proto Power West and North-West Short Line. English's Model Railroad Supply (a division of Bowser) offers mechanism kits specifically for Bachmann and Lionel locos. Precision Scale Co. specializes in O-scale gears, motors, and drive mechanisms. NorthWest Short Line offers the Flea II, a miniature motorizing unit for N to On3 scales.

Proto Power West sells top-rated repowering kits for Athearn, Bachmann, Model Power, and other locos. The kits include motor, flywheels, and wiring hardware, along with accessories (frame, flywheel cement, etc.). Proto Power West is also known for its hand-assembled, ready-to-run diesel chassis, powered by can motors.

Other manufacturers of motors and/or motor parts include F & M, Grandt Line Products, Holgate & Reynolds, Life-Like, Mantua, NJ International, Roco, and Wallace Metal Products.

Trucks. The wheels underneath most freight and passenger cars are arranged in assemblies called *trucks*, which help distribute the weight of the car evenly. Each truck has four or more wheels; the trucks of passenger cars tend to have a longer wheelbase to ensure a smoother ride.

Trucks have changed in design over the years, and your railroad will be more accurate if you choose the right trucks for the period you are modeling. Here are a few of the names of trucks you might encounter, with the period in which they were used:

- *arch bar—1860s–1925*
- *Fox—circa 1900–1930*
- *Bettendorf—introduced circa 1903*
- *Commonwealth—late steam era; usually six-wheeled*
- *Andrews—1920s–1950s; still used in work cars*
- *roller bearing—1950s–present; required for most new freight cars*

Although you can easily buy rolling stock with trucks already attached, you may want to choose your own trucks—and thereby be able to pick exactly the style and quality you want. Companies offering kits of trucks include Kadee, Athearn, Model Die Casting, and Precision Scale Co. If you want to repair or alter a truck, parts (such as wheelsets, bolsters, and side frames) are available from Kadee and Walthers.

Power trucks—trucks that contain motor units—can be installed in a passenger or freight car to help boost a heavy train. A power truck can also serve as the motor of a loco or trolley car, leaving the interior of the model free for interior detail, sound equipment, or *command control* electronics.

Couplers. A *coupler* is a device that hooks two cars together, but not all couplers are alike. Most HO model locomotives and cars

Below: A close look at two Bettendorf trucks mounted on the underside of an S-scale 50-foot steel boxcar. This styrene kit—with trucks included—is offered in many roadnames by Pacific Rail Shops. Opposite: An assortment of HO-scale trucks from Cape Line Models. Top row: On the left and right are freight and tender trucks; in the center is an old-style plain journal for passenger service. All are four-wheeled. Middle row: Six-wheeled trucks for passenger cars. On the left is a Commonwealth; on the right is a Pullman. Bottom row, left to right: A Taylor freight truck; a Commonwealth four-wheeled passenger truck; a Bettendorf freight truck.

come with plastic *horn-hook* couplers. (Horn-hook couplers are also available separately for cars that are sold without couplers.) Horn-hooks lack working *knuckles*, the part of the coupler that hooks and unhooks.

Most HO modelers prefer to replace the horn-hook coupler with an automatic knuckle coupler. With this device, two cars are automatically coupled when one is rolled against the other. This has the obvious advantage of not requiring you to interfere manually: a locomotive can push the cars together. By using a *magnetic uncoupler*, the process of uncoupling can also be automatic. A locomotive brings the cars to a *magnetic uncoupler* located between the track rails; there magnetic force causes the cars to disengage.

Kadee's Magne-Matic system is by far the most well-known system of couplers and uncouplers. Several options are available. With a permanent magnet uncoupler, cars will uncouple whenever they stop with slack over the magnet. The disadvantage to this is that the cars cannot recouple until they are moved away from the magnet. An electromagnetic uncoupler, however, will only force the cars apart when a remote-control switch is pressed; one car can then be recoupled to a different one without having to move it away from the uncoupler. This gives you more freedom in deciding where and how to link cars together.

A delayed-action uncoupler is perhaps the most versatile device. With this system, two cars become effectively uncoupled when over an uncoupler, but remain superficially joined. The cars can be pushed to any other place on the track—say, an industrial siding, where one of the cars will be left for loading. The final uncoupling does not take place until the train stops and then pulls away.

Many modelers choose to install Kadee couplers on all of their rolling stock; Kadee couplers fit virtually every brand and scale. International Hobby Corp. also has a magnetic coupling and uncoupling system, and Right-of-Way Industries offers magnetic uncouplers. Manufacturers of *horn-hook* or other couplers include Athearn, Grandt Line Products, LaBelle Industries, Life-Like, and Precision Masters Inc.

PAINTING

Your train's paint job is the first thing people see, so it pays to do it right. You can buy ready-to-run equipment with paint already applied, but doing your own painting individualizes your trains and can give old rolling stock a new identity. Each of the prototype lines had its own distinctive color scheme. By studying those color schemes—in photos appearing in magazines and manuals—you will soon know which color schemes are appropriate for the lines you want to model.

Discussed below are the paints and accessories—and, if you choose, the airbrush equipment—needed to turn from assembling trains to painting them.

Paint. Like everything else on a scale model train, the train's coat of paint has to be "scale." If it isn't ultra-thin, it will look heavy and conceal the train's fine details. The paints made by Floquil-Polly S Color Corp.—a pioneer in the industry and still thriving—provide a finish about .0002 inches thick. That is the HO-scale equivalent of the 1/64 inch thickness of a prototype coat of paint. The finish does not obscure fine detail and adheres to almost any surface—wood, metal, cardboard, plastic.

Floquil markets two lines of paints: the water-based Polly S line, and the older, more complete line of solvent-based Floquil colors. These colors match the color chips of prototype originals—Reading Green, Dela-

ware & Hudson Blue, Union Pacific Armour Yellow. Floquil also offers more generic colors—Engine Black, Reefer White, Caboose Red. Weathering colors, such as Mud, Rust, and Grime, can be used to give trains a realistic, battered appearance. Pigmented wood stains—driftwood, natural pine, mahogany, teak—can be used to simulate different kinds of wood.

Another highly-regarded line of paints is the Scalecoat line sold by Quality Craft Models. The Plasti-Kote company has made Pactra hobby paints since 1947. The Testor

Opposite, left: Two of the most widely-used colors from Floquil: engine black and plain black. Opposite, right: This display of Pactra hobby paints suggests how many choices are available to the model railroad painter. Left: Tape is an essential accessory for painting stripes and two-toned color schemes. Pactra offers both masking tape and trim tape. Above: An array of brushes—camel, sable, and ox-hair—from Pactra.

Corp. (actually a sister company of Floquil's) makes model paints for a broader market than the more expensive Floquil line. Badger produces a line of water-based paints called "Air-Opaque." These are safe for modelers allergic to lacquers, enamels, or petroleum-based paints.

Accessories. Most of the companies mentioned above offer a complete line of accessories for their paints. Thinners are a must; a retardant (a solution that slows drying time, giving you time to work) may prove convenient. A clear flat (nongloss) finish eliminates gloss on decals and protects surfaces.

Sable-hair brushes are preferred by many modelers for their versatility and their ability to hold a sharp point for fine detail work. "Camel" hair (a trade term for hairs from a variety of animals) is popular and less expensive. Bristle and ox-hair are mainly used for base coats and large surfaces. Plastic brushes are also used by many modelers.

If brush painting is too tedious for you, you may want to avail yourself of aerosol paints. These are mainly useful for primer and clear finish coats. The spray can droplets are too large and under too great a pressure to provide a fine finish.

Other useful accessories include:

● *mixing bottles (empty bottles for mixing paint),*

● *pipettes (eyedroppers)*

● *masking tape or Scotch Magic tape for painting stripes and two-color paint schemes*

● *masking fluid (such as Micro-Scale's "Micro Mask") for the same purpose*

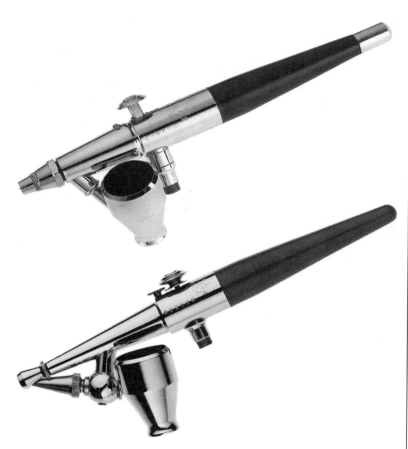

Airbrush equipment. Buying an airbrush is a big investment, but the ease of operation and the professional results may be worth the cost. An airbrush is basically a miniature spray gun that allows you to control the size, direction, and pressure of spray, from tiny dots to full coats. Compressed air is fed through a hose from an electric compressor, or from a pressurized tank. Paints can be mixed before being loaded into the airbrush, and there are no brushstrokes to interrupt the smooth finish.

Airbrushes, however, are expensive. The airbrush itself may run from $20 to $130; the electric compressor costs $110 and up. Still, most experienced modelers swear by the airbrush and consider it worthwhile. It takes some practice to learn how to adjust the air pressure and the paint-thinner blend, but that investment is also worthwhile.

Badger Airbrush, Binks Manufacturing, W. R. Brown, Paasche Airbrush, Pactra Coatings, and Polk's Hobby International all offer airbrushes for model railroaders. Some are external mix, mixing air and paint outside the gun; others are internal mix. The external mix airbrushes produce larger dot patterns; the internal mix ones produce smoother, finer effects. Single-action air-

Above, left: Paasche's double-action VL airbrush (top) and single-action H airbrush. Right, top to bottom: 1–2) Paasche's airbrush sets (such as the H, at top, and the VL), come complete with airbrush, color cup, bottle, wrench, air hose and more. 3) Paasche's BBF Bench type Economy Filter Booth accommodates the spraying of small parts. 4) Paasche D500 air compressor. Opposite, top: The Paasche 99 respirator protects modelers from paint vapor and spray mist. Opposite, middle: An alternative to the air compressor is the disposable pressure tank, such as these tanks from Paasche. Opposite, bottom: The Belvedere Hotel, an HO-scale building kit from Life-Like. This replica of a downtown Baltimore hotel comes prepainted in "weathered" colors.

brushes, such as the Paasche H, are favored by many hobbyists; others prefer the greater versatility of double-action airbrushes, such as the Paasche VL, which can handle both fine detail and broad coverage.

One useful innovation is the Chameleon color-changing system by Binks (to be used with its Raven II double-action airbrush). This system of attachments allows the modeler to store up to nine colors without having to replace a paint reservoir.

If you prefer not to buy an electric compressor, there are less expensive alternatives. A reusable cylinder tank, such as Paasche's LCT or Liquid Carbonic Tank, uses carbon dioxide as a propellant. It must be refilled by carbon dioxide suppliers. Disposable pressure tanks are another alternative. In the long run, however, a compressor may be the best value.

Large compressors need a regulator and a condenser unit to keep the airflow dry; smaller units can get by with a moisture trap. Here are some other useful accessories:

- *paint and vapor respirator—to filter out harmful paint spray mist*

- *spray booth—to contain spray*

- *turntable—to reduce the need to touch the model during painting*

WEATHERING

Unless you want your trains to look like toys, the first thing you should do with your newly assembled, freshly painted, carefully lettered train is to make it appear old and grimy. Most prototype locos and cars—along with structures—show the effects of weather, age, dirt, grease, and soot. Your railroad should simulate these effects.

There is no one way to weather model railroads. The techniques you choose will help to personalize your layout as well as make it more realistic. Fading should be part of the original paint job—done by mixing a given color with white. Plastic simulating weathered wood should first receive a base color like yellow-tan or gray-brown, then highlights of lighter grays and browns, then thin washes of black and brown. Grime, rust, mud, and so on can be added with appropriate stains or washes (a wash will be translucent and allow the original color to show through).

To simulate paint that has worn off—say, on a piece of plastic doubling for wood—first paint the plastic with weathered wood colors. Add a finish color, then use a fiberglass eraser to rub that color off in places, letting the weathered wood show.

Weathering is an art form all its own. Don't be afraid to try new tricks, and do as much original research as you can—studying photos of prototypes to see the patterns and shadings of real dust and grime.

DECALS AND DRY TRANSFERS

Like a careful paint job, decals and dry transfers are ways of giving a locomotive a distinct identity—a place and time in railroad history. Roadnames, slogans, trademarks all give life and individuality to rolling stock that would otherwise be generic and incomplete. Ready-to-run cars and some simple kits come with roadnames already applied, but you may choose to paint these over and apply new lettering. Whether the car is old or new, there are basically two ways to letter it: wet-process decals and dry transfers.

Decals. Decals usually come in sheets that group together roadnames, number series, stripes, and freight car dimensional data. The modeler cuts out an individual decal, then, using tweezers, dips it in water, holds it in place, and removes the backing. A clear, pre-decaling paint such as that offered by Microscale can help prepare a surface for decals. Decal-softening fluid makes the decal film more flexible and ensures that it adheres to small details. A light coat of clear, flat paint will hide the glossy finish of the decal film.

Champion Decal Company, Islington Station Products, Microscale, and Walthers all offer catalogues of decals. Walthers offers a "Decal Catalog and Reference Manual." Champion Decal's "Freight Car Lettering Plan Book" shows the correct way to letter and paint over 611 cars from 208 different railroads. Champion's 2500 different sets of decals include such fine detail as "WATCH YOUR STEP" signs for the steps of passenger cars.

Detail Associates, Master Creations, ShellScale Decals, Virnex, and Westerfield also sell decals.

On this page and opposite are examples of custom-made decals. This page: three decals from Rail Graphics. Opposite, top: from Microscale Decals. Opposite, middle: from Rail Graphics. Opposite bottom: from DM Custom Decals.

Dry Transfers. Dry transfer letters are applied by being rubbed directly from a waxy sheet onto a model surface using a dull pencil or an artist's burnisher. No water is required. A coat of clear, flat finish seals the letters. Because the letters are applied directly to the model surface, there is no decal film to hide. However, transferring the letters successfully requires some practice.

Clover House offers a broad assortment of dry transfer sets in HO, reproducing slogans and symbols as well as roadnames. Your Atchison, Topeka & Santa Fe boxcar can bear the slogan "Santa Fe all the way" along with a map of ATSF's routes. Regional roadnames—the Savannah, Americus & Montgomery from around 1900; the Trinity & Brasos Valley from the 1890s—are also available.

Clover House also offers brand names for rolling stock: the Armour Refrigerator Line (circa 1890), White Swan Shortening (circa 1913), and Schneider Brewing Company (circa 1933). Signs to be applied to structures and vehicles include such turn-of-the-century names as "Bull's Pills for Health" and "Elwood's Root Beer 5¢." To create your own signs or tailor existing ones, Clover House offers alphabets and stripes.

Woodland Scenics has a large assortment of dry transfers, including alphabets, number sets, and stripes in many styles and sizes, and also business and product signs in full color. Islington Station Products specializes in dry transfers for HO tank cars carrying products such as Hubinger corn syrup, Schaefer salt, and various toxic chemicals. Vintage Reproductions also sells dry transfers.

CUSTOM SERVICES

All of the procedures described in this chapter have to do with customizing your railroad: making it your own, in the course of making it realistic. But, for various reasons, you may not want to do all the work yourself. You may not have the resources or the skills; you may simply not have the time.

If so, there are companies that will do some of the work for you. Custom decal services are perhaps the most frequently used custom services. DM Custom Decals offers a range of specifications from which to design your own decal; the decal is then prepared according to your request. You can also provide camera-ready artwork from which DM will prepare your design. Arlington Consulting & Engineering (ACE), Champion, and Rail Graphics also provide custom decal services.

ACE, the Modelmaker, Walker Model Service, and Yellowstone Custom Service do custom painting. Pope Imagineering, Track One, Trackside Specialties, and Yellowstone are among the companies that build custom models. Precision Scale Co. will create custom detail parts in brass or plastic, following your master pattern, descriptive information, or pictures.

Opposite and right: HO-scale decals from Microscale Decals for a variety of cars and lines, including New York Central cab diesel locomotives, Missouri Pacific cabooses, and assorted freight cars and reefers.

CHAPTER FOUR
Making Connections

Below: A modeler at work on his homemade Centralized Traffic Control (CTC) board. Opposite: The train at the top of the picture is composed of #1-scale equipment from Märklin. These cars loom large compared to the Märklin HO-scale train at bottom of the page.

ost of us regard electricity as a mystery rivalled only by plumbing and the law. No wonder then that wiring can be the most intimidating part of model railroading. The instructions that come with the average train set are simple enough, but what happens when you start designing more complex layouts and running more than one train at a time? What happens when you add switch machines, lights, sound effects? What if you want to computerize your system? The electrical situation becomes complicated—but never impossible. This chapter will help you make sense of what is available in the electrical products market.

GETTING ADVICE

However self-reliant you are, you will need to take advice from *somebody* if you want your railroad to run well. It is up to you whether your principal source of information will be books, magazines, a trusted hobby dealer, or an expert fellow modeler. Most railroaders learn from several of these sources. In time, you may become the modeler others go to for advice.

Linn H. Westcott's *How to Wire Your Model Railroad* (Kalmbach Publishing) has initiated modelers since 1950 in the art of wiring. The book does an admirable job both in explaining the basics and outlining the many possibilities that open up as your railroad expands. Paul Mallery's *Electrical Handbook for Model Railroaders*, Vols. I and II, (Carstens) is also highly recommended. You might also look at the following books:

Wiring Your Layout (Atlas)
Easy-to-Build Electronic Projects for Model Railroaders (Kalmbach Publishing)
Basic Electricity and Electronics for Model Railroaders (Kalmbach Publishing)
34 New Electronic Projects for Model Railroaders (Kalmbach Publishing)

OTHER SYSTEMS

Most of the discussion in this chapter pertains to the two-rail, DC system that is the standard for North American model railroading. But other systems exist that have a wide following—notably Lionel's and Märklin's. Both use a three-rail AC system; consult each company's materials for more information.

G and #1 scale use the same DC two-rail system as most other scales, but have some special characteristics as a result of their large size and outdoor operation. For help on wiring those systems, consult Robert Schleicher's *Model Railroading with LGB* (Greenberg) and the magazine *Garden Railways* (Sidestreet Bannerworks).

Most trolley models can run on DC rail power, but they also present a unique modeling opportunity: receiving power through an overhead wire, just like the prototype. Bowser sells trolleys that run on rail power but can be adapted for overhead operation. An overhead wire system and trolley pole or pantograph make it possible. Precision Scale Co., Brawa, and Vollmer also sell overhead systems; Richard Orr sells traction wiring accessories and tools (phosphor bronze wire, hanger holder, tapered street poles to support wire, etc.)

POWER PACKS

When shopping for power packs and accessories, it is useful to have a basic understanding of how railroad wiring works. A power supply is connected by *feeder* wires to each of the two track rails. An electric current travels through one rail until it gets to your locomotive. It passes through the locomotive motor, causing the train to move, and returns via the other rail to the power supply. As long as you keep the power turned on, the circuit remains closed and the train moves. If you reverse the current, the train moves in the opposite direction. If you turn it off, the train stops.

The only electrical device you absolutely need to get this circuit going is a *power pack*—a device that converts your household current (110 volts AC) into the types of current a model railroad uses: 12 volts DC for the trains; 16 volts AC for the accessories (lights, switch machines, etc.). A toy train transformer that only puts out AC power (a requirement for Lionel's three-rail trains) will not do for two-rail trains: your locomotive will just sit there and the motor may burn out.

A power pack comes with almost any train set, but it may not have the features or the quality you want. A good basic pack for running one HO or N train is Model Rectifier Corp.'s (MRC) RailPower 1400. The pack is U.L. listed, has a circuit breaker to protect against short circuits, and has basic *throttle* or speed controls—an on-off switch, a direction control or reversing switch, and a speed control. It also features Proportional Tracking Control, which is said to enhance handling by conveying subtle speed variations more effectively.

For a G, O, or S train a more powerful pack is needed, such as MRC's RailMaster 2400. MRC's TrainPower 6200 is especially

designed for G-scale trains. For the delicate circuits of Z scale, Kadee markets an MRC 1100 power pack modified to have a voltage output of only 10 volts. Starr Enterprises' Starr-Tec Hogger is a multi-scale pack delicate enough for N but powerful enough for G. The Hogger features "walk-around" throttle controls, described in the section on "Controlling Your Layout" below.

Note that a pack's capacity is sometimes described in terms of the scales it can power (as are those mentioned above), sometimes in amperes or amps. Bachmann's Spectrum line of power packs, for example, includes the 2.5 amp Ultra Plus and the .9 amp Magnum. An N-scale engine motor requires about one-half amp, an HO motor one-half to one, an O motor as much as three or four.

Lionel's locomotives require AC power such as that provided by MRC's TrainPower 027. Lionel also sells transformers that supply AC power for its O-27 gauge trains.

If you have a toy train transformer and want to use it on a DC railroad, A. J. Fricko Company offers the "Transverto," which changes the output of a toy train transformer from 18 volts AC to 18 volts DC. Circuitron and Train Tronics also make AC to DC converters. To provide the AC power that runs lights, switch machines, and other accessories, you can either use the AC terminals of your power pack or buy a separate transformer.

The biggest differences between power packs are in the throttle or speed controls. A prototype train does not accelerate from 0 to 60 miles per hour any more than a car does. Because the train is massive, and because passengers and cargo need to be protected from the strain of acceleration, a prototype train only slowly builds up speed; when it comes to a halt, it does so gradually. On a model railroad, this effect is simulated by carefully adjusting the voltage so that the train takes its time speeding up and slowing down.

The simplest packs use a variable resistor or rheostat to adjust the voltage. More sophisticated packs use transistors to achieve realistic *momentum control* (a feature that simulates the gradual changes in speed of a prototype train).

Another feature that distinguishes power packs is the ability to power more than one train. MRC's DualPower 2800 can run two HO or N locos with independent control. Independent control is needed so that each train on the layout will run at its own speed. Without independent control both trains would run at the same time at the same speed—a rather "unprototypical" sight.

If, however, you have several locos powering a single, very long train, you will want the locos to run at the same speed. In that case you might want MRC's Loco-Motion 1500, which can run up to three HO locos without independent control. The Engineer Throttle by Dallee Electronics is a high-quality, heavy-duty unit especially useful for multiple-unit diesel trains where all the diesels are powered. It has a variety of monitors and features, including momentum effects and adjustable pulse; its high amperage is sufficient to handle any normal combination of models from large to small scales.

For experienced modelers who want to monitor a pack's output, some power supplies, such as MRC ThrottleMaster 550, feature *ammeters* and *voltmeters*. Some packs, such as MRC's ThrottleMaster 500, come with "pulse power" or "pulse injection," which is a way of ensuring smooth motion at very slow speeds—a useful feature when coupling cars or diagnosing track problems.

Some modelers choose to build their own transistorized throttles. Some of NTRAK's resource booklets describe how to build simple throttles for your N-scale layout, using parts available from Radio Shack.

Once you are running several trains, the need arises for a way of coordinating all the activity on your layout. That need is met by building or buying a *control panel* or *control system*. The control system is necessary to control not only locomotives, but the electrical blocks, remote control turnouts, signals, and other features that make up a model railroad.

WIRES

Wiring for an oval of track without loops or turnouts is fairly simple. All you need are two wires, each connecting the power pack and a *terminal track*—a section of track with attachments for wire. Terminal track is available from Atlas, Roco, and other track manufacturers. You may also use terminal joiners such as those made by Atlas to connect wires directly to the rails—or you can *solder* the wires on (see the next section).

Electrical "hook-up" wire, connectors, and wiring accessories are available from many sources—A-Line, Belden Wire Company, Brawa, Con-Cor, LaBelle Industries to name a few. You may have old wire lying around the house, but don't use it if it is brittle, hard to strip, or badly oxidized. Also, make sure it is the right gauge for the electrical demand (see box on wire gauges next page). Buying wires in an assortment of colors and then color-coding them will make it easier to trace connections.

You'll notice some wire is *stranded* (made up of strands) and flexible, some solid and stiff. The choice is yours. Solid wire fits better under screw terminals and won't fray, but stranded wire is easier to bend and maneuver.

Opposite; top: MRC's Tech II Loco-Motion 1500 power pack, which can run up to three HO locomotives. Opposite, bottom: MRC's Train-Power 6200 is designed to power G-scale trains, but will also handle O and HO scales. Below: Special care is needed to protect the wiring of a garden layout. Here Eric Lloyd inspects his Lloyd County Railway in Wrexham, Wales.

ELECTRICAL SOLDERING

Soldering was already defined in Chapter Three as the process of heating and melting a piece of filler metal until it forms a bond between two surfaces. But soldering electrical connections is very different from soldering parts of a train. First, it is essential that you use a *non-corrosive, non-acid-based* flux (the material that chemically cleans the surfaces to be joined). Acid fluxes (including those with zinc chloride) will eventually corrode your electrical connections and cause the wires to fall off the terminals. Solder with a resin or rosin core flux is considered safe for electrical soldering.

Second, you might consider using a *eutectic* solder (solder with a very low melting point); these solders typically have 53 percent tin rather than 60 percent tin (the remainder of the solder being lead). Eutectic solders are easy to use because they form a bond quickly and require less heat than solders with higher melting points; however, they are more expensive and the bond is not as strong. If you are new to soldering, they are certainly worth trying.

Third, make sure you get the right diameter of solder for the job. Solder is sold in rods of different diameters; .025 inches is not too small for delicate electrical work.

Finally, don't use a torch or soldering iron that is too big for the job. For electrical work, the best choice is a soldering pencil rated at about 25–40 watts (such as those made by Ungar and Weller) or a soldering gun (such as those made by Weller). Wahl makes a cordless, rechargeable soldering pencil that is convenient for crawling under layouts. On either a pencil or gun, a built-in light is handy to help you see what you're doing.

H & N Electronics offers several solders that have received good reviews, along with a non-corrosive flux that can be cleaned up with water. Other companies offering solder and fluxes for electrical work include Kester, Ersin, and Radio Shack.

BLOCKS

Wiring becomes more complex as soon as you add a *turning track*—a track, such as a *wye* or *reverse loop*, that enables a train to turn around and start traveling in the direction from which it came. The polarity on such a track when a train crosses it will be *opposite* to that of the rest of the railroad (the mainline).

When a *westbound* train enters a reverse loop, the polarity on that loop must match the polarity on the approaching track (the track from which the train just came). As it travels around the loop, the train turns end for end

and leaves the loop going *eastbound*. In order for the train to return to the mainline track in what is now an eastbound direction, the mainline polarity has to have been reversed—without affecting the polarity on the reverse loop. (You could have reversed the polarity on the mainline without placing the train on the reverse loop, but then the train would simply have gone backwards—caboose forward.)

Since the polarity on the turning track has to be controlled separately from the polarity on the rest of the railroad, the turning track will have to be electrically isolated from the rest of the railroad. (If it were not, it would cause a short circuit.) Such an isolated section is called a *reversing block*.

A block is electrically isolated by means of plastic insulating rail joiners, available from track manufacturers such as Atlas and Kato. You can also cut the gaps yourself with a razor saw or motor tool, then add an insulator such as Ambroid cement to keep it from closing when hot weather causes the rails to expand.

Once gaps are cut to isolate a section of track, that section or block becomes insulated from the flow of current. A train that reaches that block will stop dead. To keep the train moving while it is in the block, the block must have its own feeder wires running from the power source, independent of the wires running to the rest of the track.

Turning sections or reverse blocks are only one kind of electrically-isolated block. Another type is the *control block*, used for independent control of more than one train. As long as each train is always in a different block from all the other trains, you can have one train move faster than another, have one make stops while another continues, etc. There are also *signal blocks* (containing signals or other devices); *interchange blocks* (electrically connected to adjacent blocks when turnouts are thrown); and *stopping blocks* (a short block that forces a locomotive to stop when power is disconnected there). Each of these blocks requires gaps disconnecting it from the rest of the railroad, wires feeding power, and switches to control it.

WIRE GAUGES

Wire comes in gauges graded on the American Wire Gauge (AWG) scale. The larger the AWG number, the thinner the wire is—and the smaller the number of amps the wire can carry. You need a thick wire (measured as a *small* AWG number) to carry a large number of amps. Don't try to feed more power than a wire is rated to carry—it'll overheat and might start a fire. Eighteen gauge wire is a standard size for most layouts; for O or G scale 12–14 gauge might be needed. For a G-scale garden railway, you may also need a conduit to protect wires buried underground.

AWG Number	Amps
22	2
18	4
16	5
14	8
12	10

For large layouts you will need a thicker gauge of wire than that indicated here. That is because a very long wire will act as a resistor and reduce the flow of power to the track. You will have to feed more power to keep the train going—requiring a thicker wire.

ELECTRICAL SWITCHES

Model railroaders use the word "switch" in two ways. It is the place where two diverging tracks join (called in this book a *turnout*) and it is the electrical device—a toggle, a button, a lever, a slide—that turns current on and off. You will use this latter kind of switch as you isolate blocks on your railroad, add lights, install turnouts, etc. Ready-built control systems can eliminate the need for some switches (see "Controlling Your Layout" below). But most modelers install switches at one time or another.

Some useful types of switches to know about:

● **SPST** *(single pole, single throw)*—the simplest type of switch; turns power on or off*

● **DPDT CO** *(double pole, double throw, center-off)—controls two separate sets of electrical contacts; two positions besides off, with off in the center; used for reversing flow of current and allowing two-train operation*

● **wafer or multigang**—*controls a large number of sets of electrical contacts; many possible positions (8PDT, 6P12T, etc.)*

● **momentary contact**—*a spring restores the switch to normal position (usually "off") as soon as you let go; useful for controlling twin-coil switch machines*

● **magnetic reed**—*placed out of sight (e.g., inside a locomotive or car body) to control lights or other accessories; turned on and off with an external magnet; useful in preserving realism*

Switches of various kinds are available from MRC, Roco, Atlas, Arnold, Bowser, Brawa, Circuitron, NJ International, Scale Shops, and Train Tronics. Ten Industries has a full catalogue of electrical accessories, including switches and relays (coils that operate switches). Atlas sells groups of switches in parallel that can be easily coupled together—useful for reversing sections, sidings, and other areas.

*A *pole* is a moving metal contact, a *throw* is a position. An SPST controls only one set of contacts and has one position besides off.

TURNOUTS AND SWITCH MACHINES

A model railroad turnout has to do two things: it has to move the switch "points" so that the train is guided onto the correct track, and it has to carry electrical current so that a train can operate as it crosses the turnout. If you are running only one train, you can buy *fixed-control* turnouts that keep electric current flowing to *both* diverging routes: that way your train never ends up on a "dead" route without current. Most snap-together lines of sectional track feature fixed-control turnouts.

However, as you add trains to your system, you will need *selective-control* or route-selective turnouts (such as those made by Shinohara). These transfer power to one branch or the other when the switch points are moved, leaving the other branch "dead." The switches turn sidings on or off automatically, making wiring easier. Turnouts of both kinds are available from the track manufacturers noted in Chapter Two. Fixed-control turnouts can often be converted to selective control when you're ready to use them that way.

A remote control turnout is one that you activate from some place *away* from the turnout. The mechanism for remote control does not have to be electric. A hand-operated choke cable (similar to the ones used as brake linkages on a bicycle) can cause the switch points to move. So can a "ground throw" kit such as that marketed by Right-of-Way Industries. This kit simulates the kind of manual switch machine used by the railroads; it is meant to be mounted on top of a layout near the turnout.

If manual machines are not convenient for you, electrically powered remote-control turnouts are available. The mechanism here is an electrical switch machine or switch motor mounted either beside the track or under the table. The switch machine is controlled by a pushbutton or momentary switch mounted nearby or in a control panel. Switch machines like those made by Atlas and Rix are usually "dual-" or "twin-coil" devices that can only be exposed to momentary voltage; to activate them, use only momentary contact switches such as the Atlas #56 switch control box. Switch machines are powered from the accessory terminals of a power pack.

The points of a turnout often fail to provide a good electrical connection. Oxidation or dust can interrupt the flow of current. You can, however, install electrical contacts separate from the *points* that will maintain a reliable connection. The same switch machine that moves the points can also move the electrical contacts. Such contacts are

valuable even if you choose to operate your turnouts manually. Many electric switch machines have these contacts built in.

The disadvantage of dual-coil switch machines is that they work too fast. The motion is unrealistically abrupt and may tangibly shake the layout. To get a slower, more realistic motion, use a switch motor. These tend to be more expensive, but they too can be mounted under the layout and run off the power pack (though they require DC rather than AC power). Some switch motors, like the ones made by Switchmaster, are "stall-outs" that need to have continuous power. Others, like those made by Scale Shops, are "auto cut-outs" that can take power either continuously or momentarily. Cut-outs require somewhat more complex wiring than stall-outs; however, they don't draw as much current, since they only use current when changing the position of the turnout.

You may want a mounting bracket for your switch machine or switch motor. Rix offers Rix Rax, a convenient mounting bracket that will work with almost any switch machine. Atlas also makes mounting brackets for their line of switch machines.

SIGNALS AND DETECTION UNITS

Like automobile traffic signals, a railroad signal turns red or green to tell drivers (or engineers) whether to stop or proceed. But unlike a traffic signal, a railroad signal may be linked to a *detection system*—a way of telling where a train is on the track. If Train A reaches that point, the signal will turn red, informing trains that might be on a collision course of Train A's presence.

On model railroads, detection systems operate in several ways—magnets that activate reed switches; sensitive electric series relays; mechanical sensors; and current sensors. Circuitron's "Opto-Sensor" detection system uses an opto-electronic method—photocells mounted between rails. The detection kit offered by N-Way Products is adaptable to all signals and yields two detection units for two different locations. The Trigor detection unit (available from Walthers) is a special track that activates signal circuits when a train is present.

Integrated Signal Systems (ISS) manufactures a variety of "operating" signals in HO. ("Operating" means that it turns red or green in response to a change in current.) Electrical accessories detect the presence of a train and operate LEDs in signal heads and on panel boards. The signals can be designed to your specifications as to type, mast height, type of head mounting, etc. You can also buy partially assembled kits at a re-

Opposite: More power packs from MRC. Clockwise from top of page: 1) The DualPower 027 allows independent control of two AC powered O-gauge trains. 2) The RailPower 1250 handles HO and N scales. 3) The Tech II RailMaster 2400 can power any size locomotive from G to N scale.

duced price. The systems can be used to signal diverging routes, sidings, crossings, and yard entrances. ISS's block occupancy detector detects the presence of a train and sends a signal to the controller.

Right-of-Way Industries makes operating brass signals for O scale. Other manufacturers of signals include Circuitron, Dallee, Life-Like, Mann-Made, Model Power, N-Way, NJ International, Oregon Rail Supply, Roco, Tomar, Tru-Scale, and Walthers.

CONTROLLING YOUR LAYOUT

As you isolate blocks, run trains independently, add electric switch machines and signals, your layout will necessarily become more complex. Each block needs its own feeder wires; each switch machine needs its own electrical switch to activate it. It soon becomes hard to tell which pushbutton or lever performs which function—unless you design an organized control system.

You have several choices for such a system: you can build one or more *control panels*, use *walk-around control*, buy or build an electronic *command control system*, or put together some combination of all three. Here are the options presented one by one.

Control Panels. This is an old-fashioned but still effective solution to the problem of control. Typically made of a wooden frame with a Masonite® or metal panel, the homemade control panel consolidates in one easy-to-reach place the power pack and the switches for all the different blocks and devices installed throughout the railroad (or throughout a given area of a large railroad). Each of the switches (or buttons or levers) on the panel is clearly marked so that you know what will happen when you press it—whether it is to stop a train in its tracks or switch a train from Route A to Route B.

The control panel should have a schematic diagram of the layout, either painted on or applied with drafting tape. Each switch is installed at the point on the diagram corresponding to the section of track that the switch controls. Wires run from the back of the control panel to a terminal strip (available from MRC, Arnold, Acme, and others) and from there to the rails, switch machines, or accessories on the layout.

A control panel need not be entirely scratchbuilt. Arnold sells a variety of control panels, from an inexpensive one that operates turnouts to a sophisticated starting and braking system for multi-train operation.

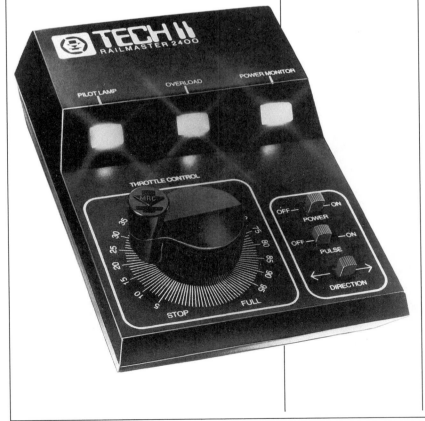

Walk-Around Control. Suppose you don't want to sit at a panel all day, flipping switches and sending your trains into faraway corners of the layout. Suppose you want to get up and follow your trains as they travel. The answer is *walk-around control.* In this system electrical switches for blocks and turnouts are placed not on a central control panel but on the edges of the layout near the operations they manage. You walk around with a portable throttle control in your hand (connected by a wire to the power pack), flipping switches on the layout when necessary. This system is particularly appropriate if you have a single train on a shelf layout that runs along all four walls of a room.

To achieve walk-around control, you need a hand-held throttle with a long cable. Dallee's Engineer Throttle, mentioned above, comes with an optional Walk-a-Round hand-held controller. Dallee's Yardmaster is a hand-held electronic throttle that can be wired directly into a control panel; it requires input power from a transformer or power pack.

Starr Enterprises sells the Starr-Tec Hogger (also mentioned above), a combination power pack and walk-around control system for scales N through G. It provides up to 100 volt-amperes of power along with memory, momentum, and braking controls. The controls can be hand held or become part of a one-piece console. Standard telephone cables and jacks keep the system connected.

Rix Products offers a 4-amp hand-held transistor throttle with a track voltage lamp and mounting rack. Scale Shops and MRC also produce hand-held throttles.

Command Control Systems. Thanks to solid-state electronics, there is an alternative to block wiring as a way of controlling trains: command control. In these systems, a throttle or *cab* (held by the operator or mounted in a control panel) transmits electronic messages through the rails to a locomotive. The loco carries a *decoder* which decodes the message and translates it into action—whether it is slowing down or speeding up, starting or

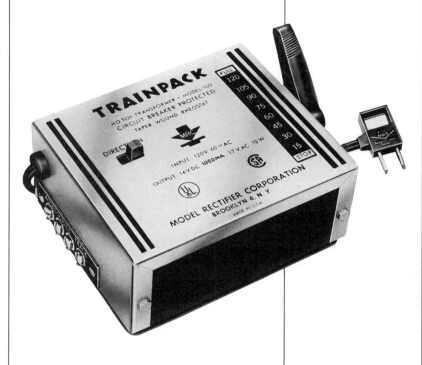

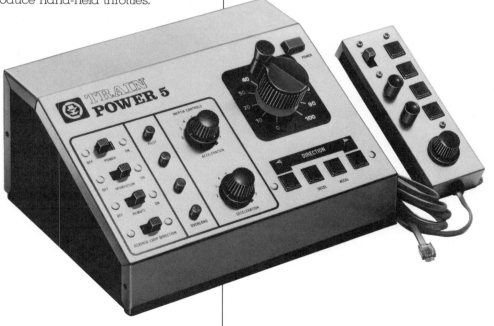

Above: MRC's Train-Pack 100 power pack uses a rheostat instead of transistors to control speed. Left: MRC's TrainPower 5 power pack allows sensitive speed and momentum control for trains from G scale to N scale.

stopping. If there is a second locomotive, it receives a separate set of messages from a separate cab, transmitting on a different frequency (or *channel*). Each channel is used to control one and only one train. Depending on the system, as many as sixteen to sixty-four channels can be in operation at any given time—controlling sixteen to sixty-four trains.

The beauty of command control is that very little block wiring is needed to control trains. Wiring is greatly simplified; the railroad runs more smoothly; the operator doesn't have to spend as much time doing things that are not done on real railroads (such as throwing block switches). However, some block wiring may still be needed to control turnouts and signals.

Command control can be very expensive. The cheapest and most common approach is to build the system oneself, using circuit boards and other parts that are commercially available. If you'd like to try this route, consult *CTC:16e: A Model Railroad Command System You Can Build* by Keith Gutierrez (Kalmbach Publishing). The CTC-16 system uses sixteen channels (though some people extend it to thirty-two or even sixty-four channels). It is not proprietary, meaning anyone can build it and sell parts for it. This is an advantage over trademarked systems that you buy "ready-to-run": if the manufacturer goes out of business, how will you find parts for it?

Of course, not everyone is an electronics whiz. If you want to buy a "ready-to-run" command control system and are willing to spend a few hundred dollars, there are several excellent ones available. The Digipac Phase III/MTC system from Mann-Made Products supports up to sixty-four walk-around cabs, each transmitting digital commands on a separate channel and each connected by cable to a command station/ power station. The system is designed for HO- or N-scale layouts.

If you have a personal computer, the Märklin Digital system will enable you to control your trains directly from the keyboard. This system is available in HO for both Märklin's AC three-rail system and the more common DC two-rail system. With a Basic Digital Set, decoders in up to four locos and four turnouts or signals receive messages from a central control panel. Decoders can be installed in existing locos, or you can buy digital-equipped engines from Märklin in HO, G, and Z scales.

Power Systems, Inc., (PSI) makes Dynatrol, an 18-channel independent train control system for O through N scales. All cabs are walk-arounds that plug into a common line, and can be installed in existing layouts.

If you want a system that controls both locos and sound effects, consider Keller Engineering's "Onboard" sound and control system. Handheld keypads (actually miniature computers) serve as cabs to control up to twenty locomotives, with sound equipment (simulating steam or diesel) mounted in the loco or tender. Onboard can handle scales N through O; a radio adapter permits direct radio control of O- and G-scale equipment.

Automatic Train Control. Whatever control system you use, your control will be limited by how many trains you can stay aware of. Even two or three trains may be too many for a single person to run efficiently. If you run trains with friends on a big layout, you can run many more trains. But what do you do when you're alone in your basement?

One thing you can do is *automate* one or more of your trains while you run another manually. To do this, you can take advantage of the fact that many prototype trains follow preset routes and make predetermined stops. A train picking up and unloading ore from a mine on a regular schedule, a passenger train making stops at a number of stations, can be run automatically—adding interesting background activity to your layout.

To run trains automatically, a control system must incorporate detectors (see "Signals and Detection Units" in this chapter). Circuitron's Automated Reverse Circuits send a train back and forth on the same section of track until the throttle is turned off— simulating the movement of a commuter shuttle, for example. Circuitron's Time Delay Circuit provides an adjustable delay period so that a train can make automatic stops, just as passenger trains and some freight trains would. An Automatic Slowdown Circuit and an Automatic Turnout Control circuit are also available—as is the Turnout Direction Alternator, which causes a train to travel alternate routes as it circles a layout. Used together, the circuits can produce complex effects that do not require hands-on control.

Peerless Industries makes a solid-state automation system for point-to-point operation (to simulate mines, lumber mills and other scenarios). Control units are fully assembled with color coded wires: all you have to do is cut gaps in the rails. The control units for N, HO, and O offer automatic direction reversing, delayed reversing, and intermediate stops. (Automatic direction reversing for large scale is also available.)

LIGHTS

The AC power in your power pack can operate a few accessories besides turnouts. Perhaps the most popular are lights. Locomotives and rolling stock are often sold with working lights, as are streetlamps, crossings, signals, buildings and vehicles. You can also add lights of your own. Light bulbs for model railroading are sold in several sizes and colors (amber, clear, green, red). It's good to have an assortment around to replace bulbs that burn out; for a large layout it may even pay to buy in bulk packages.

The most common small bulb is a grain-o-rice bulb (12–18 volts). Micro-bulbs (1.5 volts) and "angel hair" bulbs (1.2 volts) are even smaller. Fluorettes are tiny incandescent lamps in the shape of fluorescent tubes. LEDs or light emitting diodes (offered by Circuitron, Walthers, Scale Shops, and Train Tronics) operate off low-voltage DC supplies. Fiber optics (such as those offered by BL Hobby Products and Train Tronics) are handy for vehicles, flashers, signals, and other uses. A dual filament bulb simulates the "mars light" or gyrating beacon seen on many locos. Panel lights are used for interiors of structures and as control panel indicators.

Some bulbs can be mounted in sockets; others have tiny pigtail wires that must be soldered into the circuit. Pay attention to voltage ratings (6v, 12v, etc.). If a lamp is rated for less than the voltage in the circuit it will burn out quickly unless you wire the lamps in a series or use dropping resistors (such as those sold by Arnold and Cir-Kit Concepts) that waste some of the voltage.

Bulbs are available from many companies, including Arnold, Acme, Brawa, La-Belle Industries, Cir-Kit Concepts, G-R-S Model Brass, Life-Like, Model Power, NJ International, Precision Scale Co., Scale Shops, Roco, and Walthers. Plastic model lamps (with bulbs) are also widely available.

LIGHT EFFECTS

F & M Enterprises offers an alternative to plastic lamps with its line of fine imported brass lamps made by the West German company Hans Liebl. The lamps come in scales Z through G; wire, connectors, and other accessories are available with them. The Busch line of lamps for HO, N, and Z scales, also imported by F & M, includes city traffic lights and a miniature Christmas tree with lights.

To simulate the flickering light of bonfires and campfires, consider G-R-S Model Brass's "Flamemakers." The lights can also simulate larger fires, such as those of a blast furnace or burning structure.

Other interesting light effects are the Signs of the Times "neon sign" kits sold by Quality Products Company. The signs are not actually neon but clear dyed plastic; edge-lights with a flashing capability give the effect of neon. The signs represent actual brand-names for store windows or entrances ("Chevrolet," "Schlitz on Tap," "Enjoy Coca-Cola," "Zenith Radio-TV") as well as more generic names ("Beer," "Open," "Pawn Shop"). Clocks with neon signs are also available.

Headlight kits for a loco are available from companies such as Walthers, Bowser, and LaBelle Industries. To light the tail end of a passenger train, Tomar Industries sells lighted drumhead kits in scales N through O. The full-color signs are available in many train names—among them Super Chief, Amtrak, California Zephyr, Corn Belt Route. Tomar also offers a red tail light kit and marker lights for observation cars.

Circuitron's battery-operated strobe flashers in HO and O can be installed on locos, police and emergency vehicles, and as beacons on tall structures. Circuitron's alternating flashers cause two lights to flash on and off alternately. Other companies making flashers include Train Tronics, Walthers, G-R-S, and Quality Products.

To light the interior of structures, Walthers sells frosted tubular bulbs in insulated sockets. These can be cemented to the ceiling of a car or building to give uniform, diffuse lighting. Bachmann, Brawa, Faller, LaBelle Industries, and Life-Like also sell structure lighting kits.

Model railroad lights can be operated either by batteries or by external power. Tomar makes battery hook-up kits and slide-switches for those who prefer battery power. If you are using track power for car or loco lights, a constant intensity light source or constant brightness kit may be desirable. This keeps lights from dimming when there is a change in current and protects bulbs from over-voltage. Arnold, Circuitron, G-R-S Model Brass, Modeltronics, Tomar, and Walthers offer a variety of devices to keep brightness constant.

After you've window-shopped for everything that's available, remember that some of the best lighting effects can be achieved in relatively low-tech ways. To simulate a day-night cycle, all you need is a light-dimming switch and a timer to dim the room lights at regular intervals, while streetlights and headlights appear on your layout. A few blue bulbs high above the layout can simulate moonlight when the room lights are off.

Opposite: One lighting option that modelers would be amiss to overlook is ambient light. In this small trackage diorama, Stafford Swain merges his layout with an actual prairie sunset to create a Canadian country scene out of the mid-1950s. As his 2-8-2 hand-painted and lettered steam locomotive pulls away, the wood-crib grain elevator is dramatically illuminated by the skies at dusk.

SOUND EFFECTS

What lights do for the eye, sound does for the ear. A few sound effects devices can contribute greatly to the overall realism and interest of your layout. Choices range from basic steam whistles and diesel horns, such as those made by Train Tronics and Circuitron, to the sophisticated Onboard sound and control system offered by Keller Engineering (see Command Control Systems above).

As you shop for sound effects, let your own ear be your guide. Prototype crossing bells, for example, are sometimes simulated by a real miniature bell and sometimes by electronic circuitry. Make sure the "bell" you buy sounds right to your ear. Circuitron's "bell-ringer" contains a real bell mounted on a printed circuit board. Starr Enterprises's Crossing Signal System for G scale has all-electronic flashing lights and sound. Train Tronics's crossing system incorporates both electronic sound and a track detector for crossing control.

Steam and diesel sound systems are usually mounted in a box car or tender. Starr's sound systems for scales HO and larger include American and European whistles, "a rich chuff sound" for steam engines, and turbo and horn sounds for diesel. Starr's Tri-Tec sound systems are more expensive and elaborate, using radio frequency transmitters and speakers.

For background noises, New England Hobby Supply sells cassette tapes that can be played near a layout. Some of the scenes that can be evoked are a metal factory, freight yard, harbor, farm, forest, and city.

Right-of-Way Industries produces digital sound effects for O scale. These include "idle" sounds for steam and "air pumps and dynamo" for locos. Layout sounds include animals (cow, horse, dog), buzz saw, passenger station, and water tower.

Sound effects kits and systems are also available from Faller, Modeltronics, N-Way, Pacific Fast Mail, and Scale Shops.

Right: A realistic diesel horn is the last touch needed for a locomotive such as this HO-scale Athearn F7 diesel. The layout was built by the Convair Club in San Diego, California.

Top: At the Menomonee Falls depot by Oregon Rail Supply, passengers await the oncoming mainline trains. This plastic HO-scale model of the depot features original details like the clock and French doors. **Above:** A black hopper and orange-and-black engine sit at this small branch line terminal in a late 1940s layout by Bruce Cameron. The tank car, at far right, has just been repaired by the crew. The track for this 2 × 12 foot layout was hand laid by Willard Jones. **Left:** In this HO-scale creation of the Port of Arapahoe by Gil Freitag Jr. and Sr., gondolas are readied for transport up the river. Note the truss bridges crossing the upper half of the layout, allowing additional access for freight trains into the port. A summer touch is provided by the boys fishing at the pier below.

Top: To re-create the "neon age" on your miniature Main Street USA, Quality Products offers these realistic-looking neon-like signs for all major scales. These selections, from their "Signs of the Times" collection, feature family storefronts, like the Bake Shop and Shoe Repair, as well as nationally-known signs of the age like Zenith Radio-TV and Hires Root Beer (not shown). The signs are hand-made of acrylic plastic and dyed in neon-like colors. When the sign is assembled in a building, it is edge-lighted to give the effect of a neon sign. **Above:** A steam engine travels over a thru bridge along the water in this HO-scale layout of the Canadian prairie by Stafford Swain. **Right:** A freight train crosses a stone arch bridge at Shingle Springs in this HO-scale layout by the Freitags.

Top: This finely detailed HO-scale freight station is made from a kit designed and produced by C.C. Crow. A precise replica of Southern's Kinston, North Carolina, freight station, it features Hydrocal® wall castings, prototypical truss construction, full rafters, and a mock "tin roof." **Above:** In this HO-scale layout of Black Gap by the Freitags, bridges and mountains provide the focus. A backdrop of mountains creates the far view; prototypically correct mountains were constructed throughout the body of the layout. In the rear, a freight train travels across Stony Creek Bridge over the Gap; in the front, a steam locomotive travels over a sec-

ond bridge leading to a tunnel. **Left:** Classic American styles of urban architecture are celebrated in these high-quality HO-scale injection-molded styrene building kits from City Classics. Both buildings are based on actual prototypical structures, and have clear styrene window glazing and cast metal chimneys. 101 Grant Street (left) represents a five-story iron-front building that was made of prefabricated cast iron parts. 102 Penn Avenue (right), also five floors, is distinguished by its styrene replication of a fired ceramic front. The front can be painted in a variety of colors, like the real thing.

Above: The Milton Lumber Company at Arapahoe is represented in this HO-scale layout by the Freitags. Note details like the sakrete sign on the fence in front. **Right:** This HO-scale layout features a steam locomotive approaching Eagle Mountain station, as boxcars sit on the other tracks. The parked cars situate the layout circa mid-1950s to mid-1960s. Note the truss bridge at the upper right. **Below:** Boxcars are being loaded from the conveyor at the stamp mill and Bozman Casting Company at Eagle Mountain in this HO-scale layout.

Above: In another view of the Eagle Mountain HO-scale layout, the focus is the switcher working the stamp mill. Note the smart 1940s coupes and the Stony Creek train awaiting pickup. **Left:** The freight house and chemical plant in the town of Arapahoe. **Below left:** A Walthers backdrop of the Norfolk Coal Company provides the setting for these industrial switching lines in an HO-scale layout by Bruce Cameron. The trains in this and his earlier layout view are part of Cameron's Cornet Line, named for his part-time occupation as a cornet player. At bottom, by the Athearn engine cab, a maintenance-of-way crew works on a switch. At top, on the industrial level, trains wait to be loaded. The middle level of track, marked by an Atlas through truss bridge, runs between two switching areas.

Below: A steam locomotive passes near the slough in the Canadian prairie in this HO-scale layout by Stafford Swain. Right: This HOn3 autumn layout of a late 1930s train station at Vance Junction, Colorado, was scratch-built by Jeff Reynolds from models of the actual station. Reynolds, a member of the Los Angeles Philharmonic, created a model of the Galloping Goose, part of the well-known train line that built its locos and rolling stock from trucks and buses. The station is flanked by sheds made from old freight cars and passenger cars. At front, notice the occupied outhouse. Bottom: In this HO-scale layout of the freight house at Stony Creek, viaducts, a pier bridge, and several freight trains cross the mountains. Note the lines of evergreens along the mountaintops and the carefully built rock faces.

Right: This 1953 Chevrolet Belair two-door hardtop from Magnuson Models is made of clear polyester casting and has all of its details molded in place, including its abundant chrome trim.

Left: Nothing marks a busy street scene more than a maze of taxis like this variety from Magnuson Models. These 1959 models are based on a prototype used for decades, and will fit into layouts dated from the 1960s to the 1990s. Decals for Yellow Cab, Checker, or Veteran Taxi are included in the kit.

Above: These two classic American Flyer streamliners span the two World Wars. The pre-World War II O-gauge Pacific B&O is blue; the post-World War II S-gauge Pacific B&O is red. Both bullet-nosed 4-6-2 locos are prize collectibles. **Right:** This Ives O-gauge New York Central clockwork (wind-up) locomotive was introduced in 1921. Note the details in this early train: the headlight, bell, rivets, grabirons, lettering, and key that winds the spring that sets the train in motion. The train is now a favorite of collectors. **Below left:** these reproductions of two-rail 2⅛-inch Lionel electric train cars were based on trains produced around 1903–1905. The original trains ran on dry cell batteries, which were developed in 1900 by Lionel founder, Joshua Lionel

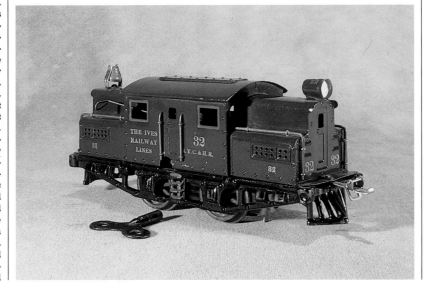

Cowen. Originals of these large-gauge trains are all but impossible to find today. **Below right:** This reproduction of Lionel's handsome standard-gauge 1912 Special electric locomotive is an example of a popular—and expensive—brass collectible. Reasons for the high demand for these locos include the hand-worked details and high quality of materials. The train runs on the then-newly developed (1907) three-rail 2⅛-inch Standard gauge track, which was produced by Lionel until 1939.

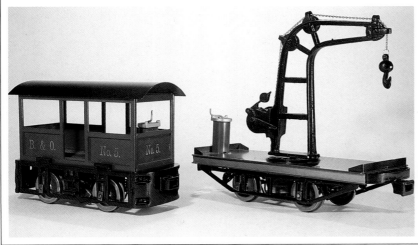

VIDEO

An interesting electric accessory for the fan of home video is Lionel's RailScope—a video system for scales HO through G that gives you an engineer's-eye view of your layout. A RailScope loco comes equipped with a black-and-white TV camera, installed in the locomotive and powered by a 9-volt DC battery. The camera transmits television signals through the rails to a TV set. The focus ranges from 4 inches to infinity, keeping near and distant objects in focus; the circuitry automatically adjusts to lighting conditions.

The battery lasts only 30 to 45 minutes, but if you're really interested, it is possible to wire a track-powered supply. (See Don Hansen's "RailScope Battery-Saver" articles in the Fall 1989 and January/February 1990 *Classic Toy Trains*.)

COMPUTER-ORGANIZED TRAIN OPERATIONS

In a prototype railroad, trains don't just move in circles. Shippers call for cars to be sent to their sidings so that products can be loaded and sent off; passenger trains move on regular schedules. A few industrial sidings, with yards for sorting and switching cars, are the raw materials for a realistic model railroad. But to use these materials, you need a system for deciding which cars to couple into a train, what stops it has to make, and perhaps what products it has to load and unload.

A standard way of simulating realistic car movements—putting cars together into a train for a particular purpose—is a "card-order" system. Each car on the layout is represented by a 3 × 5 inch index card; "waybills" indicate what kinds of cars are needed for particular purposes. The "operation-unlimited" system described in Schleicher's *The Model Railroading Handbook* is an example. The system is inexpensive, requiring only basic stationery supplies, and many clubs use it for their operating nights; but it is time consuming, heavy on paperwork, and can become repetitive if not done properly. It is also hard to keep the system current as new cars or industries are added to the layout.

Computer programs have made it possible to organize traffic quickly, update records easily, and maintain a realistic degree of unpredictability in traffic demands. In effect, the computer serves as both the railroad's main office and its customers. It prints out waybills and switch lists and performs other functions that would otherwise require hours of paperwork.

Mil-Scale offers a number of programs for

managing traffic, most of them no more expensive than a new hardcover book. They include "Manifest" (for loop or out-and-back operation), "Switch" (for additional switching maneuvers at industrial sidings and multiple yards), and "Loco" (which assigns each loco to the kind of train for which it is appropriate).

Computer programs can also help you keep track of *fast time*. Just as model railroads condense space, model railroad operators often condense time. For example, a 60-mile distance, covered by a prototype train traveling 30 miles an hour, would take 2 hours to cross. But few model railroads have even a tenth of the track necessary to cover the scale equivalent of 60 miles. (To model it accurately, you would need a room over ten times bigger than what you are using.)

So modelers speed up the clock, and have their train reach the destination "60" miles away in only 15 minutes. Timetables are written in which each station on a route takes a given amount of "fast time" to reach—but a much smaller amount of real time. By using a faster than normal clock, a whole "day" of operations can be condensed into three real hours—an evening's work at your local model railroad club.

You can mechanically speed up a clock so

Above: With Lionel's RailScope,™ what the "engineer" would see is what you get. A video camera mounted in the O-gauge GP9 diesel in the foreground transmits an image of the locomotive up ahead.

that an "hour" on the clockface passes in five to ten minutes. You can also get the Mil-Scale program "Clock," which does this electronically and displays scale times and distances. "T/D Calc" helps you calculate scale distance and times. Other Mil-Scale programs include "Maintenance Manager" and the "RailstaRR" programs, which combine the features of the other traffic-generating programs and more. Some Mil-Scale programs run on a Commodore 64 computer; others can be used with IBM/compatibles or the Apple II.

MISCELLANEOUS SOFTWARE

For those who really want to get their home computer involved in their hobby, other railroader's programs are available. Abracadata sells "Design Your Own Train," a soft-

ware package that allows you to build and test model layout simulations before laying track. The layouts can include up to four trains, twenty-six turnouts, and a variety of automatic sequences. Other Abracadata programs—"MacInooga Choo Choo," "Run Your Own Train," "Train Library"—allow you to turn your home computer into a detailed, colorful "railroad" that exists in electronic space rather than in your basement.

Computer software and services are also available from Arlington Consulting and Engineering, Data Train, James R. Hunt, Model Rail Link, and TCI. Ten Industries offers custom computer programming and "Scratchbuilder's Scaleware" to help you convert from and to any scale.

See also Chapter Five on CompuServe's® computer network for model railroaders.

Below: The Märklin digital system enables modelers with personal computers to control trains directly from the keyboard. The train in the background is part of the Märklin HO-scale Digital Starter Set.

ELECTRICAL MISCELLANY

To close the chapter, here is a sampling of other electrical accessories that might contribute to the smooth running of your railroad:

● *Tomarshoes (Tomar)*—renowned for improving current flow to locomotives. Mounted under locos, they help keep rails clean and eliminate stalling. (For HO, HOn3, Sn3, and some S.)

● *Power boosters (Circuitron, Train Tronics)*—increase the load capacity of a power pack or device, such as a detection unit.

● *Tapewire (Cir-Kit Concepts, Inc.)*—an alternative to ordinary wire. Tapewire is a flat, adhesive-backed Mylar tape containing electrical conductors. It can be run nearly invisibly under grass mats or other ground coverings. No soldering is required; brads or pins connect Tapewire to conventional wiring systems.

● *The Zapper (J & M Laboratories)*—addresses a common problem in model railroad operation: stalled operations because of poor contacts somewhere in the circuit. The Zapper provides lightning-fast pulses of up to 250 volts that are quick enough not to harm the motors but strong enough to get the train moving. It is not for use with command control or track powered sound systems.

● *Printed Circuit Mounting Track or PCMT (Circuitron)*—an extruded plastic assembly that provides easy snap-in mounting for all of Circuitron's printed circuit boards.

● *Motorized blinker (Faller)*—emits pulses that can be used for rhythmic switching, blinking, or church bells.

● *Two-way radios (Maxon)*—for communication with other engineers on large layouts.

Above: Another view of the control units used in the Märklin Digital system. The electric locomotive in the lower right is a German Federal Railroad class 111 for passenger traffic.

CHAPTER FIVE
The Wider World of Railroading

he world of model railroading extends far beyond trains, kits, and track. It includes the written world of books and magazines, the electronics world of videos and photos, and especially the human world, the people you meet through shows and conventions. This chapter provides a brief look at the expanse of the model railroading community.

CLUBS AND ORGANIZATIONS

The most well-known and broad-based organization for model railroading is the National Model Railroad Association. Headquartered in Chattanooga, Tennessee, it was founded in 1935 and now has a membership of 25,000 hobbyists in all scales and gauges. As stated in its constitution, the goals of the NMRA are:

● *"to promote the art and craft of model railroading and the preservation of its history, science and technology"*

● *"to establish standards to promote cooperation and understanding between manufacturers, distributors, dealers, consumers and the general public"*

● *"to develop the skills of modelers and promote fellowship and education about modeling and prototype railroading"*

● *"to promote the hobby."*

The NMRA publishes a monthly magazine, the *Bulletin,* and holds regional and national conventions annually to discuss changes in model railroading practices.

Another major national club is NTRAK. Founded in the mid-1970s, it was the first major organization to promote model railroading in the then-new N scale. It succeeded in doing so by encouraging N-scale modelers to use the portable modular concept. The club produces a bi-monthly newsletter and helps to coordinate NTRAK layouts for public shows. (See Sources for addresses of these and other clubs and organizations mentioned in this chapter.)

Local and Specialized Clubs. It is not an exaggeration to say that we could devote an entire book to railroad clubs and societies. Railroad and modeling fans are legion, and so are their clubs, where members meet to share techniques, parts, and layouts. These clubs and societies are the best way to become acquainted with fellow modelers interested in the gauge or rail line in which you model or collect. A few of the more well-known national organizations include:

● *the LGB Model Railroaders Club in Decatur, Georgia*

● *the Lionel Operating Train Society, founded in 1979 for operators of Lionel O and O-27 gauge trains; the Society publishes a bi-monthly magazine called* Switches, *holds an annual convention, and sponsors at least four local meets*

● *the National Association of S Gaugers*

● *the Teen Association of Model Railroading (open only to members aged between 12 and 19)*

● *the Toy Train Operating Society, for Lionel and*

Below: At a meeting of the New Jersey Live Steamers in Basking Ridge, New Jersey, member Fred Bouffard places his 1½ inch-scale/7¼ inch-gauge New York Central Hudson on the transfer table, en route to the main line. Opposite, top: Bob Hornsby oils his 1½ inch-scale/7½ inch-gauge Pennsy E6 Atlantic at a New Jersey Live Steamers meet. Opposite, bottom: Tom Rhodes drives this 2½ inch-scale Fitchburg & Northern 0-4-2-T train in Saratoga Springs, New York. Rhodes built this train from a kit, which he modified to meet his specifications.

American Flyer operators, among others; its benefits include two bi-monthly magazines, one a listing of buy-sell-trade items.

Collectors' Clubs. Because collectors have different concerns about their model trains than modelers, there are specialized clubs, which include:

● *the American Flyer Collectors Club, in Pittsburgh, Pennsylvania*

● *the Lionel Collectors Club in LaSalle, Illinois*

● *the National Collectors Club in Ramsey, New Jersey*

● *the Toy Train Collectors Society in Rochester, New York*

● *the Train Collectors' Association, in Strasburg, Pennsylvania*

Railfan Clubs. For those who want to celebrate the railroads themselves rather than the activity of modeling the railroads or collecting the models, there is an array of railfan organizations:

● *the American Southwest Railroad Association, in Lakewood, California, for those who love the rails of the southwest*

● *the Central Electric Railfans' Association, in Chicago, Illinois, focusing on rapid transit and electric railways*

● *the National Railway Historical Society, in Ho-Ho-Kus, New Jersey, which offers annual conventions, a bi-monthly magazine, and excursions*

● *the Pacific Railroad Society, in San Marino, California*

● *the Railway and Locomotive Historical Society, in Westford, Massachusetts, the leading rail history society in America since 1921, has five chapters across the country and publishes a journal, Railroad History, which recounts railroad events from the 1870s to the current day, as well as a quarterly newsletter*

● *the Railroad Enthusiasts, Inc., devoted solely to the studies of prototype railroads, in West Townsend, Massachusetts*

Prototype Historical Societies. Some railfans want to concentrate their study on one or two prototype lines, rather than all prototype railroads. For these people are the prototype historical societies and special interest groups, each devoted to a different line. Here are just a few of the many regional and national clubs:

• *the Baltimore & Ohio Railroad Historical Society, which produces a magazine*

• *the Chesapeake & Ohio Historical Society, for C&O fans of Virginia, West Virginia, Kentucky, Ohio, Michigan, and Indiana; produces a monthly magazine, the Chesapeake & Ohio Historical Society Magazine, and has a research library*

• *the CN Lines Special Interest Group*

• *the Great Northern Railway Historical Society, which produces a newsletter*

• *the Illinois Central Historical Society, which pro-* duces a newsletter, magazine, and holds swaps

• *the Missouri Pacific Historical Society, which offers a newsletter*

• *the New York Central System Historical Society, Inc., which, among other activities, produces an annual New York Central Calendar*

• *the Santa Fe Railway Historical Society, which produces a quarterly magazine*

• *the Shore Line Interurban Historical Society, which produces a newsletter, First & Fastest*

• *the Soo Line Historical & Technical Society, which produces a quarterly magazine*

• *the Union Pacific Historical Society, which produces a quarterly magazine*

In addition to the groups' abovementioned activities, each of these societies holds annual meetings for members to share ideas and history.

Opposite: An F-series Kansas City Southern diesel, one of the many prototypes that can be researched through historical societies and libraries. Left: You can study the SD-series diesels through the Santa Fe Railway Historical Society.

RESEARCHING PROTOTYPES

To achieve realism, model railroaders often need to find out more about the prototypes they are modeling. One excellent source for this information is the A.C. Kalmbach Memorial Library in Chattanooga, Tennessee. Founded in 1986, it is operated by the National Model Railroad Association and is a major research source for prototype information, photographs, modeling techniques, and model railroad manufacturing and publishing.

For modelers with computers, another worthy source is Mil-Scale's "Dilocron," which provides complete historical information and profiles of over fifty types of diesels. The file can be revised as new data becomes available, and can tell you whether a particular diesel could possibly have been in use in a given year (thus preventing anachronisms in your railroad).

Opposite: Research this Soo Line switcher through the Soo Line Historical & Technical Society. Left: A Lehigh Valley 166 S-4 traveling through Manchester, New York. Below: A Louisville & Nashville F-series diesel.

MAGAZINES

To attest to the growing interest in trains, there are dozens of magazines on model and prototype railroading. Some magazines are general and cover all aspects of a line or gauge; others are more specialized. Here are just a few, listed according to areas of interest:

Modeling Magazines

● *Model Railroader, a national monthly publication featuring modeling in all scales (Kalmbach Publishing)*

● *Model Railroading (Eastwood Publishing Co., Inc.)*

● *Prototype Modeler (Green Lantern Press Ltd.)*

● *Railroad Model Craftsman, with detailed presentations and tips (Carstens Publications, Inc.)*

● *Railmodel Journal, with articles on all scales (Golden Bell Press)*

● *Narrow Gauge and Short Line Gazette, with information on narrow gauge prototypes, modeling techniques, plans, and product reviews (Benchmark Publications)*

● *³⁄₁₆ "S"cale Railroading, covering both S-standard-gauge and S-narrow-gauge modeling; topics from prototypes to painting to decals to commentary from an S-scale modeler named "S"pike are included (³⁄₁₆ "S"cale Railroading)*

● *48/ft. O Scale News (ControlAbility, Inc.)*

● *Freight Cars Journal, for those interested in the history and modeling of North American freight cars; it includes information on design and evolution, reviews, and spotter's guides (Freight Cars Journal)*

Right: A few of the many magazines. *Model Railroading* keeps you up-to-date on modeling techniques. *Railfan* serves the armchair traveler who celebrates the glory days past and present of prototype railroads. *Model Railroader* is one of the basics: It offers modeling tips and plans, plus listings of shows and conventions throughout the country.

TRAILER TRAIN HISTORY • MODELING A TR2

RAILROAD MODEL CRAFTSMAN®

$2.95/JULY 1990
CANADA $3.95 47803

REVIEW OF LIONEL'S INTERMODAL CRANE

FROM THE EDITORS OF
Model Railroader

CLASSIC TOY TRAINS
FOR THE COLLECTOR AND OPERATOR

$3.95
August 1990

MADISON HARDWARE'S WARTIME PRODUCTION

LIVE STEAM

JULY 1990 $3.50

614

614

614

The Last of the C & O Northerns Restored

• Garden Railways, called "the magazine for the outdoor modeler," with information on all aspects of building and running an outdoor layout (Sidestreet Bannerworks)

• N-Scale magazine (Hundman)

• O Scale Railroading (Vane A. Jones Co.)

Video Magazines. The *RPO Fast Mail Video Magazine* (available from Yampa Valley Mail Production Company) contains stories about railroading as a business, as a hobby, and from a historical viewpoint. Each issue features several well-known railroad lines from past and present.

Prototype Magazines. Leading magazines that feature prototype lines, past and present, include:

• *Rail Classics, which is devoted to the history and current operation of rail lines, electric interurban buses, and trolleys (Rail Classics)*

• **Railfan and Railroad** *(Carstens)*

• **Trains** *(Kalmbach Publishing), which features photo essays on all types of prototype lines*

• **Trolley Talk,** *a quarterly newsletter about prototypes and models (Trolley Talk)*

Left: *Live Steam* **is geared to fans and operators of scale steam-powered trains big enough to ride.** *Railroad Model Craftsman* **offers instructive articles by and about modelers on building layouts and scratchbuilding models.** *Classic Toy Trains* **is the magazine for lovers of Lionel, American Flyer, and other collectibles.**

Above: Rare models of trains like this early nineteenth-century prototype train, the John Bull, are featured at many of the museums listed below.

MUSEUMS

When planning your next vacation, remember there's more to life than Disney World (though their railroads are worth riding, too). Sprinkled throughout the country, railroad and model railroad museums allow you to make your hobby part of your holiday. Here are a few favorites:

● *The A & D Toy-Train Village and Railway Museum in North Middleboro, Massachusetts, has thirty-five exhibits of toy trains from twenty-one countries from the past 150 years.*

● *The California State Railroad Museum, in Old Sacramento, offers the Milepost Book and Gift Shop and many displays.*

● *The Colorado Railroad Museum, located twelve miles west of Denver, offers valuable looks at the historic standard and narrow gauge prototype lines.*

● *The Cranbrook Railway Museum in British Columbia offers a restored version of the Trans-Canada Limited of 1929.*

● *The Frisco Railroad Museum, in Ash Grove, Missouri, has over 1500 items of Frisco and Frisco-related memorabilia on display.*

● *The New York Transit Museum, in Brooklyn, New York, is for urban transportation fans and collectors; periodically, it holds tag sales and auctions of such items as uniforms, turnstiles, and station globes.*

● *The North Carolina Transportation Museum in Spencer, North Carolina, was originally the site of the Southern Railway's largest steam repair facility for trains. It has been transformed into a museum that offers a three-mile ride around the Southern Railway's repair facility.*

● *The Old Depot Museum, in Dassel, Minnesota, once a depot for the Great Northern line, is now a collection of lanterns, signs, signals, bells, whistles, handcars, china, telegraph equipment, and more.*

• The Park-Lane Model Railroad Museum is located near the Wisconsin Dells, in Reedsburg, Wisconsin. It offers several operating layouts, including a Western Pacific Z-scale layout.

• The Portola Railroad Museum, located fifty miles west of Reno, Nevada, in the high Sierras, has the West's largest collection of diesel locos.

• The Railroad Museum of Pennsylvania, in Strasburg, Pennsylvania, offers a large collection of vintage motive power and rolling stock, interpretive exhibits, and special events.

• The San Diego Model Railroad Museum, in Balboa Park, features four scale model railroads and a toy train exhibit covering 22,000 square feet.

• The Shore Line Trolley Museum, in East Haven, Connecticut, presents a Lionel layout built inside an operable 1899 Brooklyn Rapid Transit car made by the Laclede Car Company.

• The Toy Train Museum, in Strasburg, Pennsylvania, operated by the Train Collectors Association, offers hundreds of locomotives dating from the 1800s to the present and has "a large action exhibit of toy tinplate trains our dads and granddads played with."

• Travel Town, in Los Angeles, California, is a transportation museum containing airplanes and steamrollers as well as trains. Among its train exhibits are a 1902 Pacific Electric Steeple Cab, an 1899 Baldwin 2-8-0 loco, and a 1904 Alco Santa Fe loco. Next door to the display is a park featuring the Los Angeles Live Steamers club, which offers rides on steam trains on Sunday afternoons.

CATALOGUES

Model railroading catalogues are among the few types of catalogues that offer more than product listings. Many companies feature valuable modeling techniques and historical background in their catalogues that can be invaluable to modelers.

For serious modelers in Z, N, HO and large scale, there are the extensive catalogues produced by Walthers of Milwaukee, Wisconsin. More like compendiums than catalogues, the three collections—*The World of N and Z Scale*, *The World of HO Scale*, and *The World of Large Scale Trains* offer information and price listings for thousands of products from hundreds of manufacturers. They are available through your hobby dealer or from Walthers.

Catalogues from individual companies often include detailed descriptions of products and practical modeling tips. Some of these catalogues are free; others charge a

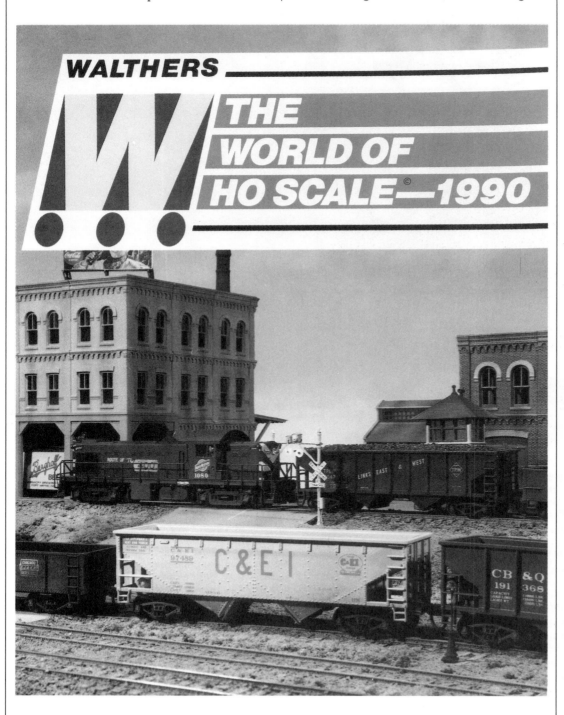

Left: The world of model railroading that Walthers presents is wide. The wishbook of modeling presents the latest in rolling stock, locos, accessories, books, videos, and railroadiana from several hundred manufacturers from the United States and abroad. Walthers and most of the other catalogues mentioned offer modeling tips and background as well as listings of products. For example, the Clover House catalogue presents suggestions on scratchbuilding; Con-Cor and Woodland Scenics on working with scenery; and Kadee on the workings of couplers. Opposite: Walthers specializes in companies whose products are otherwise difficult to obtain.

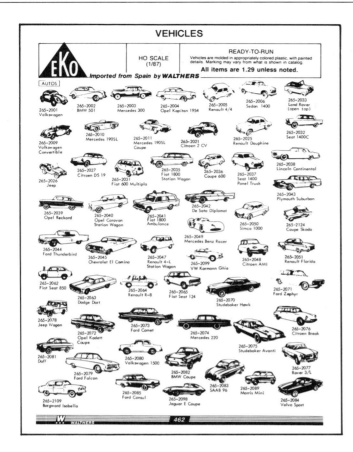

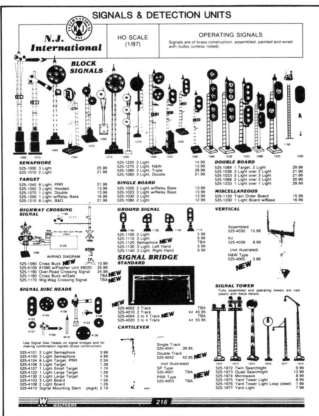

nominal fee. Because many model railroading companies cannot mail catalogues at no cost, query each company first and include a self-addressed stamped envelope for response. Here are some of the companies (see Sources for company addresses) offering catalogues:

- *Clover House* (scratchbuilding tools and supplies)
- *Con-Cor International* (HO and N trains and equipment; railroadiana)
- *Floquil-Polly S Color Corporation* (paints and supplies)
- *Kadee Quality Products Co.* (couplers for all gauges, trains and equipment)
- *Life-Like Products, Inc.* (structures, ground cover, tunnels, and related supplies)
- *Mil-Scale Products* (craftsman kits and computer software)
- *PBL* (narrow gauge trains)
- *Pecos River Brass* (handcrafted brass locos and cars)
- *Plastruct, Inc.* (plastic structures, figures, and related supplies)
- *Precision Scale Company, Inc.* (detail parts)
- *Westerfield* (high quality craftsman kits)
- *Woodland Scenics* (trees, ground cover, supplies)

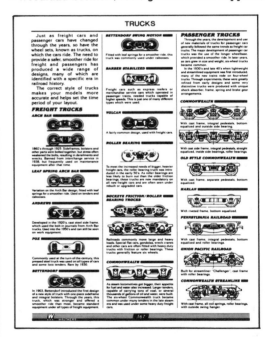

COMPUTER NETWORKS

For owners of personal computers, CompuServe® offers a computer network called Model Net. With a modem, modelers can exchange ideas, solve technical problems, and find information. The Model Rail Link is a computer system and database to locate or find a buyer for equipment, parts or other rail items. A specifications and instruction kit is available.

SHOWS, EXHIBITIONS, AND CONVENTIONS

National and regional shows are a good way to catch up on the latest or rarest model trains and equipment, and to get new ideas from other model railroaders.

National Shows. Possibly the largest annual meeting for modelers is the National Model Railroad Association's annual convention (see "Clubs and Organizations"). Usually held in a major train and modeling town (1990's convention was in Pittsburgh, 1991 in Denver, and 1992 in Columbus), the NMRA convention includes tours of local railroads and industries, technical programs, contests, and visiting with well-known hobbyists. Some convention events are cosponsored by other important railroad associations, including the National Association of S-Gaugers and NTRAK, and all are open to the general public, not just NMRA members.

Other national shows include:

● *The Chicago Model Hobby Show is an annual show focusing on recreational planes, cars, boats, trains, and games. It offers exhibits of hundreds of model and hobby equipment, and is usually held in the fall.*

● *The Great American Train Show is held in over twenty cities across the country, with over 10,000 trains and hundreds of dealers.*

● *The Los Angeles Model Hobby Show, cosponsored by the Model Railroad Industry Association, offers model railroad demonstrations and presentations on planes, cars, and boats.*

● *The National Collectors' Club annual Toy and Train Show, usually held in northern New Jersey, features new and collectable toys and trains and train "doctors" to do repairs.*

● *The National Narrow Gauge Convention focuses on narrow gauge railroads.*

Below: At a Maricopa Live Steamers meet in Scottsdale, Arizona, modeler Bob Newton stands with his 1½ inch-scale/7½ inch-gauge 2-6-0 Upper Sierra Nevada Railroad. In the forefront is a Rio Grande diesel.

Regional Shows.

Regional shows are abundant and varied. Most of them offer running trains, plenty of parking, and much buying, selling, and trading. The shows take place throughout the country at many times of the year. In the Northeast, for example, modelers can take their pick from among any of the following shows—and many more:

• The Allentown (Pennsylvania) Train Meet Associates annual train meet, features O- and HO-gauge switching contests and operating layouts.

• The Great Bergen-Passaic Toy and Train Show is held annually in northern New Jersey.

• Greenberg Shows, Inc.'s Great Train, Dollhouse, and Toy Shows are held up and down the East Coast throughout the year, offer auctions and products from dozens of dealers.

• The New Jersey Bayshore Model and Toy Train Show and Sale, said to be the largest on the Jersey shore, has layouts and movies.

• The Pennsylvania Train Show in Pittston, held since 1974, offers thousands of toy trains for buying, selling or trading, plus operating Lionel layouts.

• The Trainways of New England Annual Train Show, held since 1979 in Massachusetts, offers tinplate, LGB, scale, and toy trains.

• The Westchester Toy and Train Associates, Inc., collectors and modelers shows, is held several times per year.

To find out about local shows, talk to your hobby dealer or consult one of the many model train magazines, which provide lists of dozens of shows each month.

Finally, there are seventeen annual National Model Railroad Association Regional Conventions, each sponsored by a different NMRA region and held in a variety of cities across the United States, England, Canada, and Australia.

Above: Regional shows are often good places to find varieties of models of favorite mainlines like the Southern Pacific. Below: Historic pieces, like this 1890 combine car modeled here in HO scale by Mantua, can also be found at many shows.

VIDEOS

Given the vast array of historic information available, a railfan or modeler could spend his or her entire life in front of the television screen reliving the glory of the train eras. Videos fall into three categories—those about prototype rail and traction lines, those about model railroads, and instructional how-to modeling books. Many video companies produce tapes in all three areas. Here is a sampling:

● Berkshire Productions highlights the Nickel Plate Road steam locos in its videos.

● Cadwallader Productions features train activity in Pittsburgh and western Pennsylvania, including scenes of the CSX, Conrail, B&LE, P&LE, Union RR, N&W, and Allegheny PAT Commuter.

● Carstens Publications, Inc., offers, among many videos, a study of an HO layout in the "Alturas and Lone Pine Way Freight."

● Catenary Video Productions offer traction videos, featuring the North Shore line, the Sacramento Northern, and (San Francisco) Bay Area Rapid Transit.

● Green Frog Productions, Ltd., offers a variety of videos on subjects including standard gauge lines like the DT&I and Western Maryland, and narrow gauge lines like the Rio Grande.

● Herron Rail Services presents rare footage of various American steam, diesel, and electric lines in "Glory Machines." Among the prototype lines covered are the Pennsylvania branchlines, including the New York & Long Branch, and the Sandusky Line. Other videos highlight railroads in the 1980s and American railroading from 1928–1952.

● Hopewell Productions offers a series titled "Great Model Railroads," with three volumes published to date. Also available are "Steamin' to L.A." and "Railroads of St. Louis," which take you inside the cabs and control towers of famous rail lines throughout the West and Midwest.

● Interurban Films has a variety of color and black-and-white films on mainline and traction railroads as well as miniature railroading. Traction videos feature such trains as "Trolleys in Baltimore" and "Streamlining Chicago," showing the 1941 streetcar shoofly operation when the streets of the city were torn up.

RAILROAD VIDEO
PRODUCTIONS
Presents

THE
ORANGE BLOSSOM
SPECIAL
RF&P   RF&P
PART 3
Copyright 1989   Walter M. Berko

RAIL
PRO
Presents

P.R.R. POWER
VOLUME I
Tape No. 2
Copyright 1988   Walter M. Berko

- *Kalmbach Publishing Company offers dozens of videos on steam, diesel, and electric lines, including the Denver & Rio Grande, Western Pacific, and Union Pacific, as well as instructional videos on modeling in such subjects as weathering, layouts, and wiring.*

- *Lykos Productions follows "Steam Over China," showing locos traveling through Manchuria, Inner Mongolia, and western China.*

- *The Märklin Club offers modelers the chance to traverse Europe on various rail lines, including the Black Forest Railway through West Germany, a dozen Swiss railways, and the Orient Express.*

- *PBL Video offers a 90-minute instructional video on "The Art of Soldering" for model railroads.*

- *Pentrex celebrates stream prototypes with titles such as "Washington Centennial Steam" and "Steam to Los Angeles."*

- *Railroad Video offers a range of videos shot from the engine cab, including those featuring the following routes—Sparks, Nevada to Oakland, California on the Southern Pacific, and Glacier Park to Havre, Montana on the Burlington Northern.*

- *Sunday River Productions has gathered collections of nostalgic inside-the-cab trips along Chicago-area interurban lines—the North Shore, the Chicago, Aurora & Elgin, and the South Shore Line, as well as videos of Colorado mining lines and the New York Central.*

- *The Toy Train Operators Society has assembled nostalgic videos of 1950s and 1960s TV shows, including the "American Flyer Boys Railroad Club" and a video, "Toy Trains in Action," featuring Lionel's Cavalcade of Trains and a view of the Gilbert Hall of Science Layout.*

- *Video Classics takes rides on steam trains, including titles "Applachian Doubleheader," "The Cotton Belt," "Frisco Steam Power," and "Rocky Mountain Steam Power."*

- *Video Rails™ takes viewers for rides on great steam rail lines like the Southern Pacific 1941 in their Classic Collector's Series.*

- *World Quest Productions offers "The Orient Express: Paris to Istanbul," a five-day journey with history and legends of the old Orient Express, with rare footage.*

Opposite and left: Passenger and freight lines in action—from past and present—are represented in videos from Railroad Video. Along with providing hours of enjoyment, they can aid modelers in accurately re-creating a route for a layout.

BOOKS

Like videos, books fall into three general categories—those about prototypes, those about model railroads, and instructional how-to books. Many publishers offer all three types of books. Some manufacturers offer instructional books tied to their areas of speciality. Here is a browser's sampling of publishers, large and small:

● *AMS—a* Prototype in Railroad Color *guide allows modelers to gain better prototypical accuracy. The book includes references to well-known modelers' paints, including Floquil, Scalecoat, and Accu-Paint.*

● *Atlas—a variety of basic modeling books, including* Blueprints for Atlas Snap-Track Layouts, Wiring Your Layout, *and* Six Railroads You Can Build.

● *Badger Air-Brush Company—two books for meticulous modelers—the* Step-by-Step Modeler's Guide to Air-Brushing *and* Hobby and Craft Guide to Air Brushing.

● *Carstens Publications—lavishly illustrated studies of favorite rail lines, with black-and-white and color photos. Modeling books range from guidebooks on design, handbooks on electricity for model railroads, and books of layout plans and traction planbooks. For toy train fans, there is a book on* Toy Trains of Yesteryear. *For railroad biographical historians, there is a biography of Frank Hornby,* "The Boy who Made $1,000,000 with A Toy."

● *Chilton Book Company—modeling guides that have become standards for modelers, including the* HO Model Railroad Manual, *the* Model Railroad Handbook, Vol. 1 *and* Narrow Gauge Model Trains.

● *Custom Railway Supply—limited editions of hand-bound books on various modeling subjects, like* Firing Locomotives *and* Locomotive Water and Cooling Stations. *The* Lenahun's Locomotive Lexicon *offers HO-scale steam and electric loco production from 1920–1970.*

● *Doubleday—histories of Union Pacific, including* Union Pacific Volume I: The Birth of a Railroad, 1862–1893.

● *Dover Publications—richly illustrated railroad histories, including* Early American Locomotives

and A History of the American Locomotive: 1830–1880.

● *Faller—instructional guides for modelers, including* Scenic Modeling Made Easy, *and in German,* Z-Gauge Modeling *and* Dioramas Made Easy.

● *Golden West Books—books on all types of railroading, from steam to interurbans to famous railroad runs, like the Donner Pass and Minnesota's* Logging Railroads. *Lines represented in books include the Pittsburgh & Lake Erie and the North Shore. Of special interest to modelers may be a history/reference book called* The Beauty of Bridges.

● *Greenberg Publishing Company—price guides to collectable toy trains that have become standard reference works. These include parts manuals for Lionel and other lines, and general guides to collectable trains like Lionel, Marx, and American Flyer. The* Greenberg's Guides *are used by collectors of all ages.*

● *Newton K. Gregg Publishers—reprints of classic railroad books, primarily the plans and photos from various "cyclopedias" on railroading printed over the past fifty years. It also publishes several detailed locomotive dictionaries, including* Passenger Cars from the 1919 Car Builders Dictionary *and the* 1912 Locomotive Dictionary.

● *Heimburger House Publications—fully illustrated softcover books on several lines, and a cartoon version of the mythical* Fiddletown & Copperopolis. *Also, instructional books on such subjects as* Sn3 Modeling, Railroading with American Flyer, *and* S Gauge Building and Repair Manual.

● *Interurban Press—lavishly illustrated books on electric lines, and a retrospective called* The Last of the Great Stations. *Also available is a cookbook,* Dinner in the Diner, *with almost 300 recipes from nineteen famous railroads.*

● *K-Line—service manuals, including* The Complete Service Manual for Lionel Trains *and others for American Flyer trains, O and O-27 trains.*

● *Kalmbach Books—how-to books, including* The Practical Guide to HO Model Railroading *and* Hints and Tips for Plastic Modeling, *and a* Kitbashing HO Model Railroad Structures.

● *Ladd Publications—reprints of classic train checklists for collectors or modelers who want to re-create a running historic set. Titles include the* Lionel 1932 Dealer Catalog Reprint *and the* Gilbert HO Checklist 1938–1963.

● *NJ International—books on the trains and interur-*

Above: A famous prototype—a modern Union Pacific SD60 diesel in East Los Angeles, California, from Rail Photos Unlimited. **Left:** In his official Lionel vest, Jack Earley is one of hundreds of devoted proprietors of train stores. At his Flemington, New Jersey, store, Little Hobby's, Earley offers both new and collectible trains and accessories, as well as a wide selection of books and magazines. A recent visit revealed a showcase of Kadee couplers, a Lady Lionel, and an operating HO-scale layout on the second floor. **Opposite, top:** One of the best ways to plan your layout is with one of the many books on prototype lines. For example, this kit of perhaps the most famous of all trains, the Orient Express, in N scale from Model Power can be the starting point to building a layout that includes the mountains and valleys of Europe. To re-create this line as it was during its heyday, however, you should research the finer details of the route in a book on the subject. **Opposite, bottom:** Prototype trains, such as this DW&P switcher, are always popular topics of books and videos.

bans of the Eastern seaboard, including The Brooklyn Trolleys, the Brooklyn Elevated, and The Many Faces of the Pennsy K-4.

• *Northwest Short Line*—a pictorial look at The Northern Pacific Railway, with over 300 photos depicting the NP from the 1930s to the 1950s.

• *Precision Scale Company*—booklets of scale drawings of a wide variety of authentic material chosen for their adaptability to railroad modeling, including western buildings, logging cars, and churches.

• *Quadrant Press*—pictorial reviews of rail lines and interurbans from across the country. Lines featured include the rails along the Hudson, Long Island Railroad, Staten Island Ferry, New York trolleys, Santa Fe streamliners, and the California Zephyr.

• *R. Robb Ltd.*—narrow gauge pictorials, each with over 100 black-and-white photos.

• *TAB Paperbacks*—guides for modelers, including the ABCs of Building Model Railroad Freight Cars and Real Life Scenic Techniques.

• *Weekend Chief Publishing*—pictorial histories of eastern U.S. rail lines, including the Pennsylvania Railroad Era on Long Island, Victorian Railroad Stations of Long Island, and Brooklyn Waterfront Railways.

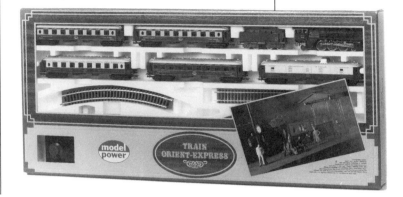

CHAPTER SIX
Collecting Trains

When you have too many trains for your basement layout or acquire some trains that are too valuable for everyday use, you have the beginnings of a full-fledged collection. By displaying your collection in a cabinet or on shelves, you can share rare and more valuable locomotives with others without having to integrate them into a layout. Collecting trains is especially appealing to those who love antique trains, those who want to hold in their hands an original Lionel or American Flyer that first circled a Christmas tree fifty years ago. It is also appealing to investors who want to hold onto an antique train—or a new, limited run loco—until it increases enough in value to be sold at a tidy profit. There is no denying that buyers will spend money for a rare train: A Märklin 1909 antique train sold for $39,000 at Sotheby Parke Bernet's London gallery in 1985.

A BRIEF HISTORY

The practice of train collecting began in the 1920s and 1930s. At that time, the most popular trains to collect were Standard gauge trains, often made of tinplate. The Lionel Blue Comet (which will be discussed later) is a good example of the kind of train most popular at the time.

Collecting grew throughout the 1940s, 1950s, and early 1960s. In the mid-1960s, it started to decline and hit its lowest level in the 1970s. One reason, says a hobby shop owner, is because other types of motorized vehicle sets—like racing car and track sets—were becoming popular. Collecting was rejuvenated in the 1980s, most say, because those who loved trains as children became old enough to afford them for themselves.

WHY COLLECT?

There are two basic reasons to collect trains—a desire to recapture the past and the desire to make a good investment. Whatever the reason, there are some basic points you need to consider before making a purchase. The first is price and what governs it—*scarcity and demand*. In most cases, look for the rarest train possible. These are often trains that are or were produced in limited numbers. Prime examples are failed past lines, like the 1957 Lady Lionel Pastel Set, which was meant to appeal to young

Above: Since 1891, Märklin has concentrated on model railroads: Here, one of their early German railroad stations and steam engines. Opposite: Some early examples of American model trains—two Clark friction locomotives from the 1900s.

female toy train operators (it was advertised as giving girls the power to "do anything *he* can do"). Also produced in limited numbers are some currently manufactured brass locos and reproductions of famous lines.

Another distinction to consider is *age versus condition*. A train magazine editor says that generally a collector's main goal is simply to get the train that is in the best condition. As for rarity, he says that if you are not serious about collecting for profit and want only to "collect the trains of your youth," rarity is not a factor. It is best to look for trains that are in original condition—that is, untouched and still in the original box. An original-condition American Flyer is worth much more than a loco twice its age that has been repainted and "customized" to make it more appealing to the eye.

Another consideration is whether you want to operate collectible trains. According to one railroad magazine editor, 50 percent to 60 percent of collectors buy collectors' trains to run them. The remaining buyers are varieties of "closet collectors," who never let their trains see the light of day or leave the shelf.

For more information on the finer points of choosing and judging collectible trains, and keeping up with trends in the field, there are several collectors' magazines. One such magazine is *Classic Toy Trains*, which has 53,000 readers. Along with articles, it lists current information on auctions, antique train dealers, and collector clubs, like the 23,000-member strong Train Collectors' Association of America, headquartered in Strasburg, Pennsylvania. Many serious collectors belong to the TCA, and more than one-half of them are Lionel collectors. Branches of the TCA have regular meetings across the United States. Other national clubs include the Lionel Collectors' Club in LaSalle, Illinois, and the Toy Train Operators Society in Pasadena, California. There are also many dozens of regional and local clubs, listed either in magazines and the phone book, or at hobby shops.

Finally, before you buy any collectible, familiarize yourself with the going prices. Perhaps the easiest to use and most comprehensive sources are the *Greenberg Guides*, published by Greenberg Publishing Company. These books, each concentrating on a different gauge and manufacturer (HO, O, S, Lionel, Standard gauge, for example), feature listings and photos of past models, with the date of issue and current price information. Antique catalogues, available from some train book publishers, are also useful.

ORIGINAL OR REPAINT?

For every collector planning a new purchase, there is a major consideration: to buy a car with its original paint job or a newly repainted model. Your decision rests on your reasons for collecting. Nearly all collectors agree that if you buy a train as an investment, buy it only in its original condition. Repainting reduces the value of the train; even an excellent repainting job causes the train to diminish somewhat in value. In fact, the Train Collectors of America, which requires collectors selling a train at its meets to not only follow strict *grading standards*—from mint to poor—also requires sellers to indicate whether a car has been restored.

But not everyone wants a train with an unrepainted, truly weathered paint job. Those who want the train to look like it did when their parents bought it for them thirty or forty years ago will appreciate a true-to-original repainting effort.

A collector may consider refinishing or customizing collectible trains, but only for commonly available items and those in very good or better shape. Hard-to-find items should not be touched, unless they are in poor shape—and then only to be brought to their original colors.

Below: A variety of New York Central Hudson locomotives. From top: an "erector" wide gauge; an O-gauge GA Lionel 700E; an American Flyer S-gauge; and an HO-scale. Opposite: Two early Märklin O-gauge clockwork trains with accessories.

A SAMPLING OF COLLECTORS' TRAINS

With the basics about collecting covered, here is a sampling of currently favorite types of trains for collectibles:

Lionel. By far the most popular—and pricey—type of collectible train is the trusty Lionel. According to one hobby store owner, it has the highest "collector value," not surprisingly, because it "relates back to childhood." "So many things were made and you wanted to buy everything," he says, and now, finally, "you are in the financial situation to buy them."

The favorite Lionels of collectors are the Santa Fe F3 freight and passenger sets. Manufactured in the 1950s, they were the models most often given as a gift. That familiarity, plus its always popular "Warbonnet" red-and-yellow paint scheme, account for their popularity with collectors.

Another popular Lionel is the Blue Comet, manufactured in the late 1920s and 1930s in tinplate. It was made in standard gauge; a Blue Comet Junior appeared in O gauge. One reason for the train's popularity, aside from historical interest and the attractive namesake blue color scheme, is its scarcity. There are not many Blue Comets left. The even more scarce Red Comet is also a much desired collectors' item.

But the Santa Fe and Blue Comet are not the most expensive of the Lionel trains. One more costly item is the Lionel Hudson. Among the reasons are that it was originally a more expensive model than the Santa Fe and that it was produced in smaller quantities.

Another expensive train is the Lionel State Set. This highly detailed set, first produced in 1929 in standard gauge, has an electric outline engine, a 4-4-4 steam locomotive, and 21-inch cars named after the states of the union. Today, original sets can run into several thousands of dollars.

American Flyer. The American Flyer, first manufactured in Chicago in the 1920s and 1930s, was originally an O-gauge train called the Chicago Flyer. When the New York-based A. C. Gilbert Company bought out American Flyer in the 1930s, it was renamed the American Flyer and manufactured in S gauge.

The Flyer, once the Gimbel's to Lionel's Macy's, was not always popular for collectors. At first, collectors wanted only Lionel; but as Lionel became harder to find, collectors "discovered" American Flyer. Over the past five or six years, the popularity of American Flyer has rivaled that of Lionel. As with other trains, the most popular collecting period is the post-war era through the late 1960s. The most popular American Flyer trains are the PA with Santa Fe or Northern Pacific markings.

Marx. These tin trains in O gauge were lower priced sets, most popular in the early 1950s for, as one dealer put it, "the kid whose parents could not afford to put a Lionel set under the tree." Until the past decade or so, interest in collecting these trains was not high. Now, it is popular, particularly for collectors who don't want to spend as much as serious Lionel buyers, or who want to complement a Lionel collection. Marx trains should not be ignored, however: "They've got beautiful lithography," says a train magazine editor.

Ives. This now-defunct company, whose trains appeared on the market before Lionel, in standard and O gauge, has fewer trains available in the collectibles market because they were a smaller company with a shorter life span, and have a smaller following in shops and magazines. One dealer suggests the best way to track what is available is through the *Greenberg Guides*.

Opposite: A variety of American electric collectibles. From left: a Lionel 1902 2⅞ inch-gauge trolley car; a 1908 Voltamp 2-rail 2100 2 inch-gauge loco; a Lionel standard gauge 381E; and an Ives 1918 O-gauge 1125. Above: An all-metal limited edition 1-gauge model of a German State Railroad Company prototype (Class EG-589-594) from Märklin. The locomotive features two motors that power six axles, and that can be powered from the track or catenary. The built-in electronic circuit plate operates a true-to-prototype whistle.

THE LURE OF THE POSTWAR LIONEL: 20 FAVORITE SETS*

by Joe Algozzini, *Classic Toy Trains*

Everyone has a favorite train set. Usually it's one you got as a kit, or maybe one you saw at a friend's house or in a catalogue and could only dream about. Here are my 20 favorite Lionel sets. The list is strictly chronological, and I've generally selected the first year the trains were available.

No. 1—1945. This is the first postwar catalogued set and the only one listed for the year. This is the unique 1945 set headed by a no. 224 steamer. The set is unique because it's a mix of pre-war and post-war parts blended together into something that's both enjoyable and collectible.

No. 2—1946. Next would come the set that contains a no. 726 Berkshire (with all the trimmings) pulling the three no. 2625 Irvington passenger cars.

No. 3—1948. The "Electronic Set" had "at your fingertips control" and could unload and uncouple cars anywhere on the track. It included a coal elevator and other accessories, and sold for the unheard-of-price of $199.95!

No. 4—1948. The no. 671, four-car freight set, which came with the operating log and milk cars as well as a lighted caboose, is next. Why this set? It was my very first train set!

No. 5—1950. This year, when Lionel celebrated its golden anniversary, provides two more sets: a no. 2023 yellow Union Pacific Alco pulling the Plainfield, Westfield, and Livingston passenger cars. Collectors have long prized this set, which they refer to as the "Anniversary Set."

No. 6—1950. Another memorable passenger set is the no. 773 Hudson. It included the nos. 2625 Irvington, 2627 Madison, and 2628 Manhattan passenger cars with silhouetted people in the windows.

No. 7—1954. The Santa Fe Super Streamliner with the baggage car wins my vote. This is the first version of the Super Streamliner to include the "Brand New in 1954 Classic," the no. 2530 baggage car.

No. 8—1955. The Pennsylvania RR *Congressional* is next. Here it's shown with a no. 2340 Tuscan Red GG1; the next year it had a no. 2360 GG1. Both locomotives are true classics.

No. 9—1956. The no. 2328 Burlington passenger set was a four-car set that had distinct red stripes.

No. 10—1956. The no. 2341 Jersey Central Train Master, with the wide channel aluminum passenger cars, is one of the most sought-after engines of the post-war era and is often duplicated.

No. 11—1957. A year later Lionel offered a train set just for girls, and it's become a true

classic. It was listed as the "Lady Lionel;" collectors have now named it "The Girls Train."

No. 12—1957. The Canadian Pacific set is another well-made and good-looking set.

No. 13—1958. The 1625 0-4-0 pulling three flatcars with military loads is next. The toy military vehicles were made for Lionel by Pyro and, because they were quite fragile, are usually found broken or even missing. The caboose, no 6017-85 painted gray, is hard to find.

No. 14—1958. When the Budd set was first catalogued in 1957, it contained two identical 2559 commuter cars. The 1958 version included the 2559 passenger car and the 2550 baggage/mail car.

No. 15—1958. The Virginian Rectifier freight set has the hard-to-find no. 6556 Katy stockcar and no. 6427-60 Virginian caboose.

No. 16—1960. The uncatalogued no. 1882, or what collectors call the "Halloween set," has become a classic. One source says the 1882 was "made for Sears probably in 1960." Another source refers to the set as a "Macy special General." I've heard still others refer to it as a "Wards Set."

No. 16½—1960. The "over-and-under set" or the "father-and-son set" is actually two sets in one: an HO empire on ground level and an O gauge layout above. Because of the HO element I probably shouldn't consider

it one of the top 20, but the O gauge set includes the scarce 6357-50 Santa Fe caboose and probably should be listed.

No. 17—1960. The "New Land-Sea-And-Air Gift Pack" is unique because all the cars have Khaki Marine Corps markings and because it has the scarce U.S. Marine Corps helicopter.

No. 18—1961. Although the red-striped, Santa Fe *Super Chief* set first appeared in 1959, I prefer the four-car passenger set shown in 1961.

No. 19—1962. 1962 is the first year for the gold-striped Presidential passenger set. The set came with four cars: one no. 2523 President Garfield Pullman, two no. 2522 President Harrison Vista Domes, and one no. 2521 President McKinley observation.

No. 20—1964. My final entry never appeared in a Lionel catalogue. The Sears no. 9820 "Military Train Set" includes the scarce "flat car with tank," no. 3666 cannon boxcar, and no. 347 cannon firing range set and toy soldiers.

*Excerpted from "Lionel's top 20 postwar train sets," by Joe Algozzini, *Classic Toy Trains* (Summer 1989), © 1989, Kalmbach Publishing Co.

Below: A one-time HO-scale limited edition freight locomotive with tender from Märklin, based on a Borsig design for the German State Railroad. This loco and tender have four axles, four traction tires, and working headlights.

LIMITED EDITIONS

Like other limited edition items, some currently produced limited edition trains make good collectibles; that is, they increase in value.

One type of limited edition is the reproduction of old trains from original castings. For example, Williams, which is licensed to use the Lionel name, produces exact replicas of Lionel tinplate trains. They have manufactured replicas of both standard gauge Blue Comet and State sets of the 1920s, and have also reproduced favorite Lionel tinplate trains in O gauge, popular in the 1930s, like the Hiawatha and 700E. One of Williams' recently produced trains increased $1,000 in value in the course of one year. Lionel itself manufactures reproductions of old trains, including a recent four-part State Set, which featured two fully-detailed passenger and one observation cars.

Another type of limited edition is the highly detailed brass model that does not reproduce an old toy train but accurately follows a prototype design. Companies offering these trains include Pecos River Brass (N- and HO-scale custom-painted trains); W&R Enterprises (hand-built N-, HO- and O-scale trains); MTS Imports (custom-painted HO- and O-scale trolleys and locos); and Trackside Specialties (O-gauge locos and cars from a variety of companies). Newly designed plastic-and-metal limited edition trains are offered by Bachmann and Lionel.

Who collects limited edition trains? It is often *not* the collector of old trains. Although there is some overlap between collectors of original model trains and collectors of newly produced collectibles, most members of each group are interested only in their particular domain. Another reason for the break between the two types of limited edition collectors is simple: money. According to the Train Collectors Association, many collectors cannot afford the original; but can find satisfaction with a convincing reproduction or new collectible.

One note: It stands to reason that not all limited edition trains yield thousands of dollars in profits, as did those mentioned in the examples. However, with judicious buying and selling, some profit might be made. On average, however, most collectors would do as well financially with an insured bank savings account; but they wouldn't have as much fun.

Below: A group of British brass steam-fired locomotives made by Steven Dockyard in the 1890s. These trains can be run on floor or rail. Opposite: A 1912–1913 Knapp Electric Company 2"-gauge 2-rail locomotive 222, made in the U.S.

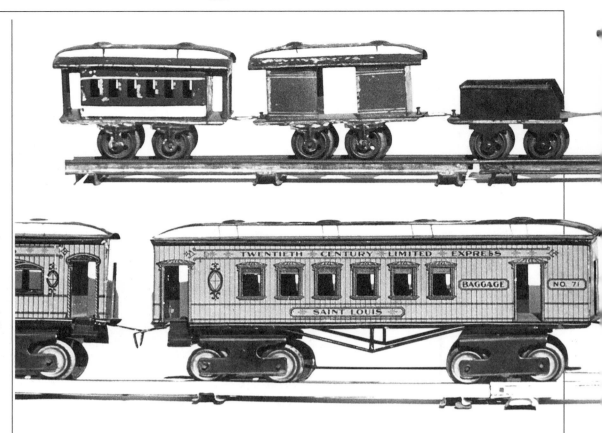

DEALERS AND SOURCES

There are five basic ways to find the collectibles you want: garage sales and flea markets, classified ads, auctions, swap meets, and hobby shops.

Garage Sales and Flea Markets. Once rich lodes of hidden train treasures, garage sales and flea markets are more chancy sources these days. One reason is that sellers have become more knowledgeable about the worth of collectibles and rather than offering valuable items at flea markets, take them to professional auctioneers. Or, if desirable items are available at flea markets, they are snatched up quickly by the flea market regular, who may not even be a train lover but instead someone who wants to sell the loco at a profit to a hobby shop dealer. The other reason for the relative scarcity of collectible trains at garage sales is the fact that the supply is dwindling. Much of it was already sold (or trashed) in the 1960s and 1970s, as post-war kids grew up and abandoned their trains. Much of what is left is in the hands of train collectors, who, if they want to sell or trade, do so at swap meets.

Classified Ads. These ads in train magazines are the most direct way to reach buyers and sellers in print. Every month, in *Model Railroader, Classic Toy Trains,* and other train magazines, there are ads for Lionel

Postwar trains, American Flyer, Lionel replacement parts, and other exotica.

Hobby Shops and Dealers. Many train shops devote a portion of their floor space to collectible trains. Among the leading shops offering collectibles are:

● *Choo Choo Works in Oak Lawn, Illinois, offers prewar and post-war O- and S-gauge and standard-gauge trains, and train service.*

● *Dougs Train World in Des Moines, Iowa, offers Lionel Collectors' items and limited editions of all kinds.*

● *Anthony J. Dudynski Supply Company in the Bronx, New York, offers O-gauge limited edition Lionel train sets, collector boxcars, limited Bachmann editions, and historic American Flyer S-gauge trains and sets.*

● *Grand Central Ltd. in Lincoln, Nebraska, offers a variety of collectors' trains, plus collectors' editions of American Flyer.*

● *Joseph A. Grzyboski, Jr., in Scranton, Pennsylvania, offers specialty limited edition trains and collectors' train sets, including Blue Comet and mint cars.*

● *Jerry's Train Gallery in Chatham, New Jersey, offers a complete assortment of Lionel trains and accessories, including new and investment sets, and rare American Flyer sets.*

● *John's Train Shop in St. Louis, Missouri, offers a large selection of new and used trains, specialized in Lionel and LGB.*

● *Leventon's Hobby Supplies in Chehalis, Washington, offers only American Flyer in HO, S, O, and*

Above: Some rare, early Ives 1902–1904 O-gauge and 1-gauge clockwork trains.

standard Gauge.

- *Little Hobby's in Flemington, New Jersey, offers collectible Lionels dating back to 1900, American Flyer, and new trains in all scales and brands. Owner Jack Earley, who opened the shop 14 years ago, says he loves his job because "it makes everyone happy."*

- *Mikes Train House in Columbia, Maryland, offers Lionel Collector lines.*

- *The Red Caboose in New York, New York, offers a wide selection of post-war O-gauge, standard-gauge, American Flyer, and pre-war Lionel collectible trains.*

- *Charles Ro Supply Company in Malden, Massachusetts, the self-proclaimed "America's Number One Lionel Dealer," offers rare Lionel pre- and post-war cars and commemorative collector series, and American Flyer.*

- *Charles Siegel's Coins and Trains in Erie, Pennsylvania, offers Lionel consumer catalogues from the past 40 years.*

- *Sommerfields in Milwaukee, Wisconsin, opened several years ago by Mark Sommerfield, a past and current lover of Lionel ("I'm addicted to Lionel," he says), offers a wide selection of new and original Lionel collectibles.*

- *Train 99 in Glen Mills, Pennsylvania, offers new Williams, American Flyer, and Lionel.*

- *Train World in Brooklyn, New York, and Trainland in Lynbrook, New York, offers a wide variety of American Flyer and Lionel original collectibles and limited editions, along with Williams.*

- *Underground Railroad Shoppe in New Castle, Pennsylvania, offers older MPC and post-war Lionel, American Flyer, and Marx trains.*

Swap Meets and Auctions. These sources can also be fruitful, especially if you have a desirable train to trade and if you know what you want and what condition you want it in. Some of the top U.S. swap meets include:

- *Lionel Collectors Club of America in Rockford, Illinois, holds annual meets.*

- *Lionel Operating Train Society in Cincinnati, Ohio, holds conventions, annual shows, and swap meets, and publishes a magazine, Switches, which contains a "Track Changes" swap section.*

- *Lionel Railroad Club in Brookfield, Wisconsin, holds all-gauge swap meets, one in Cudahy, Wisconsin.*

- *National Collectors Club in Montvale, New Jersey, holds a toy and train show.*

- *Toy Train Collectors Society in Rochester, New York, is a not-for-profit organization that holds ten train shows and swap meets each year in several upstate New York towns, including Rochester, Syracuse, and Niagara Falls. Show participants include dealers and hobbyists; show features include test tracks, running layouts, and a sick train clinic.*

- *Train Collectors Association meets (for TCA members and guests) are held twice yearly in York, Pennsylvania, Timonium, Maryland, Santa Clara, California, and near Philadelphia, Pennsylvania. The meets, which routinely attract 8,000 collectors, are said to be the biggest collectors' meets held in the country.*

- *Toy Train Operators Society holds well-attended meets similar to those mentioned above.*

Right: Examples of antique alcohol "spirit fired" live steam trains of all gauges, from German, English, French, and American makers.

DISPLAY CASES

To store your collection of trains, there are a variety of carrying cases and display cases. Here is a sampling:

To transport cars and locos, Proto Power West makes Tote-All, a storage and carrying system, combining corrugated boxes and a nylon carrying case. The storage containers for HO- and N-scale equipment consist of boxes made of heavy corrugated cardboard, which have been diecut and scored for assembly. Each 27 × 6¾ × 3 inch tray holds about 16 HO 40-foot cars of 72 N-scale 40-foot cars. The foam pad at the bottom of the tray keeps the models from moving; the top cover protects the cars from dust.

To store your collection at home, Rail-Safe offers the Rail-Safe. It is constructed of 200-pound corrugated cardboard with a diecut urethane foam insert that will accommodate seven pieces of rolling stock. Each slot in the safe measures 10 × 1⅜ × 2¾ inches.

Other makers of display and carrying cases include A-Line, Boxes Plus, Brass Locomotive Company, Gauge One America, and Kibri.

To display your collection, Rail Rax makes an aluminum display shelf called, appropriately, Rail Rax®. Available in 6-foot sections in combination HO/S gauge, O gauge, and combination O/#1/standard gauge, it is engineered to support the heavier toy train locomotives and has been heat treated for strength. The anodized finish is durable and easy to maintain. Rail Rax can be fastened to the wall with #10 × 1½-inch sheet metal screws.

A FINAL NOTE

To keep a separate record of your collection, Virnex Industries makes a Model Train Inventory Record Book. It allows you to list every particular of your collection—make, model, date purchased, where purchased, price paid, and any additional data—and search for them by category (locomotive, freight car, etc.). The book is especially valuable if your collection is lost or stolen, and also useful when attending a swap meet or sale.

Depending on where you live, security may be important. Guard your collection as you would any other valuable. One New York collector whose basement had been burglarized, with his entire collection stolen, had this advice for railroaders: "Invest in a good lock."

CHAPTER SEVEN
Railroadiana

Even in a perfect world, you can't be running your trains all the time. For those times when you have to surface from your basement, you can take a little bit of your railroad with you, through railroadiana. The vast array of railroadiana available allows you to make it part of your kitchen, office, art collection, and wardrobe. Even those people who never see your layout will know you are a devoted model railroader.

There are two general types of railroadiana—items related to the prototypes and their history, and those related to model trains. For example, a painting of a nineteenth-century locomotive coursing across the Great Plains recalls the railroad itself; the ceramic mug inscribed "I am a model railroader's widow" speaks directly to the modeler. This chapter will present a wide choice of both kinds of railroadiana.

ARTWORK

There is a full variety of railroad artwork—from prints to plaques—to display on your walls. From Con-Cor are brightly colored ready-to-frame railroad prints. These 14 × 18 inch photographic prints show prototypes from all eras in their glory, moving along the tracks. Duo-tone prints of classic steam, diesel, and electric prototypes like the Texas & Pacific, the Nickel Plate Road, and the Rio Grande are available from M. F. Kotowski. From Gil Reid are the "Great Trains of America" and "Emperors of the Road" series of full-color prints showing famous steam, diesel, and electric trains in action. The prints, which are either 16 × 22 or 25 × 19 inches, have a white border and are ready for framing. Narrow gauge prototypes are featured in the full-color prints from Chama Graphics Lines, like the Colorado & Southern and the Rio Grande Southern. Full color glossy prints of steam and traction lines of the 1950s and 1960s are available from Answer Railway Visuals Division. The prints can be mounted on heavy backing at an additional cost. Lionel offers three full-color train posters: two represent prototype trains of a bygone era; the third depicts a sleeping boy dreaming of Lionel trains.

Con-Cor offers railroad plaques, each silkscreened in prototype colors with a famous logo, like the Union Pacific or Rio Grande. The plaques are approximately 12 × 18 inches and are made of ⅛" Masonite. Signal Signs also produces railroad logo wall plaques. Made of tempered hardwood, these 11 × 14 inch plaques are silkscreened in prototype colors and represent over 100 train lines—including the C & O, Soo Line,

and the Rock Island. Cardboard roadname signs are available from Creative Screen Process. Types of signs range from the standard railroad crossing to logos for lines such as the Chicago & North Western and famous trains such as the California Zephyr.

Railroad and railroad historic product signs are available from Phil Derrig Design. The 8-inch color porcelain/enamel signs feature such views of the past as the American Flyer logo and an ad for Fincks's "Detroit-Special" Overalls. Railroad and model railroad-inspired porcelain signs like American Flyer and Lionel are offered by the Painted Post Calliope Co.

To recall the past most vividly, nothing is as immediate as a photograph. You can choose from over 4,500 steam, diesel, electric and trolley photos in the collection of Railroad Avenue Enterprises. Most photos are 8 × 10 inches and have detailed information about the train on the back. Charly's Slides offers slides of mainlines, industries, trolleys, short lines, and old-time steam lines; Rail Photos has over 1,500 slides and color prints representing 275 companies. Audio-Visual Designs has color slides of prototype railroads; EVDA Slides offers slides of American and foreign prototypes and trolleys. Historical railroad photos of the Union Pacific line from 1934–1971, either 5 × 8 or 11 × 14 inches, are available from Stan Kistler. Other leading sources for prototype photos and slides are the Kalmbach Memorial Library (see Chapter Six), Alco, Historic Photos, and the State Railroad Museum of Pennsylvania.

Finally, for lovers of toy trains, there are authentic cancelled Lionel stock certificates, framed under glass.

NOTE CARDS AND CALENDARS

For the office, for gifts, or at home, there is a wide selection of calendars and note cards with railroad scenes and logos. These items are also an inexpensive way to surround yourself with some of the impressive paintings, sketches, and lithographs of both bygone and active train lines.

Con-Cor offers several 8½ × 11 inch prototype wall calendars, including:

- **a New York Central Calendar**, *representing the steam, diesel, and electric periods*
- **a basic Railroads Calendar**, *with both steam and diesel trains*
- **Those Magnificent Trains Calendar**, *with an array of trains in action (also available as a desk calendar)*
- **Don Ball's Calendar**, *with twelve photographs by the well-known railroad photographer*

In an 11 × 14 inch format from Con-Cor is *The Art of Model Railroading Calendar*,

Opposite: This full-color 21 × 27 inch reprint of classic original Lionel Trains artwork evokes memories of the famous Lionel steamers.

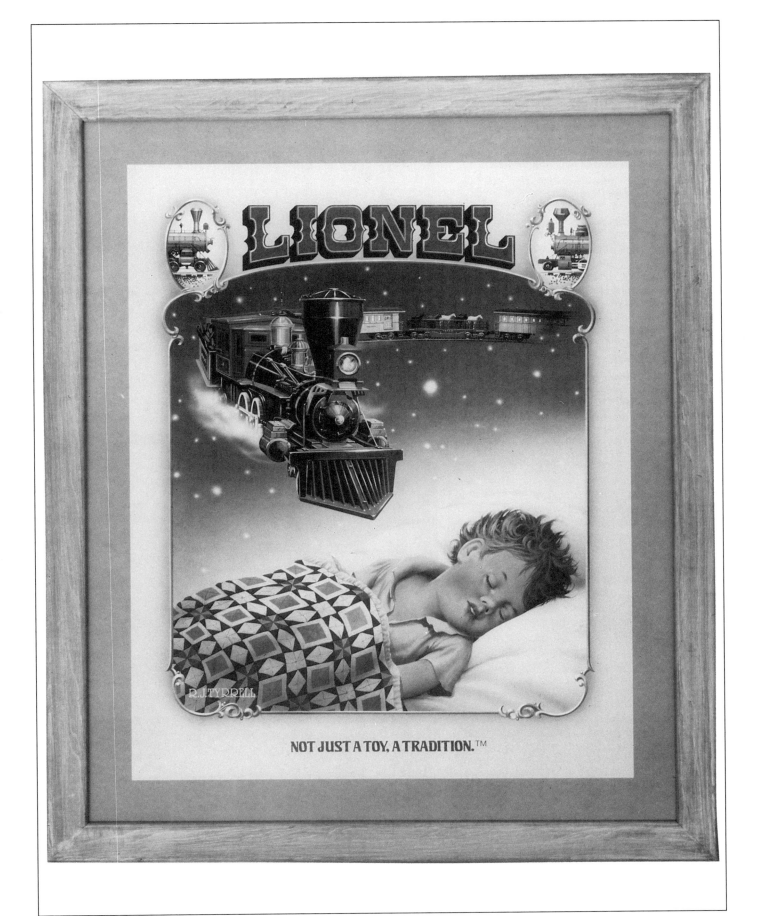

with some of the country's most lavish and realistic model railroad layouts. From other manufacturers are calendars that feature the following:

- *garden railway scenes in the "View from the Bird-water and Raspberry" calendar, with six drawings by railway artist Bruce Bates*

- *two black-and-white calendars, one celebrating Santa Fe steam trains, another Southern Pacific steam trains, from Whistle Stop Publications*

- *color paintings of prototypes in the New York Central Calendar and the Pennsy Calendar, from Audio-Visual Designs*

- *an all-color Big Boys calendar, featuring action shots of a variety of 4-8-8-4s, from Video Rails*

- *a Long Island Railroad calendar, with fourteen full-color views of steam, diesel, and electric trains, from Long Island Sunrise Trail Chapter NRHS.*

- *station sketches from major railroads in a calendar from Rideau Graphics*

- *cabooses in a full-color photo calendar from American Railroad Photography*

- *steam locomotives in pen-and-ink drawings in a calendar from the Shade Tree Press*

- *A Rocky Mountain Railroad calendar, with fourteen steam color views of narrow gauge lines, from Sundance Publications Ltd.*

- *two full-color poster-size calendars from Märklin—one called "Powered by Steam," the other "Childhood Dreams." (Note: These and all Märklin products listed in this chapter are available only to Märklin Club members. See Appendix for more information.)*

For quick notes, Lionel offers a set of 3 × 5 inch note pads imprinted with the Circle L logo. Note cards with railroad, train station, and prototype scenes are offered by Mountain State Model Works. Nineteenth-century railroad engravings are reproduced in note-cards from American Bank Note Railroad Cards. Color postcards of past and present trains are available from Audio-Visual Designs. Trolley postcards are available from Dover Publications.

JEWELRY AND ACCESSORIES

Whether you're a male or female railfan, there are more than enough ways to express your love of model railroading with jewelry. To match an official LGB tie, from Lehmann-Gross-Bahn are LGB tie tacks and lapel pins. Lionel presents three kinds of lapel pins, plated with brass, nickel or gold: the Circle-L logo, the American Flyer logo, and the rectangular Lionel logo. Steel railroad pins of all types are available in true-to-prototype color from Sundance Marketing. A full selection of railroad heralds, name train logos, locomotive number plates and logos is available. Sundance can also create custom pins for railroads or railroad historical societies and clubs.

From Con-Cor, there are two types of key chains—leather and metal, stamped with logos of famous prototypes. Lionel also offers a solid brass key chain stamped with the Lionel logo and a Lionel train.

From C&J, a dozen different lines are represented in cast metal belt buckles. All buckles have a pewter finish, detailed engraving, and a brass clasp. Some of the trains represented are the Broadway Limited and the Super Chief. Belt buckles featuring rapid transit lines are offered by H-R Products.

Leather belt buckles, stamped with train logos and rimmed in brass, are also available from Con-Cor, as are true-to-prototype color fabric logo patches for jackets and jeans. To complete the looks, Con-Cor offers brass railroad watches, complete with second hand, snap-down cover, and watch fob. The case itself is stamped with a scene of an oncoming steam locomotive.

A gold-tone pocket watch, its case en-

Top: For the musically-inclined modeler, Railroad Tie Express offers this brightly-colored tie with a replica of a steam engine. The tie contains an electronic device that, when pressed, plays "I've Been Working on the Railroad." Above: Sundance Marketing accurately depicts famous heralds and logos in tiny cloisonné railroad pins—perfect for hats, jackets, and coats.

Right, top: Carry your childhood memories with this solid brass die-cast Lionel key ring. The Lionel logo is stamped into the medallion. Right, bottom: You can keep to your train schedule with this nickel-plated Lionel pocket watch. The cover features an engraving of a C&ARR locomotive. It protects an old-fashioned wind-up watch with a sweep second hand. The red Lionel logo is marked on the watch face. Below: A one-size-fits-all engineer's cap in trusty hickory-striped railroader denim, from Lionel.

graved with a steam locomotive, is available from Foster-Trent, Inc. Time in Motion offers men's quartz watches with a second hand consisting of a famous steam train like the C&NW "400". Lionel also offers a wind-up nickel pocket watch with a C&ARR General locomotive engraved on the back.

Finally, to mark yourself as a train lover while you travel, Lionel offers a 10 × 18 inch nylon tote bag, in Lionel red or American Flyer blue, each embossed with its representative logo.

CLOTHING

A wide variety of railroad-inspired clothing is available for the well-dressed railroad fan. For example, Con-Cor sells roomy T-shirts and polo shirts for men and women, embossed in the colors of a favorite train line, such as the Pennsy or Chessie System. Matching caps are also available. T-shirts, sweatshirts, and nightshirts embossed with the logos of fallen flags and other train lines like the Western Maryland, the Erie Lackawanna, and Clinchfield are available from Fallen Flaggs RxR Wearables. Conductor caps, railroad jackets, and vests are available through Rolling Stock. Märklin also offers a red baseball club cap with the official company logo. Other novelty railroad caps are available as well, embossed with phrases like "The headlight's on, but no one's in the cab!," "Narrowminded and proud of it," and "I'm a Model Railroad Widow." Blue and white hickory-striped engineer's caps are also available from Con-Cor, Walthers, Rolling Stock, NJ International, Merit, Lionel, and Greenberg Publishing Co. Perhaps most novel is a musical engineer's cap, which plays "I've Been Working on the Railroad," available from New Liberty Enterprises. Some companies offer sizes for children as well as adults.

Bright red or blue cotton/poly Lionel sweatshirts and T-shirts with the Lionel logos are available in adult's and children's sizes. From Märklin are official Märklin sports shirts, emblazoned with the company crest, and 100 percent cotton Märklin T-shirts, in white with the official logo on black and red. Both items are available in adult sizes; the T-shirt also comes in children's sizes.

For women from Con-Cor are large square fashion scarves, embossed with dozens of popular train lines. From Lehmann-Gross-Bahn, there is the official LGB tie, in solid red, with the LGB emblem on the lower right side. Lionel also offers silk-blend navy blue ties and bows for men and women. A musical railroad tie that plays "I've Been Working on the Railroad" can be ordered from Railroad Tie Express, Inc.

Right: This comfortable 50% cotton/50% polyester official Lionel T-shirt features the traditional "Circle L" logo, and is perfect for weekend wear. Below: Historic Atcheson, Topeka & Santa Fe Mimbreño china is re-created by Nostalgia Station. Following the original Santa Fe designs, this hotel grade, high-fire vitreous china reproduces the service used on AT&SF dining cars for nearly a century.

HOUSEWARES

To bring your world of trains into the kitchen, Con-Cor offers an array of ceramic mugs, stamped with nineteenth-century line drawings or humorous sayings. From Lionel, mugs of black ironstone, with the logo in 22-karat gold trim, are available, as are frosted glass mugs and polyurethane "Colder Holders" to keep drinks at their proper temperature. Märklin's 10-ounce mug is perfect for hot coffee, while their intricately inscribed beer stein is for a more potent drink. CM Shops give railroaders a choice of dozens of rail line logos in their ceramic mugs, from New Jersey Transit to the Texas-Mexican Railway. For traveling, there is also the 22-ounce multi-color Thermo Travel mug, embossed with railroad logos like Santa Fe and Chessie System.

From Con-Cor, there are also ceramic ash trays with quips, cocktail napkins stamped with train logos, and playing cards with scenes of famous prototypes in action.

For elegant entertaining, reproductions of the dining car china from the Atchison, Topeka & Santa Fe line are available from Nostalgia Station Ltd. The high-fire vitreous hotel china comes in shapes matched as closely as possible to the prototype pieces, including fruit dish, celery tray, and teapot. For an historic touch, actual Pennsylvania Railroad dining car china and glassware is available from Right Track Trading Co.

Finally, for your patio, there are brass wind chimes in the shape of tiny locomotives and a Lionel director's chair in natural wood with canvas seats and back. To check the temperature, there is an antique reproduction working thermometer from Gaus Enterprises, which features an old advertisement for the Platte Valley Route of the Union Pacific.

FOR THE OFFICE OR WORKPLACE

To bring your hobby to your desk, Con-Cor offers several brass paperweights in the shapes of locomotive tanks or dining car. The brass replica is mounted on a decorative hardwood base. For signing important documents, there are desk pen sets, with hand-finished bases made from pre-1880 Santa Fe Railroad oak boxcar floors. They can be ordered from Santa Fe Railroad Pens.

To keep correct office time, Con-Cor also offers modern wood wall clocks, the faces stamped with the logos of favorite lines, like the Burlington Route. A battery-run railroad crossing digital alarm clock with bells that ring and red lights that flash can be part of an on-time office; it comes from the Train Station.

From Merit are a variety of office and travel accessories, including wood and brass wall clocks, barometers, table and desk clocks, travel alarm clocks, and a mini-

Above: This Z-gauge Märklin model of the Santa Fe is one way to distinguish your desk as a modeler's workplace. As seen earlier, a Z-gauge layout is even small enough to fit into your briefcase.

Left: For your next modeling-oriented vacation, take along this 10 × 18 inch water-repellent, Oxford nylon American Flyer tote. Below: Whether scratchbuilding or weathering a model, this two-pocket, 10 × 18 inch cotton duck official Lionel carpenter's apron is useful for toting tools or train parts. Both items are available with either Lionel or American Flyer logos.

calculator with case. Each is embossed with the logo of one of a dozen or more classic prototypes and model railroads, like the AT&SF, Missouri Pacific, and American Flyer.

Blue Lionel door mats are available in heavyweight rubber and vinyl. They measure 18 × 27 inches and have nonslip backs.

For the contractor or handyman, a 10 × 18 inch carpenter's apron, inscribed with the Lionel or American Flyer names is available. It has two pockets for tools. To fill the apron is the official Märklin tool kit, with five screwdrivers and tweezers.

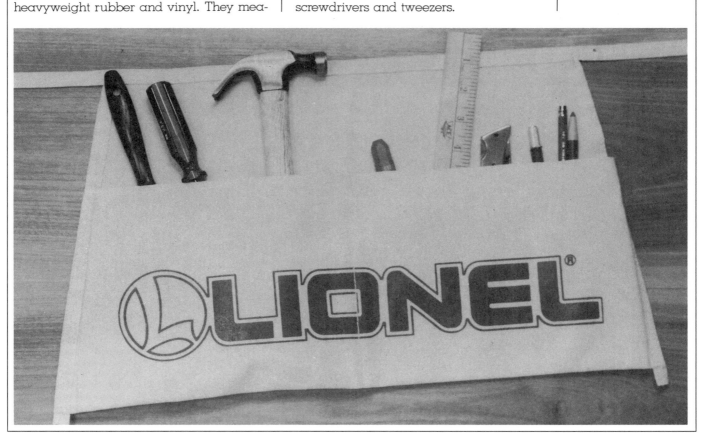

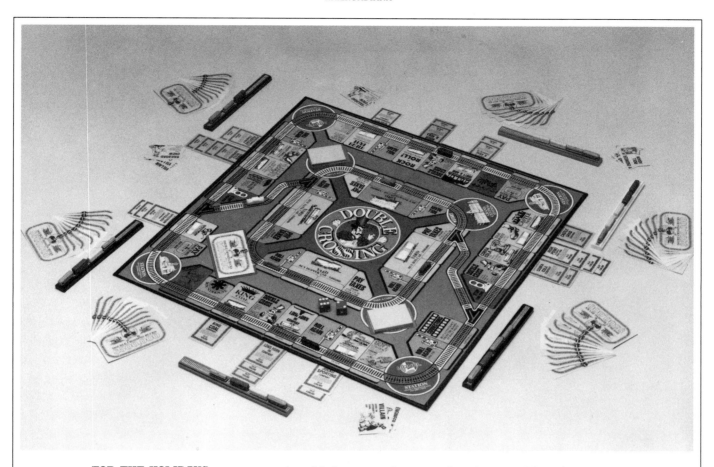

FOR THE HOLIDAYS

A railroad-inspired Christmas tree is easy to create with the variety of railroad ornaments available. Con-Cor offers three types, including tiny wooden locomotives, gold-covered locos and cars, and golden bulbs imprinted with classic and modern railroad scenes. Christmas cards featuring paintings of famous prototypes like the Burlington Twin Cities Zephyr and the Santa Fe Super Chief are available from the Leanin' Tree.

MISCELLANEOUS

For children, Greenberg Publishing Company offers a number of coloring books, including books devoted to LGB- and G-gauge trains. For a children's room, TEN Industries offers plastic switchplate covers, in engine and caboose designs.

Sets of garden railway picture cards are also available through *Garden Railways* magazine. These 2½ × 1¼ inch cards feature photos and descriptions of various steam locomotives, engines, and rolling stock, printed on acid-free stock. They recall the free picture cards that were created in all subject areas and distributed at the turn of the century by tobacco and tea companies. Cards are sold in sets of twenty with their own album.

Modern employee railroad timetables, with line-by-line instructions and speeds for such lines as the Soo Line System 1986, are offered by Carl Loucks. Original historic timetables—and menus—from famous lines like the Burlington Route and Union Pacific are available from Graylord Station.

A record featuring "Great American Train Songs (Vol. 1)," featuring well-known train tunes sung by Johnny Cash and Jerry Lee Lewis, is available from Roundhouse Records.

From Lionel is a fast-paced board game for the entire family called "Double Crossing." The goal of Double Crossing is to build a railroad empire, avoid financial and mechanical pitfalls, and be the first to reach Grand Central Station. "Empire Builder," a board game about building your own rail dynasty and pitting it against others, is available from Mayfair Games. If trivia is more to your liking, the Rail-Triv Software game is available from Mil-Scale Products. It offers hundreds of questions and is compatible with the Commodore 64 computer.

Finally, no hobby would be properly represented without bumper stickers, and Creative Screen Process offers a wide variety, including "I Love HO Scale," "I Love N Scale," "I Love O Scale," and simply, "I Love Model Railroading."

Above: Take time from modeling to build a different kind of railroad empire in "Double Crossing,"™ a new railroad board game from Lionel. By purchasing train cars, winning contracts, and avoiding tariffs and opponents, you may become the railroad to reach Grand Central Station first—and win the game.

APPENDICES

Glossary

ABS Plastic—plastic used by some scratch-builders; harder than styrene

ACC—see *cyanoacrylate*

air brake—a brake operated by compressed air

airbrush—a miniature spray gun that allows the painter to control the size, direction, and pressure of spray

alignment gauge—when using flexible track, a plastic or metal gauge that fits between rails to show whether a section of track maintains a particular radius

alternating current (AC)—current that reverses its direction of flow at regular intervals

articulated locomotive—a large steam locomotive with two sets of driving wheels and cylinders pivoted together for ease in negotiating curves

backdrop—flat painting, lithograph, or collage of background scenery (such as sky and mountains) for use in extending the horizon of a layout

ballast—small rocks or stones that support and stabilize track ties, and provide drainage

benchwork—the wooden frame that supports a layout

bi-level commuter coach—coach with an upper gallery for commuter runs; first built by Pullman-Standard for use in the Chicago area in the 1950s

block—commonly used as a synonym for *section*; more properly, a designated length of track, often protected by signals, used by the prototype to control train movements and to avoid collisions

boiler—the horizontal tank section of a steam locomotive in which water is heated to produce steam

bolster—transverse beam in the body of a piece of rolling stock where the truck attaches; also the main transverse beam of a track

boxcar—box-shaped, covered car typically used to transport products that need protection from the weather or vandals

brake cylinder—a cylinder containing a piston that is moved by compressed air to apply an air brake

branchline—a part of a railroad that branches off from the mainline to service a town or industry or connect with another line

brazing—soldering with a filler metal whose melting temperature is above 840°F.

bridge unit—a signal that announces an oncoming train from a road overpass or signal bridge

bulkhead flatcar—a flatcar fitted with walls on the ends, to prevent shifting of loads

bunk car or camp car—a car used to house railroad personnel during major repair or construction projects

cab—enclosure in a locomotive that shelters the engineer; also, an electrical control panel in a cab control system

cab control—model railroad control system in which trains are operated from a fixed panel

cab-forward—a steam locomotive design in which the cab is at the front

caboose—last car on a freight train; used as living quarters for the crew; usually with an elevated cupola or bay window from which workers could monitor the cars ahead

cafe car—a food car with limited, quick service

carrier control—see *command control*

catenary—a compound overhead wire system used by some streetcars and most heavy electric-powered railways

center-cab—a locomotive in which the cab is in the center

coach—a passenger car with windows and seats

code—height of scale train rail, to model the different heights of rail used on prototype railroads; the digit that gives a particular code its name (e.g., Code 83) represents x/1000 of an inch (.083-inch high)

combine—a car divided into two or more parts to fulfill different functions, such as coach and baggage

command control system—a control system in which coded electronic messages are transmitted through the rails to locomotives equipped with decoders, allowing several trains to be independently controlled without complex track wiring

constant intensity headlights—locomotive headlights that don't change brightness when the train starts or stops

container car—a specialized flatcar carrying a standardized container or large steel box; the container can also be carried by ship or truck

control panel—a panel containing all the controls for a railroad or a section of a railroad

conversion kit—a kit that enables a modeler to convert one model into another

cook's car or kitchen car—the car where food is prepared for a maintenance-of-way crew during major projects

coping saw—a ribbon-shaped saw used for cutting intricate patterns; also called a scroll saw

coupler—a device that hooks two cars together

covered hopper—a hopper with a roof; used to carry sugar, flour, and other bulk items that need protection from the weather

cowcatcher—see *pilot*

craftsman kit—an advanced kit that may require extensive cutting and fitting of parts

crossing—the place where two tracks cross each other

crossover—a pair of turnouts allowing a train to transfer from one parallel track to another

cyanoacrylate—a glue that sets in seconds and can be used on virtually all materials (also called *ACC* or "super glue")

decal—lettering or images applied to a train or structure by being dipped in water, removing the backing and placed on the surface of the train or structure

detail part—small parts, such as rails, steps, lamps, and valve gear, that are attached to a model to make it more true-to-life

detection unit—a device that senses the presence of a train or locomotive at a certain point or section of track

diesel-electric—a locomotive that burns diesel fuel to generate electricity to drive a train; usually called a diesel

dining car—a passenger car with a kitchen at one end and tables at the other, served by waiters

direct current (DC)—current that flows continuously in one direction

directional headlights—two headlights, one mounted on each end of a locomotive, that turn on or off depending on the direction of the train's motion (e.g., the one on End A goes on when the train moves in direction A, while the one on End B goes off); also called *reversing headlights*

dome car—a passenger car with a raised, glassed-in roof section for viewing the scenery

DPDT CO (double pole, double throw, center-off)—switch that controls two separate sets of electrical contacts; the switch has two positions besides "off," with "off" in the center; often used for reversing flow of current or allowing two-train operation

dribbler—a nineteenth-century, steam-driven British toy train of solid brass, so-called because it left a trail of water on the floor; also known as a piddler

driving wheels—the wheels that drive a steam locomotive; connected by rods, the wheels transform steam power into pulling power

dry transfer—letters or images applied by being rubbed directly from a waxy sheet onto a surface

dwarf unit—a small ground-based signal usually used either to control movement or to indicate track conditions in trainyards, where clearance will not permit full-height signals

electric outline—a toy or model train modeled after an electric-powered prototype

electric railway—see *traction*

eutectic solder—a solder alloy with the lowest possible melting point

fast time—condensed time for a model railroad line

feeder wire—wire connecting a power supply to track rails

firebox—the part of a steam locomotive where fuel is burned

flange—projecting edge on the inside rim of a car or locomotive wheel that keeps it on the rail

flat finish—a clear, nonglossy coat of paint to eliminate gloss on decals and protect a model's surface

flatcar—a car with no sides used for carrying lumber, machinery, pipes, and other materials

flexible track—track that can be bent into curves

flux—material that chemically cleans the surfaces to be joined through soldering or brazing

flywheel drive—a locomotive containing a relatively heavy wheel to help smooth the flow of power and promote realistic starting and stopping

frog—the part of a turnout where rails cross, facilitating passage of the train wheels

gauge—the width of track measured as the distance between track rails; may be used to indicate trains that are toys rather than accurate scale models (e.g., O-gauge trains as opposed to O-scale trains)

gondola—open-top car used to haul scrap metal, pipe, and other bulk commodities

grabiron—a short hand-rail along the side of a car or locomotive

grade crossing sign—a sign that warns motor vehicles or pedestrians of railroad track

grading standards—listings developed by the Train Collectors of America to indicate the condition of a collectible train

ground throw—manual switch machine used by the railroads; model version is mounted on top of a layout near the turnout and manually operated

Homasote®—brand name of a home insulation board made of recycled newspapers; often used in building benchwork

hopper—a car that unloads through doors on the bottom; used for granular or loose items

horn-hook coupler—common HO coupler lacking working knuckles, used by many manufacturers; also called X2f coupler

Hydrocal®—a brand name molding plaster used for constructing mountains and other scenery

interurban—an electrified railroad line connecting cities or towns, usually only for passengers

kitbashing—altering a kit or combining parts from two or more kits to create a new model

knuckle—the part of a coupler that hooks and unhooks

LED (light-emitting diode)—an electronic device used in signals and flashing lights; the same device used in digital watches and calculators

left-hand turnout—a turnout that allows a train to go straight ahead or to the left

live steam—scales of trains that are steam-powered and big enough for people to ride; the most popular are ¾ inch, 1 inch, and 1½ inch scales

loco—a locomotive

magnetic coupler—a type of coupler that can be automatically uncoupled by use of magnets

magnetic uncoupler—a device located between the track trails that unhooks cars through the use of magnetic force

mainline—a long-distance, heavily used route

miter box—a device for cutting wood or plastic at a precise angle

model train—see *scale train*

modeler's license—the right of a modeler to adapt a prototype railroad, taking into account space, aesthetics, skills, and time

modeler's pins—pins for holding parts in place during gluing

module—a segment of a layout that conforms to a set of established standards, so that several such segments can be assembled into a complete layout

momentary contact—a switch with a spring that restores the switch to normal position (usually "off") as soon as you let go; useful for controlling twin-coil switch machines

momentum control—a throttle feature that simulates the gradual changes in speed of a prototype train

MOW ("maintenance of way")—general term for cars used by a crew repairing rail or laying new tracks; often adapted from old or obsolete rolling stock

multigang—see *wafer*

multiple-unit train—a train with several locomotives for increased pulling power and better handling

narrow gauge—prototype track that is narrower than is standard in the United States (i.e., 4 feet 8½ inches); a scale representation of such a prototype

NMRA Standards Gauge—device used to check wheels, track, coupler height, and clearances on a layout; available for O, On3, OO, S, HO, HOn3, and N scales

non-revenue equipment—rolling stock that does not produce revenue for the railroad; such as cabooses or maintenance of way cars

observation car—passenger car placed at the end of a train with an open or enclosed compartment at one end, usually used for first-class passengers

office or business car—non-revenue car used by company officials while on inspection tour of a line

pantograph—a hinged device that picks up current from an overhead wire and transmits it to an electric loco or trolley

piggyback flatcar—a special flatcar carrying highway trailers

pilot—a plowlike structure placed at the front of a locomotive to clear the rails of obstructions; sometimes called a *cowcatcher*, especially on old-time steam locos

pilot wheels—the small forward wheels that guide a steam locomotive

pin vise—vise for holding small drills or parts

points—the moving rail sections of a turnout

pole—in electrical switches, a set of independent contacts

polycarbonate—a clear plastic used for making windows; also called Lexan®

power pack—a device that converts household current (110 volts AC) into the types of current a model railroad uses (12 volts DC for most trains, 16 volts AC for accessories)

prototype—a real train

prototypical—of the prototype; realistic; accurately reproducing the proportions, detail, or activity of the prototype

pulse power—electrical current fed in pulses; useful in running trains at very low speeds

rail "detector" car—in prototype railroads, automatically records the condition of the track surface alignment or locates flaws in the rail

rail nippers—pliers for cutting rail

razor saw—very fine-toothed miniature saw

ready-made track—see *sectional track*

ready-to-run—a locomotive or car that is sold completely assembled and ready for operation

reed switch—switch that is placed out of sight (e.g., inside a locomotive or car body) to control lights or other accessories; turned on and off with an external magnet; useful in preserving realism

refrigerator car ("reefer")—insulated car capable of keeping perishables cold; ice was used from the 1880s to the early 1960s; mechanical refrigeration became the norm after that

relay—an electrical switch thrown by remote control

remote control turnout—turnouts that are activated from a location away from the turnout

rerailer—a plastic wedge that moves cars onto rails; a piece of sectional track including such a wedge

retarder—a compound that slows the drying time of plaster, giving the modeler more time to work

reverse loop—a balloon-shaped track that forces a train to turn around and return to the main track, heading in the opposite direction

reversing headlights—see *directional headlights*

rheostat—a component in a power pack or throttle that adjusts current; also called a *variable resistor*

right-hand turnout—a track switch that allows a train to go straight ahead or to the right

roadbed—raised support on which tracks are laid

roadname—the name of a railroad line; usually painted on the sides of rolling stock

rolling stock—all vehicles on a railroad except for locomotives; the cars a locomotive pulls

roundhouse—storage and maintenance facility for steam engines, usually designed around a turntable

sandwich effect—in building benchwork, the effect made by laminating a sheet of Homasote® between two layers of pine or plywood

scale—the proportion of a model train to the original

scale train—a miniature train that accurately reproduces the proportions and details of a prototype train; also called a model train

scratchbuilding—building models from raw materials, such as detail parts and sheets of wood, plastic, or metal

scriber—in scratchbuilding, a device for scoring styrene sheets in preparation for breaking

section—an electronically isolated length of railroad track, permitting one train to be operated independently of another

sectional track—track sold in pieces that can be connected together; available in straight and curved sections; also called *ready-made track*; see also *flexible track*

selective compression—the technique of condensing the details of a prototype railroad to accommodate the space and time limitations of a model railroad

shortline—a short-distance route

siding—track area used to meet or pass trains

signal—equipment used to control the movement of trains by advising the driver of whether the line ahead is occupied, whether the train will be switched to another route, or other concerns

signal bridge—a structure that supports several signals above two or more tracks; used in congested areas

sleeping car—a car with beds

smoke generator—an electrically powered device mounted in the smokestack of a model locomotive to generate smoke when heated

smokebox—in a steam engine, the forward part of a boiler directly beneath the smokestack

smokestack—in a steam engine, an iron or steel chimney through which smoke and steam are discharged

smoothside—passenger cars with smooth rather than fluted sides built by Pullman Standard; made of normal rather than stainless steel; used in the 1940s and 1950s

soldering—joining metal parts by heating a piece of filler metal (solder) until it melts and forms a bond between two surfaces

SPST (single pole, single throw)—the simplest type of switch; turns power on or off

spur—track leading from a mainline to a factory or yard

starter set—a basic train set meant to get a railroader started in a particular scale; usually includes locomotive, four to six cars, a snap-together oval of track, and a power pack with connections

steam outline—a toy or model train patterned after a steam-powered prototype

stock car—car used to carry livestock; has open, horizontal slats to allow circulation of air

stopping block—short block that forces a locomotive to stop when power is disconnected there

styrene—popular, easily cut plastic used in making trains; sold in sheets, rods, and other shapes for scratchbuilding

switch—electrical device for turning current on or off; also a track switch or *turnout*

switch machine—remote control electrical device, usually twin-coil, that moves the points of a turnout from one route to another; runs on AC or DC power

switch motor—electrical device for remote control operation of turnouts that provides slower, more realistic motion than a switch machine, runs on DC power

switcher—a locomotive designed primarily for switching cars from one track to another in the yard

switchman—in prototype railroads, the person who operates turnouts

switchstand signal—a signal indicating a turnout's position

tank car—a cylindrical, watertight car for transporting liquids such as milk, corn syrup, chemicals, and oil

tap—a device for creating threads to receive screws

template—a standard planning piece that serves as a stencil for where the parts of a layout will fall; may be paper, metal, or plastic

tender—the car permanently coupled behind a steam locomotive in which fuel and water are stored

terminal track—a piece of sectional track with attachments for wire

three-way turnout—a track switch that allows a train to go straight, right, or left

throttle—an electrical device for controlling a train's speed and direction

throw—in electrical switches, the number of active positions, i.e., Single Throw, Double Throw

ties—the beams of wood, steel, or concrete to which the rails are secured

tinplate—name originally applied to toy trains stamped from tin; also a general term for toy trains as opposed to scale trains

toy train—a stylized train that does not strictly reproduce the proportions and details of a prototype; also called *tinplate*

track cleaner—a solution or device to keep track clean and maintain electrical conductivity

track plan—a paper blueprint of a layout, reflecting the design as well as the measurements for track, buildings, and scenery

track radius—a measure of the curve in curved sections of track; if curved sections were assembled to form a circle, the distance from the center of the circle to the centerline of the track would be the track radius

track switch—a turnout

traction—a railway system in which electricity is carried to a locomotive by means of a third rail or an overhead wire; includes trolleys, trams, subways, and some mainline and interurban railroads; also called *electric*

tractive power—a locomotive's ability to pull a train

train set—a collection of model railroad components (cars, power supply, track, etc.) sold as a package; see also *starter set*

transition track—short sections of track that permit the connection of different codes (or heights) of track; see *code*

truck—one of the wheeled carriages on which a piece of rolling stock rests; helps distribute the weight of the car evenly

tunnel portal—the entrance to a tunnel

turning track—a track, such as a *wye* or *reverse loop*, that enables a train to turn around and start traveling in the direction from which it came

turnout—the place where two tracks diverge; allowing a train to go onto a different route; also called a *track switch*, though turnout is preferred by most modelers to avoid confusion with electrical switches

turntable—a rotary platform that allows a locomotive to turn around completely or directs it to a specific roadhouse stall or track

uncoupler—a device that disengages the coupler on model train cars; see also *magnetic uncoupler*

valve gear—in a steam engine, the mechanism that directs steam into and out of cylinders in order to propel the locomotive

variable resistor—see *rheostat*

wafer—type of electrical switch that controls a large number of sets of electrical contacts; many possible positions (8PDT, 6P19T, etc.); also called *multigang*

walk-around control—a control system in which the throttle or cab is placed in a portable box with a cable or infrared connection to the layout; electrical switches for blocks and turnouts can be placed on the edges of the layout near the operations they manage or placed on a fixed panel

waybill—a document describing the destination, route, and type of car required for a shipment of goods

weathering—the process of treating a model with paint, washes, and other techniques to simulate the effects of weather

well car—a container car with two containers stacked atop each other; a depressed central section or well gives the car extra clearance when going through tunnels or under bridges

wet-process decal—lettering or images applied to a train or structure by being dipped in water and held in place while the backing is removed

wheelset—a pair of wheels secured to an axle

white glue—polyvinyl glue best used with wood or paper

wye—an arrangement of track with three turnouts used to reverse cars and locos

wye switch—a Y-shaped turnout that allows a train to go either right or left but not straight ahead

yard—multiple-track location where trains are assembled, serviced, or stored

yellow glue—aliphatic resin glue best used with wood or paper

Sources

Listed below are the companies—manufacturers, publishers, and retailers—named in the text, with the addresses where you or your dealer can reach them. When writing directly to companies for product or price information, include a self-addressed stamped envelope.

We have included some phone numbers in this list; however, the best way to order from almost any of these companies is through your local dealer. Ordering through your dealer helps ensure that the dealer will always be there as a source of supplies, advice, and service. It will also make life easier for the many small companies that cannot afford to maintain a large direct-mail business with the public.

Convention and trade show information changes from year to year. Check model railroading and collectors' magazines for information on these events.

Note that the products for many companies are principally (or entirely) distributed by Walthers; these should be reached "c/o Walthers" at the address given for Walthers.

A & D Toy-Train Village and Railway Museum
49 Plymouth Street
North Middleboro, MA 02346

A-Line/Proto Power West
3432 Lucero Avenue
LaVerne, CA 91750
(714) 596-9045 or (714) 593-2003

Abracadata Ltd.
P.O. Box 2440
Eugene, OR 97402

Access Models
P.O. Box 1514
Baltimore, MD 21203
(301) 732-6119

Ace Balsawood Co.
P.O. Box 2170
Upland, CA 91785
(800) 523-8322

Acme Model Engineering Co.
654 Bergen Boulevard
Ridgefield, NJ 07657
(201) 943-7650

AIM Products
P.O. Box 290092
5011 Barbagello Drive
St. Louis, MO 49508
(314) 892-1949

A.J. Fricko
See Andrew J. Fricko Co.

Allegheny Model Products
906 Barley Way
State College, PA 16801

Alloy Forms
851 Washington Street
Peekskill, NY 10566
(914) 737-6633

Alpha Models
P.O. Box 118
Rocky Point, NY 11778

Ambroid Co., Inc.
P.O. Box 164
Lynnfield, MA 01940
(617) 692-9300

America's Hobby Center, Inc.
146 W. 22nd Street
New York, NY 10011

American Bank Note Railroad Cards
Brattleboro, VT 05345-0420

American Eagles, Inc.
2220 N.W. Market Street
Seattle, WA 98107

American Flyer Collectors Club
Box 13269
Pittsburgh, PA 15243

American Models
10088 Colonial Industrial Drive
South Lyon, MI 48178
(313) 437-6800

American Railroad Photography
P.O. Box 1339
Silver Lake, OH 44224

American Southwest Railroad Association
P.O. Box 4028
Lakewood, CA 90711-4028

AMI, Inc.
P.O. Box 11861
Clayton, MO 63105
(314) 872-8146

AMS Inc.
7549 S. Country Manor Road
Salt Lake City, UT 84121

AMSI Scale Model Supplies
P.O. Box 750638
Petaluma, CA 94975-0638
(800) 821-4852

Andrew J. Fricko Co.
P.O. Box 43276
Cincinnati, OH 45243

Answer Railway Visuals Division
P.O. Box 5509
Spring Hill, FL 34606

Anthony J. Dudynski Supply Company
2036 Story Avenue
Bronx, NY 10473

Arlington Consulting & Engineering (ACE)
P.O. Box 461
Arlington Heights, IL 60006-0461

Arnold
c/o Walthers
(414) 527-0770

Athearn, Inc.
19010 Laurel Park Road
Compton, CA 90222
(213) 774-9347

Atlas Tool Co., Inc.
378 Florence Avenue
Hillside, NJ 07205
(201) 687-0880

Audio-Visual Designs
P.O. Box 24
Earlton, NY 12058-0024

Bachmann Industries, Inc.
1400 East Erie Avenue
Philadelphia, PA 19124
(215) 533-1600

Badger Air Brush Co.
9128 West Belmont Avenue
Franklin Park, IL 60131
(312) 873-3199

Baltimore & Ohio Railroad Historical Society
Box 13578
Baltimore, MD 21203-3578

Benchmark Publications
P.O. Box 26
Los Altos, CA 94023

Berkshire Car Shop
P.O. Box 151
Audubon, PA 19407

Berkshire Productions
P.O. Box 575
Brunswick, OH 44212
(216) 225-0303

Binks Manufacturing Company
9201 West Belmont Avenue
Franklin Park, IL 60131
(312) 671-3000

BK Enterprises
12874 County Road 314
Buena Vista, CO 81211

BL Hobby Products
P.O. Box 307
623 6th Street
Maxwell, IA 50161
(515) 387-1332

Bond Adhesives Co.
301 Frelinghuysen Avenue
Newark, NJ 07114

Bowser Manufacturing Company
21 Howard Street
Montoursville, PA 17754-0322
(800) 327-5126

Boxes Plus
25452 S. Cass
P.O. Box 176
Canby, OR 97013

Brass Locomotive Co.
4901 Morena Boulevard, Suite 511
San Diego, CA 92117
(414) 527-0770

Brawa
c/o Walthers

Russ Briggs Designs
17 Linda Lane
Plymouth, MA 02360

W.R. Brown Co.
2701 N. Normandie Avenue
Chicago, IL 60635

Builders in Scale
c/o Walthers

Busch
c/o F&M Industries

C & S Scale Industries Ltd.
1135 Lonsdale Avenue
North Vancouver, BC V7M 2H4
Canada
(604) 980-8818

C.C. Crow Fine Hydrocal Castings
P.O. Box 1427
Mukilteo, WA 98275

Cadwallader Productions
Box 211
Turtle Creek, PA 15145

California Model Company
1426 South Ritchey, Unit A
Santa Ana, CA 92705
(714) 972-9361

California State Railroad Museum
111 I Street
Old Sacramento, CA 95814

Campbell Scale Models
P.O. Box 121
Tustin, CA 92680
(714) 546-3380

Cannon & Co.
3947 Freedom Boulevard
Aptos, CA 95003
(408) 684-0447

Cannonball Car Shops
188 East Second
Roanoke, IN 46783
(219) 672-3753

Cape Line Models
P.O. Box 493
Wilbraham, MA 01095
(413) 596-9595

Carl Loucks
199 Wayland Street
North Haven, CT 06473

Carson Home Video
Box 42582
Philadelphia, PA 19101

Carstens Publications, Inc.
P.O. Box 700/Dept. 4671
Newton, NJ 07860-0700
(201) 383-3355

Central Electric Railfans' Association
P.O. Box 503
Chicago, IL 60690

Central Time Inspection Co.
P.O. Box 1067
Homewood, IL 60430

Chama Graphics Lines
c/o Walthers
(414) 527-0770

Champion Decal Company
P.O. Box 1178
Minot, ND 58702
(701) 852-4938

Charles Ro Supply Company
347 Pleasant Street
Malden, MA 02148

Charles Siegel's Coins and Trains
3133 Zuck Road
Erie, PA 16506

Charly's Slides
4255 Elk Park Road
Lake City, PA 16423

Chemco Resin Crafts/ETI
P.O. Box 365
Fields Landing, CA 95537

Chesapeake & Ohio Historical Society
P.O. Box 79
Clifton Forge, VA 24422

Chilton Book Co.
201 King of Prussia Road
Radnor, PA 19089
(215) 964-4000

Choo Choo Works
9734 Southwest Highway
Oak Lawn, IL 60453

Chooch Enterprises Inc./Div. of Michael's Ltd.
P.O. Box 217
Redmond, WA 98052
(206) 881-7725

Cir-Kit Concepts, Inc.
407 14th Street, NW
Rochester, MN 55901

Circuitron
P.O. Box 322
Riverside, IL 60546
(312) 749-9010

City Classics
2270 Noblestown Road
Pittsburgh, PA 15205
(412) 922-8303

Classic Toy Trains
see Kalmbach Publishing Co.

Clover House
P.O. Box 62
Sebastopol, CA 95472

CM Shops
P.O. Box 49
Newfoundland, NJ 07435

CN Lines SIG
c/o Mike Christian
2488 Paige Janette Drive
Harvey, LA 70058

Color-Rite
c/o Walthers
(414) 527-0770

Colorado Museum
17135 44th Avenue
Golden, CO 80402

CompuServe®
5000 Arlington Center Boulevard
Columbus, OH 43260

Con-Cor International
1880 S. Research Loop Drive
Tucson, AZ 85710
(602) 721-8939

ControlAbility, Inc.
P.O. Box 399
Glen Ellyn, IL 60138

Cranbrook Railway Museum
Box 400
Cranbrook, BC V1C 4H9
Canada

Creative Screen Process
555 East Airline Way
Gardena, CA 90248

CTT
c/o Walthers

Custom Railway Supplies
c/o Walthers
(414) 527-0770

Dallee Electronics
P.O. Box 1291
Reading, PA 19603

Darr's Scale Models
P.O. Box 1648
Grass Valley, CA 95945

Data Train
1415 Golden Gate
Carrollton, TX 75007

Delton Locomotive Works
120 Maple
Delton, MI 49046

Derrig, Phil, Design
P.O. Box 814
Park Ridge, IL 60068

Design Preservation Models
P.O. Box 280
Crestone, CO 81131
(719) 256-4255

Detail Associates
P.O. Box 5357
San Luis Obispo, CA 93403
(805) 544-9593

Details West
P.O. Box 5132
Hacienda Heights, CA 91745

Diamond Scale Construction
P.O. Box 691
Oakridge, OR 97463

Dimi-Trains
c/o Walthers
(414) 527-0770

DM Custom Decals
2127 S. 11th Street
Manitowoc, WI 54220
(414) 684-8688

Doubleday & Co.
666 Fifth Avenue
New York, NY 10019

Dougs Train World
6585 University Avenue
Des Moines, IA 50311

Dover Publications
31 East Second Street
Mineola, NY 11501
(516) 294-7000

Dremel/Div. of Emerson Electronic
4915 21st Street
Racine, WI 53406-9989
(414) 554-1390

East Tennessee Rail Fan Association
P.O. Box 1341
Kingsport, TN 37662

Eastern Car Works
P.O. Box L624
Langhorne, PA 19047
(215) 757-4448 or (215) 757-9348

Eastwood Publishing Co., Inc.
2901 Blake Street
Denver, CO 80205

EVDA Slides
1724 Suhulte Hill Street
P.O. Box 1183
Maryland Heights, MO 63043

Evergreen Scale Models, Inc.
12808 N.E. 125th Way
Kirkland, WA 98034
(206) 823-0458

F & M Enterprises
2318 E. Loma Vista Drive
Tempe, AZ 85282

Fallen Flaggs RxR Wearables
824 Elysian Avenue
Toledo, OH 43607

Faller
c/o Walthers
(414) 527-0770

Felix V. Bass & Co., Inc.
Westgrove Industrial Park
P.O. Box 266
Westville, NJ 08093

Finestkind MDL's/Jaks Enterprises
P.O. Box 26654
3500 Commerce Street
Dallas, TX 75226
(214) 824-2227

Floquil-Polly S Color Corp.
Rt. 30 North
Amsterdam, NY 12010-9204
(518) 843-3610

Form-a-Mountain™ Products
P.O. Box 29070
Providence, RI 02909
(401) 232-1523

Foster-Trent, Inc.
Dept. 277LM
2345 Boston Post Road
Larchmont, NY 10538

Freight Cars Journal
P.O. Box 1458
Monrovia, CA 91016

Frisco Railroad Museum
Box 276
Ash Grove, MO 65604

Front Range Products
1331 Sherman Drive
Longmont, CO 80501

Funaro & Camerlengo
RD #3, Box 2800
Honesdale, PA 18431
(717) 224-4989

G-R-S Model Brass
P.O. Box 16063
Shawnee, KS 66203
(913) 422-5405

Garden Railways
see Sidestreet Bannerworks

GarGraves Trackage Corp.
RD 1, Box 255A
North Rose, NY 14516
(315) 483-6577

Gaus Enterprises
5 Pennwood Place
Greenville, PA 16125

GHB International
P.O. Drawer E
Bowie, MD 20715

Gil Reid
P.O. Box 251
Brookfield, WI 53005

Gloor Craft Models/Div. S.R. Gloor Inc.
715 North Locust Street
P.O. Box 230
Oak Harbor, OH 43449
(419) 898-6372

Golden Bell Press
3403 Champa Street
Denver, CO 80205

Gorin, Howard
see The Machinery Works

Grand Central Ltd.
P.O. Box 29129
Seward Avenue
Lincoln, NE 68529

Grandt Line Products, Inc.
1040B Shary Court
Concord, CA 94518
(415) 671-0143

Grayland Station
P.O. Box 31344
Chicago, IL 60631

Great Northern Railway Historical Society
c/o Connie Hoffman
1781 Griffith
Berkeley, MI 48072

Green Frog Productions, Ltd.
950 Bream Court
Marietta, GA 30068
(800) 227-1336

Green Lantern Press Ltd.
P.O. Box 7032
Fairfax Station, VA 22039

Greenberg Publishing Co., Inc.
7566 Main Street
Sykesville, MD 21784
(301) 795-7447

Greg Scholl Video Productions
P.O. Box 123T
Batavia, OH 45103
(515) 732-0660

H & N Electronics
10937 Rome Beauty Drive
California City, CA 93505
(619) 373-8033

hannes fischer
c/o Walthers
(414) 527-0770

Heljan
c/o Walthers
(414) 527-0770

HO-Custom Trains
4 Brighton Wood Road
Glenmont, NY 12077

Hobbies at Frederick and Nelson
Fifth and Pine
Seattle, WA 98111

Hobby Craft Specialties
505 Woodlawn, Suite 136
North Belmont, NC 28012
(704) 825-2854

Hobsco
c/o Walthers
(414) 527-0770

Holgate & Reynolds
1000 Central Avenue
Wilmette, IL 60091
(312) 251-2455

Hopewell Productions, Inc.
1714 Boardman Road, Suite 15
Poland, OH 44514

House of Balsa, Inc.
20134 States Road
Cerritos, CA 90701

HR Products
Dept. D
2963 Avenue V
Brooklyn, NY 11229

Huff Video Productions
23 East Hebble Avenue
Fairhorn, OH 45324

Hundman Publishing
5115 Monticello Drive
Edmonds, WA 98020

I.S.L.E. Laboratories
P.O. Box 636
Sylvania, OH 43560
(517) 486-4055

Illinois Central Historical Society
865 Gen. George Patton Road
Nashville, TN 37221

Integrated Signal Systems
P.O. Box 25451
Rochester, NY 14625-0451
(716) 586-2032

International Hobby Corp.
350 East Tioga Street
Philadelphia, PA 19134
(215) 426-2873

Islington Station Products
P.O. Box 843
Islington Station, MA 02090

J & M Laboratories
P.O. Box 1105
Los Altos, CA 94022
(415) 964-1830

Jaks Enterprises
3500 Commerce
Dallas, TX 75226
(214) 824-2227

James R. Hunt
814 26th Street
Pern, IL 61354

Jerry's Train Gallery
48 River Road
Chatham, NJ 07928

John Rendall Scale Models
Box 2689
Niagara Falls, NY 14302-2689
(705) 767-2241

John's Train Shop
8151 Delman
St. Louis, MO 63130

Johnson, Rick
see O Gauge Roadbed

Joseph A. Grzyboski, Jr.
P.O. Box 3475
Scranton, PA 18505

June's Small World
P.O. Box 44
Mountlake Terrace, WA 98043
(206) 778-2372

K & S Engineering
6917 West 59 Street
Chicago, IL 60638

Kadee Quality Products Co.
720 South Grape Street
Medford, OR 97501
(503) 772-9890

Kalamazoo Toy Train Works/Div. Bangor Train
   Factory
P.O. Box 98
Bangor, MI 49103
(616) 427-7927

Kalmbach Memorial Library, NMRA
4121 Cromwell Road
Chattanooga, TN 37421
(615) 894-8144

Kalmbach Publishing Co.
21027 Crossroads Circle
P.O. Box 1612
Waukesha, WI 53187
(414) 796-8776

Kato USA, Inc.
781 Dillon Drive
Wood Dale, IL 60191

Kauffman Creative Service
P.O. Box 4
Campbelltown, PA 17010

Keller Engineering
200 San Mateo Avenue
Los Gatos, CA 95030
(408) 395-3424

Kenson Video
47 Arlene Avenue
Wilmington, MA 01887

Kibri
c/o Walthers
(414) 527-0770

Kistler, Stan
P.O. Box 977
Grass Valley, CA 95945

La Belle Woodworking Co.
205 Leonard Street
Watertown, WI 53094
(414) 261-3600

LaBelle Industries
1025 Industrial Drive
P.O Box 328
Bensenville, IL 60106

Leanin' Tree
Box 9500
Boulder, CO 80301

Lemaco
c/o Walthers
(414) 527-0770

Leventon's Hobby Supplies
11411 S.W. Johnson Avenue
Chehalis, WA 98532

LGB
P.O. Box 1247
Milwaukee, WI 53201

LGB Model Railroaders Club
3329 White Castle Way
Decatur, GA 30034

Life-Like Products Inc.
1600 Union Avenue
Baltimore, MD 21211-1998
(800) 638-1471

Limited Editions
P.O. Box 278
Spanaway, WA 98387

Lionel Collectors' Club of America
P.O. Box 479
LaSalle, IL 61301

Lionel Operating Train Society (LOTS)
7823 Hamilton Avenue
Cincinnati, OH 45231

Lionel Railroad Club
15645 Brookhill Drive
Brookfield, WI 53005

Lionel Trains Inc.
26750 Twenty-Three Mile Road
Mt. Clemens, MI 48045
(313) 949-4100

Little Hobby's
Turntable Junction
22 Church Street
Flemington, NJ 08822
(201) 782-3474

Live Steam
Dept. CC19/P.O. Box 968
Traverse City, MI 49685

Long Island Sunrise Trail Chapter NRHS
P.O. Box 507/Dept. T
Babylon, NY 11702

Lykos Productions
58 Broad Street
Gloucester, OH 45732

Lytler & Lytler
2634 Bryant Avenue South
Minneapolis, MN 55408
(612) 374-2693

M. F. Kotowski
c/o Walthers
(414) 527-0770

Mac Shops
P.O. Box 1232
Vero Beach, FL 32961-1232

Machinery Works, The
c/o Howard Gorin
101 Monmouth Street
Brookline, MA 02146

Mainline Modules
P.O. Box 21861
Chattanooga, TN 37421-1861
(615) 339-3176

Mann-Made Products
P.O. Box 27009
Cincinnati, OH 45227-0009
(513) 561-5906

Mantua Industries, Inc.
Grandview Avenue
P.O. Box 10
Woodbury Heights, NJ 08097-0010
(609) 853-0300

Märklin, Inc.
16988 West Victor Road
P.O. Box 319
New Berlin, WI 53151
(414) 784-8854

Mascot Precision Tool
P.O. Box 243
6750 Washington Avenue
Carlstadt, NJ 07072

Master Creations
P.O. Box 1378
China Valley, AZ 86323
(602) 636-5313

Maxon Systems
520 Lively Boulevard
Elk Grove Village, IL 60007

McMillan Publications, Inc.
2921 Two Paths Drive
Woodridge, IL 60517-4512

MDK, Inc.
P.O. Box 2831
Chapel Hill, NC 27515
(919) 929-4260 or (919) 929-8420

Merit
2745 W. Division Street
Chicago, IL 60622

Micro-Mark Precision Tools
340 Snyder Avenue
Berkeley Heights, NJ 07922

Micro-Metal
c/o Con-Cor
(414) 527-0770

Microflame Inc.
14857 DeVeau Place
Minnetonka, MN 55345
(612) 935-3777

Microscale Industries
1555 Palacentia Avenue
Newport Beach, CA 92663

Mikes Train House
9693 A Gerwig Lane
Columbia, MD 21046

Mil-Scale Products
P.O. Box 13612
Wauwatosa, WI 53213
(414) 774-1855

Miniplex
c/o Walthers

Missouri Pacific Historical Society
c/o Camille Chappuis
223 E. Main Street
Jackson, MO 63755

MLR Manufacturing Co.
P.O. Box 1051
Carlsbad, CA 92008

Model Builders Supply
107 Duncaster Avenue
Thornhill, Ontario L3T 1L6
Canada
(416) 881-6288

Model Die Casting
3811 West Rosecrans Avenue
Hawthorne, CA 90250
(213) 678-3131

Model Power
180 Smith Street
Farmingdale, NY 11735
(516) 694-7022

Model Rail Link
24804 Briarcliff Road NE
Suite 335
Atlanta, GA 30329

Model Railroader
see Kalmbach Publishing

Model Rectifier Corp. (MRC)
200 Carter Drive
Edison, NJ 08817
(201) 248-0400

Modelmaker, The
2013 Avenue D
Billings, MT 59102

Modeltronics
1012 Azalea Drive
Sunnyvale, CA 94086
(408) 720-1190

Monongahela Innoventions
P.O. Box 204
Myerstown, PA 17067
(717) 866-4875

Mountains in Minutes
P.O. Box 636
Sylvania, OH 43560

MRC
see Model Rectifier Corp.

MTS Imports Inc.
P.O. Box 50
Middletown, NY 10940

Mystic Valley Railway Society
P.O. Box 486
Hyde Park, MA 02136

MZZ
c/o Walthers
(414) 527-0770

N-Scale
see Hundman

N-Way Products
1650 Mayfield Lane
Madison, WI 53704
(608) 244-2216

Narrow Gauge and Short Line Gazette
c/o Benchmark Publications

National Association of S Gaugers
280 Gordon Road
Matewan, NJ 07747

National Collectors Club
Box 672
Ramsey, NJ 07446

National Model Railroad Association (NMRA)
4121 Cromwell Road
Chattanooga, TN 37421
(615) 892-2846

National Railway Historical Society
1A Rich Court
Ho-Ho-Kus, NJ 07423

New England Hobby Supply
71 Hillard Street
Manchester, CT 06040

New Liberty Enterprises
P.O. Box 1699
Tucumcari, NM 88401

New York Central System Historical Society, Inc.
Dept. D, Box 58994
Philadelphia, PA 19102-8994

New York Transit Museum
Boerum Place and Schermerhorn Streets
Brooklyn, NY 11217

Nickel Plate Road Historical and Technical
   Society
P.O. Box 444222
Cincinnati, OH 45244

NJ International
77 West Nicholai Street
Hicksville, NY 11801
(516) 433-8720

Noch
c/o Walthers
(414) 527-0770

North Carolina Transportation Museum
411 South Salisbury Avenue
Spencer, NC 28159

Northeast Modeler
c/o Central Hobby Supply
Suite 10, Burnet Plaza
3056 Burnet Avenue
Syracuse, NY 13206

Northeastern Scale Models Inc.
P.O. Box 727
Methuen, MA 01844
(508) 688-6019

NorthWest Short Line
P.O. Box 423
Seattle, WA 98111
(206) 932-1087

Nostalgia Station Ltd.
20134 Valley Mill Road
Freeland, MD 21053
(301) 343-0464

NTRAK
2424 Alturas Road
Atascadero, CA 93422

O Gauge Roadbed
19333 Sturgess Drive
Torrance, CA 90503
(213) 371-3887

Old Depot Museum
651 Highway 12
Dassel, MN 55325

Oregon Rail Supply
7212 N. Olympia
Portland, OR 97203
(503) 285-6750

Orr, Richard
6506 Western Avenue
Omaha, NE 68132

Overland Models, Inc.
5908 Kilgore Avenue
Muncie, IN 47304-4780
(317) 289-4257

P Company, The
16703 Groverdale
Covina, CA 91722

Paasche Airbrush Company
7440 West Lawrence Avenue
Harwood Heights, IL 60656
(708) 867-9191

Pacific Fast Mail
P.O. Box 57
Edmonds, WA 98020
(206) 776-3112

Pacific Rail Shops
2260 Sherman Avenue
Grants Pass, OR 97459

Pacific Railroad Society
Box 80726
San Marino, CA 91118-8726

Pactra Coatings/Plasti-Kote Co., Inc.
1000 Lake Road
P.O. Box 708
Medina, OH 44258-0708
(800) 431-5928

Painted Post Calliope Co., The
P.O. Box 88
Painted Post, NY 14870

Parkdale Hobby Products
P.O. Box 15669
Cincinnati, OH 45215

ParkLane Model Railroad Museum
S2083 Herwig Road
Reedsburg, WI 53959

PBL
P.O. Box 749
Chama, NM 87520
(505) 756-2419

PBL Video
P.O. Box 749R
Chama, NM 87520

Peco Railway Models/Pritchard Patent Product
   Co. Ltd.
Beer Seaton Devon
EX12 3NA ENGLAND

Pecos River Brass
540 Surf, Suite 133
Lewisville, TX 75067
(214) 219-0202

Peerless Industries, Inc.
7 Bedford Street
Burlington, MA 01803
(617) 273-2168

Pentrex
P.O. Box 94911
Pasadena, CA 91109

Pioneer Valley Models
P.O. Box 4928
Holyoke, MA 01041
(413) 533-5350

Plastruct, Inc.
1020 South Wallace Place
City of Industry, CA 91748
(818) 912-7016

Pola
AM Bahndamm 59
D8734 Rothhausen
West Germany

Polk's Hobby International
346 Bergen Avenue
Jersey City, NJ 07304

Pope Imagineering
P.O. Box 30318
Chicago, IL 60630

Portola Railroad Museum
P.O. Box 8
Portola, CA 96122

Potomac Chapter of the National Railway
  Historical Society
P.O. Box 235C
Kensington, MD 20895

Power Systems, Inc.
56 Bellis Circle
Cambridge, MA 02140
(617) 661-0660

Precision Masters, Inc.
P.O. Box 28094
Lakewood, CO 80228

Precision Scale Co.
P.O. Box 1262
1120-A Gum Avenue
Woodland, CA 95695-1262
(916) 662-6543

Preiser
c/o Walthers
(414) 527-0770

Proto Power West
see A-Line

Prototype Modeler
P.O. Box 7032
Fairfax Station, VA 22039-7032

Q-Car Co.
R.D. 4, P.O. Box 4345
Bangor, PA 18013

Quality Craft Models, Inc.
177 Wheatley Avenue
Northumberland, PA 17857-1699
(717) 473-9333 or (717) 473-9434

Quality Products Co.
P.O. Box 2202
Castro Valley, CA 94546
(415) 582-6381

Radio Shack Div. of Tandy Corp.
300 One Tandy Center
Ft. Worth, TX 76102

Rail Classics
P.O. Box 98
Escondido, CA 92025

Rail Craft
1130 Eagle Road
Fenton, MO 63026

Rail Graphics
1111 Beechwood Road
Buffalo Grove, IL 60089
(708) 541-2977

Rail Photos Unlimited
P.O. Box 2306
Joliet, IL 60434-2306
(815) 478-5158

Rail Rax
644 37th Avenue, Unit A
Santa Cruz, CA 95062
(408) 476-2677

Rail-Safe
P.O. Box 249
Holt, MI 48842
(417) 694-8925 (evenings)

Railroad Avenue Enterprises
P.O. Box 114
Flanders, NJ 07836

Railroad Enthusiasts, Inc., The
c/o Pomona S. Atherton
456 Main Street
West Townsend, MA 01474

Railroad History
Box 1418
Westfield, MA 01886

Railroad Model Craftsman
see Carstens Publications

Railroad Museum of Pennsylvania
Route 741
Strasburg, PA 17579

Railroad Tie Express, Inc.
P.O. Box 20810
Indianapolis, IN 46220

Railroad Video
281 Willow Dell Lane
Leola, PA 17540
(717) 656-8733

Railway and Locomotive Historical Society
P.O. Box 1418
Westford, MA 01886

Rara Avis Trains
3494 Clayton Road
Concord, CA 94519
(415) 685-6566

Red Caboose, The
16 West 45 Street
New York, NY 10036

Rex "S" Gauge Models
90 Lucy Lane
Northfield, OH 44067
(216) 467-5763

Rideau Graphics
P.O. Box 624, Station A
Toronto, Ontario M5W 1G2
Canada

Right-Of-Way Industries
P.O. Box 13036
Akron, OH 44313
(216) 867-5361

Right Track Trading Co.
Box 186
Strasburg, PA 17579

Rivarossi
c/o Walthers
(414) 527-0770

Rix Products
7707 Old Orchard Trail
Evansville, IN 47712
(812) 422-6810

Roco
c/o Walthers
(414) 527-0770

Rolling Stock
Dept. T99
7523 Benton Street
Arvada, CO 80003

Roundhouse Records
P.O. Box 210314
Nashville, TN 37221-0314

S & C Enterprises
2817 Conway Court
Sacramento, CA 95826

S.T. & L.O. Railway Co.
1130 West Shullenbarger Drive
Flagstaff, AZ 86001

San Diego Model Railroad Museum
Balboa Park
1649 El Prado
San Diego, CA 92101

Santa Fe Railroad Pens
P.O. Box 2016
Yucca Valley, CA 92286

Santa Fe Railway Historical Society
P.O. Box 92887
Long Beach, CA 90809-2887

Satellite City
P.O. Box 836
659 Laguna Drive
Simi, CA 93062-0836
(805) 522-0062

Scale Scenics Div. of Circuitron
P.O. Box 322
Riverside, IL 60546
(312) 749-9010

Scale Shops
8815 Stinson View
Linden, CA 95236-9535

Scale Structures, Ltd./A Division of Jaks
    Enterprises
P.O. Box 26654
3500 Commerce Street
Dallas, TX 75226
(214) 824-2227

Selley Finishing Touches
c/o Bowser
Box 322
21 Howard Street
Montoursville, PA 17754
(717) 368-2516

Seuthe
c/o Walthers
(414) 527-0770

Shade Tree Press
P.O. Box 383
Colorado Springs, CO 80901-0383

ShellScale Decals
Rt. 5, Box 146D
Troutville, VA 24175

Shinohara
c/o Walthers
(414) 527-0770

Shore Line Interurban Historical Society
P.O. Box 346
Chicago, IL 60690

Shore Line Trolley Museum
17 River Street
East Haven, CT 06512

Sidestreet Bannerworks
P.O. Box 61461
1040 S. Gaylord #203
Denver, CO 80206
(303) 377-4777

Signal Signs
West 727 Garland Avenue
Spokane, WA 99205

Simplex Equipment & Supply Corp.
13535 Southeast Beech
Milwaukie, OR 97267
(800) 462-4823

Sommerfields
8515 West Hampton Avenue
Milwaukee, WI 53225

Soo Line Historical & Technical Society
c/o Mike Harrington
3410 Kasten Court
Middleton, WI 53562

Starr Enterprises, Inc.
P.O. Box 170
Deerfield, IL 60015

Sugar Pine Models/Div. of Ye Olde Huff N Puff
P.O. Box 53
Pennsylvania Furnace, PA 16865
(814) 692-8334

Sundance Marketing
P.O. Box 4957
Portland, OR 97208

Sundance Publications Ltd.
250 Broadway
Denver, CO 80203

Sunday River Productions
P.O. Box 565
Concord, MA 01742
(800) 334-0854, operator 423

Switchmaster
P.O. Box 441432
Aurora, CO 80044

TCI
22 Executive Park, Suite 270
Irvine, CA 92714

Teen Association of Model Railroading
c/o Lone Eagle Payne
1028 Whaley Road, Road, #4
New Carlisle, OH 45344

Ten Industries
12 Carroll Street, Suite 126
Westminster, MD 21157

Testor Corp.
620 Buckbee Street
Rockford, IL 61108
(815) 962-6654

Thomas A. Yorke Ent.
P.O. Box 1330
Fontana, CA 92335-0421

3/16 "S"cale Railroading
1446 Fremont Avenue
Los Altos , CA 94024

Tichy Train Group
55 Kennedy Drive
Hauppauge, NY 11788

Tiger Valley Models
1070 County Road #23
Phelps, NY 14532-9769
(315) 548-9021

Time in Motion
Building 8A
Boca Raton, FL 33487

TJ Models
18 Edenfield Road
Penfield, NY 14526

TM Books
Box 279
New Buffalo, NY 49117

Tomar Industries
9520 East Napier Avenue
Benton Harbor, MI 49022
(616) 944-5129

Toy Train Collectors Society
109 Howedale Drive
Rochester, NY 14616

Toy Train Operating Society
25 W. Walnut Street, Suite 408
Pasadena, CA 91103

Track One
901 East Kimberly Road
Davenport, IA 52807

Trackside Details
1331 Avalon Street
San Luis Obispo, CA 93405

Trackside Specialties
P.O. Box 460
13 Logan Avenue
Manheim, PA 17545
(717) 272-4613

Trackside Video
P.O. Box 234
Forest Park, GA 30051

Traction Prototype and Models
2020 9th Street, S.W.
Canton, OH 44706

Train 99
333 Wilmington Westchester Pike
Glen Mills, PA 19342

Train Collectors Association
P.O. Box 248
Strasburg, PA 17579

A Train House
2020 2nd Avenue
Seattle, WA 98121

Train Station, The
P.O. Box 4923
Montgomery, AL 36103-4923

Train Tronics Inc.
206 Old Harrods Cr. Road, #4
Louisville, KY 40223
(502) 491-1307

Train World
751 McDonald Avenue
Brooklyn, NY 11218

Trainland
293 Sunrise Highway
Lynbrook, NY 11563

Trains
see Kalmbach Publishing Co.

Trains of Texas
10606 Sagewind
Houston, TX 77089
(713) 660-7115

Travel Town
115 S. Victory Boulevard
Burbank, CA 91502

Triangle Scale Models
c/o Jaks Enterprises

Trolley Talk
59 Euclid Avenue
Wyoming, OH 45215

Tru-Scale Models, Inc.
12874 County Road 314
Buena Vista, CO 81211
(719) 395-8076

Tyco Industries
540 Glen Avenue
Moorestown, NJ 08057
(609) 234-7400

Underground Railroad Shoppe
1906 Wilmington Road
New Castle, PA 16105

Union Pacific Historical Society
Box 5653
Arvada, CO 80005-0653

V & T Shops
P.O. Box 5597
Reno, NV 89513
(702) 322-5092

V-Line Locomotives Inc.
1811 South Clinton Avenue
Berwyn, IL 60402

Vane A. Jones Co.
6710 Hampton Drive E.
Indianapolis, IN 46226

Vanishing Traction Products
P.O. Box 04016
Milwaukee, WI 53204

Video Classics
84 Willow Avenue, #41
Toronto, Ontario M4E 3K2
Canada

Video Rails™
P.O. Box 80001
San Diego, CA 92138
(800) 262-2776; (619) 581-0303 in CA

Vintage Reproductions
P.O. Box 7098
Colorado Springs, CO 80933

Virginia Train Collectors, Inc.
1733 Cloister Drive
Richmond, VA 23233

Virnex Industries
S-2083 Herwig Road
Reedsburg, WI 53959
(608) 254-6256

Vista Scenic Hobby Products
c/o Walthers

Vollmer
c/o Walthers
(414) 527-0770

W & R Enterprises
P.O. Box 3235
Alhambra, CA 91803
(213) 576-5986

Wabash Valley Lines
2nd and High Streets
P.O. Box 411
Roanoke, IN 46783

Walker Model Service
5235 Farrar Court
Downers Grove, IL 60515
(312) 960-1973

Wallace Metal Products
RD #2, Box 521
Parksburg, PA 19365
(215) 857-1533

Walthers (William K. Walthers Co.)
5601 W. Florist Avenue
P.O. Box 18676
Milwaukee, WI 53218
(414) 527-0770

WB Video Productions
6447 S. Heritage Place West
Englewood, CO 80111

Westerfield
Route 13, Box 300C
Crossville, TN 38555
(615) 484-7233

Whistle Stop Publications
2490 East Colorado Boulevard
Pasadena, CA 91107

Williams Reproductions
6569 Dobbins Road
Columbia, MD 21045
(301) 997-7766

Wiltec Films
P.O. Box 135
Westminster, MA 01473

Woodland Scenics
P.O. Box 98
Linn Creek, MO 65052
(314) 346-5555

World Quest Productions
P.O. Box 518
Cornville, AZ 86325

WP Car Corp.
P.O. Box 235
Franklin Square, NY 11010

X-Acto/Hunt Manufacturing Co.
230 S. Broad Street
Philadelphia, PA 19102

Yampa Valley Mail Production Company
1020 9th Street
Greeley, CO 80631

Ye Olde Huff N Puff
P.O. Box 53
Pennsylvania Furnace, PA 16865-0053
(814) 692-8334

Yellowstone Custom Service
327 Yellowstone Avenue
West Yellowstone, MT 59758

Znic-detailZ
P.O. Box 278
Spanaway, WA 98387

Bibliography

The principal sources for this book were the many companies that sent us brochures, newsletters, and other printed information. In addition, we consulted the following sources:

Books

Carlson, Mike, ed. *NMRA 1990 Buyer's Guide to Model Railroading.* Chattanooga, TN: National Model Railroad Association, 1989.

Carlson, Pierre. *Toy Trains: A History.* NY: Harper & Row, 1986.

Con-Cor Trainalog. Bensenville, IL: Con-Cor International, 1987.

Fitzgerald, Jim, et al. *The NTRAK Module "How-to" Book.* Atascadero, CA: 1984.

Minns, J. E. *Model Railway Engines.* New York: Putnam, 1969.

Paust, Gil. *Model Railroading: How to Plan, Build, and Maintain Your Trains and Pikes.* Garden City, NY: Doubleday & Co., 1981.

Rietig, Thomas, ed. *Märklin Magazine,* Jubilee English Edition. Göppingen, West Germany: Märklin, 1984.

Schafer, Mike, ed. *Railroads You Can Model.* Milwaukee, WI: Kalmbach Publishing Co., 1976.

Schleicher, Robert. *The Model Railroading Handbook, Volume I.* Radnor, PA: Chilton Book Co., 1975.

Westcott, Linn H. *How to Wire Your Model Railroad,* fifth ed. Milwaukee, WI: Kalmbach Publishing Co., 1959.

The World of HO Scale—1990. Milwaukee, WI: William K. Walthers, 1989.

Yenne, Bill, ed. *The History of North American Railroads.* New York: Gallery Books, 1986.

Magazines

Classic Toy Trains. Waukesha, WI: Kalmbach Publishing Co.

Garden Railways. Denver, CO: Sidestreet Bannerworks.

Model Railroader. Waukesha, WI: Kalmbach Publishing Co.

NMRA Bulletin. Chattanooga, TN: National Model Railroad Association.

PBL Sn3 Dispatch. Chama, NM: Peter-Built Locomotive Works (PBL).

Railroad Model Craftsman. Newton, NJ: Carstens Publications.

Trains. Waukesha, WI: Kalmbach Publishing Co.

Pamphlets

Basic Model Railroading. Hillside, NJ: Atlas Tool Co., 1989.

Basics for Beginners: A Guide to Model Railroading, seventh ed. Baltimore, MD: Life-Like Products, n.d.

Clover House Catalogue #6. Sebastopol, CA: Clover House, n.d.

NTRAK N Resource Booklet #5. Atascadero, CA: NTRAK Publishing, 1989.

Painting Miniatures. Amsterdam, NY: Floquil Products, 1961.

PHOTO AND ILLUSTRATION CREDITS

A.M.S.I. 103 (center) (2)

Bachmann 6–7, 16–17, 17, 32–33, 46–47, 97 (bottom), 98–99 (top), 99 (bottom), 129 (bottom), 130–131, 198–199

Bozell Public Relations for Citibank 27, 82 (top & bottom), 83, 86–87

Jack Burgess 178 (top)

Capeline Models 153 (3)

Helen Chin 206 (bottom)

City Classics 136–137, 179 (left)

Classic Toy Trains 97 (center), 99 (center), 100 (top), 184 (5), 197

Beth Collette 80–81

David Cox 124

C. C. Crow 103 (top), 126 (bottom), 179 (top)

D. M. Custom Decals 159 (bottom)

Design Preservation Models 115 (2), 116 (top), 117 (bottom)

Finestkind Model Co. for JAKS Models 134–135 (3)

Floquil 154 (left) (2)

Form-A-Mountain Co. 106

Gilbert Freitag 94–95, 114, 127 (bottom), 138–139, 146, 148, 149, 177 (left), 178 (bottom), 179 (right), 180 (3), 181 (top & center), 182 (bottom)

Funaro & Camerlengo 48 (top), 51 (center & bottom), 67 (center & bottom) (3), 71 (3)

Garden Railway Magazine: Mike & Susan Decker, 108; Barbara Horovitz 89, 105, 110; Marc Horovitz 30 (top), 91, 122 (top), 167

Kenneth J. Graber 101 (bottom)

H & N Electronics 144 (right & bottom), 145 (top)

International Hobby Corp. 117 (top left & right), 119 (left & right)

I.S.L.E. Laboratories 104 (center, right), 119 (top)

Islington Station Products 140, 141 (4)

Kadee® Micro-Trains Line® 31, 40 (top), 43 (top), 50 (bottom), 51 (top), 66, 70

Kadee Quality Products® 35

Ward Kimball 107, 208–209, 211, 212, 213, 214, 218, 219, 220–221, 222–223

LaBelle Woodworking 48–49

L.G.B. 128 (right)

Life-Like 78 (bottom), 116 (bottom), 126 (top), 157 (bottom)

Lionel, reprinted with permission of Lionel Trains, Inc. 24, 25 (top & bottom), 26 (top & bottom), 28–29, 34, 36–37, 42, 46 (bottom), 46–47 (bottom), 47 (center), 52–53, 54, 55 (3), 56, 57 (2), 67 (top), 74, 75 (bottom), 102 (top), 131 (top), 185, 227, 229 (3), 230 (top), 232 (top & bottom), 233

Live Steam Magazine: John Z. Draftz for Manicopa Live Steamers, 202; Joe Rice for New Jersey Live Steamers, 190, 191 (top); Paul Zuchinno for Adirondack Live Steamers, 191 (bottom), 197

MTS Imports 43 (bottom), 44 (center), 44–45 (top & bottom), 49 (top), 63 (bottom), 68 (top), 68–69, 69 (center)

Magnuson 132, 133 (top & bottom), 183 (2)

Mantua 60–61, 98 (center & bottom), 101 (top & center right), 203 (bottom)

Märklin 11, 12–13, 20–21, 22, 38 (top), 40 (bottom), 63 (top), 64–65, 72 (top & bottom) (3), 72–73, 73 (top & bottom), 78 (top), 97 (top), 101 (top), 165, 186, 187, 210, 215, 216–217, 231

Louis A. Marre 192, 193, 194, 195 (top & bottom), 207 (bottom), 224–225

Master Creations 104 (bottom), 127 (top)

Microflame 145 (center & bottom)

Micro Mark 142 (top & bottom), 143 (top, bottom & right), 144 (left)

Microscale Decals 159 (top), 160–161

Don Mitchell 76–77, 79 (top), 88, 92, 100 (left & right), 101 (left), 102 (center left & right), 103 (bottom), 104 (left), 109, 111, 164, 176, 177 (top & right), 181 (bottom), 182 (right), 188–189, 203 (top)

Model Power 207 (top)

Model Railroader 196

Model Railroading 196

Model Rectifier Corp. 166 (top & bottom), 169 (top), 171 (3), 172 (top & bottom)

Mountains in Minutes 112 (top & bottom), 113

Nostalgia Station 230 (bottom)

Oregon Rail Supply 128 (left)

Richard Orr 84–85

Paasche Airbrush Co. 156 (6), 157 (top & center)

P.B.L. 128 (top)

Pacific Rail Shops 152

Pecos River Brass 37 (top), 38–39

Peerless Industries 169 (bottom)

Pioneer Valley Models 118

PlastiKote Co. 151 (bottom), 154 (right),

155 (left & right)

Rail Fan and Railroad 196

Rail Graphics 158 (3), 159 (center)

Rail Photos Unlimited 30 (bottom), 32 (top), 33 (top), 62, 206

Rail Rax 10–11, 58, 59

Railroad Model Craftsman 197

Railroad Tie Express 228 (top)

Railroad Video Productions 204, 205

John Rendall 129 (top)

Right of Way Industries 69 (top)

S & C Enterprises 122 (bottom)

Scale Structures 120–121

A. L. Schmidt 75 (top)

Shinohara 93

Sundance Marketing 228 (bottom)

Stafford Swain 96, 104 (top, right), 147, 150, 175, 178 (left), 182 (left)

Tiger Valley Models 102 (bottom)

Trackside Details 151 (top)

Universal Press Syndicate 79 (bottom)

Walthers 200, 201 (3)